Native American Religions

North America

Religion, History, and Culture
Selections from The Encyclopedia of Religion

Mircea Eliade
EDITOR IN CHIEF

EDITORS
Charles J. Adams
Joseph M. Kitagawa
Martin E. Marty
Richard P. McBrien
Jacob Needleman
Annemarie Schimmel
Robert M. Seltzer
Victor Turner

ASSOCIATE EDITOR
Lawrence E. Sullivan

ASSISTANT EDITOR
William K. Mahony

Native

American

Religions

North America

EDITED BY
Lawrence E. Sullivan

Religion, History, and Culture
Selections from The Encyclopedia of Religion

Mircea Eliade
EDITOR IN CHIEF

MACMILLAN PUBLISHING COMPANY
New York
COLLIER MACMILLAN PUBLISHERS
London

Macmillan Publishing Company
866 Third Avenue, New York, N.Y. 10022

Collier Macmillan Canada, Inc.

Library of Congress Catalog Card Number: 89–12086

Printed in the United States of America

printing number
1 2 3 4 5 6 7 8 9 10

Library of Congress Cataloging-in-Publication Data

Native American religions. North America.

    (Religion, history, and culture)
    "Selections from The Encyclopedia of religion."
    Bibliography: p.
    1. Indians of North America—Religion and mythology.
I. Sullivan, Lawrence Eugene, 1949–
II. Encyclopedia of religion.   III. Series.
E98.R3N38   1989   299'.7   89-12086
ISBN 0-02-897402-6

CONTENTS

MAPS AND ILLUSTRATIONS

PUBLISHER'S NOTE

Since publication of *The Encyclopedia of Religion* in 1987, we have been gratified by the overwhelming reception accorded it by the community of scholars. This reception has more than justified the hopes of the members of the work's editorial board, who, with their editor in chief, cherished the aim that it would contribute to the study of the varieties of religious expression worldwide. To all those who participated in the project we express again our deepest thanks.

Now, in response to the many requests of our contributors and other teachers, we take pride in making available this selection of articles from the encyclopedia for use in the classroom. It is our hope that by publishing these articles in an inexpensive, compact format, they will be read and reflected upon by an even broader audience. In our effort to select those articles most appropriate to undergraduate instruction, it has been necessary to omit entries of interest primarily to the more advanced student and/or to those who wish to pursue a particular topic in greater depth. To facilitate their research, and to encourage the reader to consult the encyclopedia itself, we have thus retained the system of cross-references that, in the original work, served to guide the reader to related articles in this and other fields. A comprehensive index to the coverage of Native American religions may be found in volume sixteen of the encyclopedia.

Charles E. Smith
Publisher and President
Macmillan Reference Division

INTRODUCTION

FACING FACTS ABOUT NATIVE AMERICAN RELIGIONS

"The fundamental factor that keeps Indians and non-Indians from communicating is that they are speaking about two entirely different perceptions of the world" (Deloria, 1979, p. vii). Starting from this assumption, Vine Deloria, Jr., a Native American philosopher and writer from the Standing Rock Sioux community, argues that diverse religious outlooks and practices promote distinct views of the mysteries of the universe (see also Deloria, 1973, and Ridington, 1988). Although this volume of selections from *The Encyclopedia of Religion* encourages better understanding of such distinct views by providing an accessible introduction to the religious life of Native American peoples, something harsh must be said at its beginning.

Readers must know, first of all, that accounts of Native American religious life, however harmless or entertaining they appear on the surface, have seldom been fair or neutral (Deloria, 1987). The arrival of the first colonists immediately pitched native peoples into a struggle that has not yet ended. They strive not only to preserve their land and resources, their biological well-being and material survival, but to control their own meaning and destiny (Wright and Barreiro, 1982; Sullivan, 1988). Nowhere is that destiny and meaning more clearly at stake than in depictions of Native American religious beliefs and practices.

Each community transmits distinct traditions concerning the ancestors, spirits, and powers active in its own physical landscape and social world. Through myth, art, and ceremonial life, native peoples created an authentic sense of themselves and remained agents of their own history. Against all odds, this creative process continues. But generalizations about native religious beliefs and practices always threaten to cloud the integrity of each community's religious life with depictions that are either too "savage," on the one side, or overly romantic, on the other. Don't be misled. Even the widespread romantic notion that authentic ceremonial life long ago disappeared is an ignorant prejudice that has tried to play the role of a self-fulfilling prophecy. From first contact, invaders conjured up an image of the so-called Vanishing Indian, an image that conveniently justified the expropriation of land from peoples allegedly doomed to extinction and encouraged the disregard of ideas deemed unfit to survive in the modern world (Dippie, 1982; Lyman, 1982). The fact is, every state in the union has a Native American population, and city life has drawn many Native Americans into the political process. For all that, "over half the Indian population remains settled in areas away from the eye and understanding of the white public . . ." (Bolt, 1987, p. 304).

The Vanishing Indian and other images deserve critical study because they give evidence of the ignorance, fear, greed, or guilt both of invaders and (even) of scientific researchers who have taken possession of native property and ideas. In late

1987, for example, scavengers disturbed at least 650 graves at the Slack Farm in Union County, Kentucky, the site of an ancient Native American burial ground. The diggers maintained that the remains belong to no one, as if Native Americans were no longer living groups in communion with their dead. This was hardly the view of the Native Americans who rushed to protect the cemetery. On Memorial Day, 1988, chiefs Leon Shenandoah and Vincent Johnson of the Six Nations Iroquois Confederacy reburied the remains of 114 individuals whose afterlife journey had been disrupted before their bones had completely turned to powder, the signal of their arrival in the otherworld. The matter of these and other disturbed burial grounds is now in the courts.

Such distorted images as the Vanishing American must be set aside in order to gain a clearer view of Native American religious life. The essays in this book will help readers overcome unfounded stereotypes, which are constantly created and reinforced in films and novels despite the counterefforts of Native American writers like the Kiowa novelist N. Scott Momaday (Bataille and Silet, 1980; Zolla, 1989; Momaday, 1968 and 1969).

The following fact can no longer be denied: the creative life of native peoples, from sea to shining sea, is the foundation of American history. At the suggestion of Benjamin Franklin and others, the very framework of government and the language of the United States Constitution was taken—in some places, word for word—from the documents in which American Indians had formed federated groups of independent nations among themselves. How bitter an irony it is that those same Federated Nations that served as a model for "the people united to form a more perfect union" were pitilessly attacked by the direct order of General George Washington during the American Revolution. The fate of its native communities remains the true test of America's self-image as a just and free people. Better knowledge of Native American realities will allow young Americans, of whatever cultural background, to take responsibility for their history and to assume their own creative place in American culture—to find their place in the right picture.

ONE COMMUNITY, MANY VIEWS

Complexity and subtlety exist in any community's religious life. *Sioux Indian Religion: Tradition and Innovation*, edited by Raymond J. DeMallie and Douglas R. Parks (1987), illustrates the point well. The book emerged from a meeting held at Bismarck, North Dakota, in the spring of 1982. At that gathering the Sacred Pipe bundle was put away for seven years, as the spirits suggested. The event became an occasion for reflection on the blessings brought by the pipe to the community. This community embodies many and various religious points of view, however, and it is fascinating to read reflections on the sacredness of the pipe from so many angles. Arval Looking Horse, the nineteenth generation of keepers of the pipe, offers moving testimony to the power of the Sacred Pipe in the community today. A quite different view was put forward by Mercy Poor Man, a fundamentalist Christian who preaches in the Christian Fellowship Church. Vine Delora, Sr., a Lakota Episcopal priest living in Pierre, South Dakota, is the father of Vine Deloria, Jr., the lawyer, professor, and writer whose quote opened this introductory essay. The senior Deloria sketches the history of the Deloria family and describes the religious beliefs of his own grandfather, Francis des Lauriers. There is an interview with Emerson Spider, the Oglala bishop of the Native American (Peyote) Church. Robert Stead, a more traditional religious leader and healer, also presents a statement of his religious views and practices. The book is illustrated by the Lakota artist Arthur Amiotte, who also contributed an essay to the volume. An article by the anthropologist Beatrice Medicine discusses the role of women in the resurgence of traditional ceremonials, the sacred sphere of which, she insists, must be restored. She points out, among other things, that ceremonial life maintains a creative, balanced relationship between the sexes. These diverse perspectives demonstrate how, speaking in their own voice, Native Americans have led us to new, differentiated understandings of their spiritual heritages.

CHALLENGES ON VITAL ISSUES: NEW FRAMES, NEW LIGHT

Many issues of special interest to contemporary culture benefit from the creative input of Native American communities. Closer attention to Native American views is reshaping our perception of the very nature of art, history, sports, language, and the family. Such is the case also for the study of women's religious history, to choose but one example of a vital contemporary topic (Bataille and Sands, 1984; Allen, 1986; Erdrich, 1984; Schlegel, 1979 and 1984; Talamantez, forthcoming). The reevaluation of the role of women in contemporary society has provoked a reexamination of the role of women in Native American life just as it has prompted new scrutiny of women and gender in other places and times. In turn, the views and social roles of Native American women have served as a critique of generalizations made in the field of gender and women's studies. This was the intention of Beatrice Medicine in her study of the division of labor by sex in ritual life (in DeMallie and Parks, 1987).

Marla N. Powers makes the point that Oglala myth and ceremony embody notions of maleness and femaleness as well as attitudes toward sex, marriage, and reproduction, and she notes that females appear in myth and rite as the prime movers of Oglala society. On this basis, and on the basis of close examination of daily social life, Powers challenges certain feminist theories (Powers, 1988). "A number of feminist writers view women's productive and reproductive roles as the basis for female subordination. . . . For the Oglalas, it is just the opposite. My research shows that the fulfillment of an Oglala woman's traditional role—that of wife and mother, according to those values perceived to be irrefutably Lakota—has facilitated her movement into economic and political roles modeled after Euramerican concepts of propriety, albeit in part inadvertently." (ibid, p. 6). Similarly, Powers asserts, an unwarranted early feminist assumption about the universality of male dominance has confounded the examination of much more subtle and variable relationships between men and women in the shifting contexts of Native American life. "In summary, equating women's productive and reproductive roles with subordination, plus an unfounded belief in the universality of male dominance, precludes the possibility of seeing more complex relationships" (Powers, 1986, p. 7). Christine Bolt makes similar points (Bolt, 1987, pp. 252–269).

No matter how such differences of opinion within women's studies are finally resolved, a more careful study of women's lives is providing a new focus for the study of social change; this is true in the historical study of Native Americans also. Attention to the lives of native women in nineteenth-century California, for instance, brought Albert Hurtado a new realization of the impact of social upheaval on native communities. The gold rush fired California's developing economy. Indian participation in that economy and the concomitant forceful reordering of the Indian family took an enormous toll on Indian women living on the so-called sexual frontier, the intimate border between Americans of different racial groups. The various interactions of Indian women with men on that boundary affected not only the incidence of sexual violence, concubinage, and prostitution, but also the patterns of racial segregation, marriage, child-rearing, descent, and inheritance that shaped frontier California for Indian and non-Indian alike (Hurtado, 1988, pp. 169–192). The study of women's lives is but a single example of a key contemporary issue that has become framed in new ways in the light of Native American religious histories.

CATEGORIES AND CAPTIVES: A STRANGE QUESTION?

Why did European immigrants not convert to Native American religious beliefs and practices? A similar question could be asked in regard to almost any area of the globe where European colonists settled and carried on Christian missionary activity. In the light of subsequent history, readers may find this a strange question, but why shouldn't the question be posed in exactly this way? Settlers found much to admire in native traditions. In the judgment of New England Puritans, to cite a single case, Indians displayed more civility than Catholics or Quakers (Vaughan, 1965, p. 19; Kupperman, 1980). In general, the exchange of ideas and customs between native peoples and colonials occurred on almost every plane of existence: in style and material of dress; in the tactics of war; in farming, hunting, fishing, and cooking techniques; in the cultivation of new tastes and the adaptation of cuisine to make use of native crops; in acceptance of governmental structures; in loanwords taken into English, French, or Spanish from native languages. Settlers were so impressed with Native American lifeways that they adopted them in many aspects of their lives. Why did they not do so more completely in the realm of religious belief and practice? The question may be raised in regard to many points of contact between Europeans and Native Americans. The use of tobacco is a case in point. From what we know, tobacco cultivation and use spread from native communities in South America. Over the centuries before contact, no matter how many new and different Native American groups opted to grow and consume tobacco, they always preserved its religious character as a sacred plant used for ritual purposes (Wilbert, 1987). The introduction of the plant into European hands, however, provides a striking contrast. From the first moment of contact, Europeans eagerly used tobacco and sought it as a commodity, but at the same time they divested the use of tobacco of its religious character. In some cases, tobacco became the epitome of a profane substance and its consumption a paradigmatic secular pastime. The colonists apparently lacked the capacity to understand a religiosity that included tobacco consumption, because they had no significant place on their mental maps for *religious* behavior of this kind. Therefore, they failed to perceive tobacco use as relevant to their own religious lives.

Ultimately, the settlers and missionaries gave themselves few opportunities to understand the religious lives of their hosts. Even when they had occasion to learn something about Native American ceremonies, rites, symbols, and myths, they had few categories with which to understand them. Colonists and settlers were not much better prepared than the general population is today to understand religious traditions other than their own, and thus were compelled to revert to Christian theological categories crafted to describe European heretics, apostates, schismatics, and demoniacs in order to do so. Although even now they are still applied to Native American religions, these terms and evaluations have *nothing* to do with native traditions. They shed little or no light on Native American religion and culture.

With regard to the settlers' refusal to embrace native religions, we should take note of an incredible fact only recently brought to light by historians: large numbers of settlers who had ample opportunity to know intimately the native religious traditions in fact opted to join the native community. James Axtell's remarkable book *The Invasion Within: The Contest of Cultures in Colonial North America* (1985) recounts the lives of hundreds of European settlers who had been taken to live with native communities and who, in spite of considerable resistance from relatives and friends, yearned for continued association with their former "captors," so enamored were they of native peoples, lifeways, and relationships. In New England, at least fifteen percent of all individuals "captured" by Native Americans before 1782 elected to remain with their new Indian families. They became "full-fledged Indians," fully acculturated in custom and ceremony (Axtell, 1974, p. 276; Bolt, 1987, p. 17). Countless other "captives" found the parting painful when it was imposed on them by their "rescuers." "The Indians' conversion of hundreds of 'civilized' captives to 'savage' life tore from the hands of the colonists, however briefly, their sharp conceit as the 'chosen people' of God and their unexamined faith in the superiority of their own customs and opinions. With Montaigne, we can only regret that the invaders, stripped bare and defenseless, did not seize the moment for self-understanding, tolerance, and true humiliation" (Axtell, 1985; p. 333; see also Morrison, 1984).

LEARNING SOMETHING NEW

North American educators have expressed a growing desire to include the religions native to North American soil within the school curriculum. Failure to follow through on this desire would only further the criminal ignorance that undermines the goal of liberal education: to free citizens from the misunderstandings that keep them in the dark about themselves and that spawn injustice toward those around them. In spite of this desire to learn and teach, we must admit frankly that we still suffer from a lack of understanding and adequate teaching materials. By providing both a place to start and the resources for continued study, this volume narrows the gap between the willingness to learn about Native American religions and the practical preparation required to do so. As a reliable and accessible resource for teachers and students in courses in Native American studies, as well as in Western civilization, American history, anthropology, and religious studies, this volume aims to encourage the inclusion of Native American life in the study of the humanities and the social sciences. At the end of each article are concise recommendations for further reading, and within each essay are cross-references to other pertinent pieces found in *The Encyclopedia of Religion*, each one with its own bibliographic suggestions. By directing teachers and students to reliable resources this volume can serve as guide and centerpiece for a larger sequence of courses on Native American civilization (see also Churchill and Jaimes, 1988).

The presence of Native American religions (and of other cultures whose religious lives have been excluded from consideration in a too-narrow reckoning of human history) in our curricula admits something truly new into our educational offerings. By paying better attention to the creative religious wellsprings of cultures that have flourished in countless variety beyond the scriptural traditions of the "great world religions" we may renew our sense of humanity and our study of the humanities. It was this conviction that prompted Mircea Eliade to pursue his lifelong study of such religions and to insist on ample treatment of them within the encyclopedia. Close acquaintance with Native American religions can alter one's preconceptions about the relationship of religion to culture, society, political order, or art. Among Native American peoples, religious life is not necessarily a private affair or a set of doctrines to which one assents in faith, nor is it a set of beliefs about a supernatural life apart from this visible world. Religious life recognizes the vitality and power that fill the ordinary, concrete world. Religion breaks fertile ground for the performing and fine arts, including music, drama, dance, poetry, visual design, architecture, or plastic image. It is the basis for spirituality, both individual and communal, as well as for hunting, agriculture, the sciences, even the conceptualization of humanity, space, time, law, nature, and land.

This book can only sample such riches. North America is home to hundreds of native communities, each with a distinctive religious life of its own. Not all of these peoples could be adequately portrayed in a single volume. Here we must be content to select several different approaches to Native American religious life, ranging in scale from the general overview to regional surveys to specific examples of communities or important religious expressions.

In addition, a separate article details how the religious life of Native Americans has been studied throughout American history. The scholarly study of native peoples is itself a formidable undertaking, a hindrance as well as a help in obtaining a true picture of Native American peoples. The image that most Americans now have of Native Americans is no longer even based on the testimony that fed earlier generations of Americans—reports taken directly from frontierspeople, military personnel, miners, trappers, explorers, settlers, and ranchers, all of whom at least had a passing acquaintance with native people. Incredible as it may seem, Native American historical characters have been completely reinvented for the last several generations. They appear before us mostly on the silver screen, as figments in some film director's imaginary world (Bataille and Silet, 1980). Michael Dorris, a member of the Modoc tribe and professor at Dartmouth College, emphasizes that "flesh and blood Native Americans have rarely participated in or benefited from the creation of these imaginary Indians, whose recognition factor, as they say on Madison Avenue, outranks, on a world scale, that of Santa Claus, Mickey Mouse, and Coca Cola combined. . . . It is little wonder, then, that many non-Indians literally would not know a real Native American if they fell over one, for they have been prepared for a well-defined, carefully honed legend. . . . For five hundred years Indian people have been measured and have competed against a fantasy over which they have had no control. They are compared with beings who never really *were*, yet the stereotype is taken for the truth" (Dorris, 1987, pp. 99–100). In the past generation, anthropologists and historians of culture have said little in the public domain to dispel these illusions. Even those scholars who have tried to bring new understanding to a general audience have often suffered from biases and blinders when it came to religion. Raymond Fogelson's article on the history of study of this field helps us recognize these shortcomings and makes us aware of the need to face our own limitations in coming to grips with the truths expounded in tribal myth and ritual.

These truths need not be either mystical or ancient. Native American peoples are witnesses to modern history as it has taken shape in both beneficial as well as destructive forms. The Ghost Dance, the Native American Church, the writings of Native American intellectuals, and the attempts to gain legal rights to sacred land through the U. S. courts are all responses to modern situations. They are interpretations of the world we inhabit.

Fortunately, Native Americans themselves continue to come to the fore as public spokespersons for their points of view. This has always been true within native communities and in the sad "trail of broken treaties" that makes up the history of Indian-white negotiations over the past centuries, but such effective leadership is more than ever present in universities, in the courts, in publishing and the press, and in the sphere of political leadership both on the intertribal level and in the wider public domain. When Native Americans are allowed to interpret their own religious life in their own terms, both the complexity and coherence of a community's religious experience strike us in new ways. We learn something new, not only about others but about ourselves and about our educational, legal, and public information systems.

CHERISHING THE PARTICULAR AND CARING FOR CONSEQUENCES

This book, then, offers more adequate categories with which to understand Native American religions. In an overview of this scale, general comparisons are a necessity and broad interpretive statements are a virtue. At the same time, we should heed Peter Nabokov's warning against the dangers of "compressing all tribal experience into one North American Tao, forcibly distilling from widely different tribal traditions a mystical or theological essence that can then be demonstrated as fundamentally identical to other Ways, denying tribal cosmology and sovereignty through a sort of backhanded homage to what is presumed to be the one, true Indian spirit. . . . [By seeking peace, goodwill, and fraternity in this way, the] question remains of whether the legacy of this brand of romantic universalism might bequeath exactly the opposite consequence to the problem of ongoing protection of Native American sacred sites across the country" (Nabokov, 1986, p. 483). An overly romantic view of the traditional past often disguises indifference to the present economic and political plight of Native American communities (Philip, 1986). Discrete and multiple tribal worldviews can be overwhelmed by broad academic interpretations that are then uncharitably manipulated in court to achieve a new mode of postcolonial conquest. Gerald Vizenor, professor of Native Studies in Berkeley and a member of the Chippewa tribe, dubs the scholars' overly general and romantic images of traditional tribal culture a kind of "colonization in print" (Vizenor, 1987, p. 181). "But as legal cases deciding the fate of Yurok, Cherokee, Hopi, Navajo, Lakota and other tribal sacred places come into courts of law, and scholars are increasingly subpoenaed to testify on behalf of Indian realities, translating them into concepts and terminology which can make sense to an Anglo judge or jury, what gets concocted in academia, or in the consciousness of a seeker-scholar hunting for the common denominator to mystical experience, acquires lasting legal and political muscle" (Nabokov, 1986, p. 484).

How American society understands Native American religions carries practical consequences. It is important to recognize that Native American religiosity bears directly on rights to land. Professor Henrietta Whiteman expressed such a point regarding her own Cheyenne community: "In brief, Cheyenne history is a continuum of sacred experiences rooted into the American landscape, with Bear Butte [near Sturgis, South Dakota] as their most sacred and most powerful place. Their continuity as a people requires that they maintain their way of life. Specifically, they must maintain their traditions, beliefs, spiritual life, and, through their ceremonies, maintain their sacred mission to keep the earth alive" (Whiteman, 1987, p. 169). Not only may specific shrines, ceremonial grounds, sanctuaries, or buildings (Nabokov and Easton, 1989) be quintessentially holy places central to religious and social life, but the vast spaces that provide specific aesthetic conditions (for example, the awe in meditating, just as one's first ancestor did, on the first rays of sunlight streaming through a specific mountain pass) as well as the areas that ground economic activities (such as fishing, hunting, farming, and other income-producing labor) are integral to the ritual cycle of feasts and festivals that extends across the community's calendar year and the life cycle of the individual. The centrality of particular holy places and the need to respect the religious integrity of native American lands was emphasized in an important friend-of-the-court brief submitted to the U. S. Supreme Court during its October 1987 term (*Lyng v. Northwest Indian Cemetery*, 1987): "Sacred sites and sacred geography function as fundamental ingredients of ritual in American Indian religions" (Walker, 1987, p. 21).

No generalization about "sacred space" can do full justice to the uniqueness of the specific physical geography sacred to an individual community. In studying Native American religions, general interpretations serve as necessary guideposts on a path toward new understandings that, once arrived at, help us see and cherish what is distinctive in each community and place.

REFERENCES AND SUGGESTIONS FOR FURTHER READING

Allen, Paula Gunn. *The Sacred Hoop: Recovering the Feminine in American Indian Traditions.* Boston, 1986.

Axtell, James. "The Scholastic Philosophy of the Wilderness," in *The School upon a Hill: Education and Society in Colonial New England.* New Haven, 1974.

———. *The Invasion Within: The Contest of Cultures in Colonial North America.* New York, 1985.

Bataille, Gretchen, M., and Kathleen Mullen Sands. *American Indian Women; Telling Their Lives.* Lincoln, 1984.

Bataille, Gretchen, M., and Charles C. P. Silet, eds. *The Pretend Indians: Images of Native Americans in the Movies.* Ames, Iowa, 1980. With a foreward on "American Fantasy" by Vine Deloria, Jr.

Bolt, Christine. *American Indian Policy and American Reform: Case Studies of the Campaign to Assimilate the American Indians.* London, 1987.

Churchill, Ward, and M. Annette Jaimes. "American Indian Studies: A Positive Alternative," *The Bloomsbury Review* (September/October 1988). Suggests several thematic, interdisciplinary courses and recommends further readings.

Deloria, Vine, Jr. *God is Red.* New York, 1973.

———. *Behind the Trail of Broken Treaties: An Indian Declaration of Independence.* New York, 1974.

———. *The Metaphysics of Modern Existence.* San Francisco, 1979.

———. *A Sender of Words: Essays in Memory of John G. Neihardt.* Salt Lake City, 1984.

———., ed. *American Indian Policy in the Twentieth Century.* Norman, Oklahoma, 1985.

————. "Revision and Reversion," pp. 84–90 in Martin, 1987.

Deloria, Vine, Jr., and Sandra L. Cadwalader. *The Aggressions of Civilization: Federal Indian Policy Since the 1880s*. Philadelphia, 1984.

Deloria, Vine, Jr., and Clifford M. Lytle. *American Indians, American Justice*. Austin, 1983.

————. *The Nations Within: The Past and Future of American Indian Sovereignty*. New York, 1984.

DeMallie, Raymond J., and Douglas R. Parks, eds. *Sioux Indian Religion: Tradition and Innovation*. Norman, 1987.

Dippie, Brian W. *The Vanishing American: White Attitudes and U. S. Indian Policy*. Middletown, Conn., 1982.

Dorris, Michael. "Indians on the Shelf," pp. 98–105 in Martin, 1987.

Erdrich, Louise. *Love Medicine: A Novel*. New York, 1984.

Hurtado, Albert L. *Indian Survival on the California Frontier*. Yale Western Americana Series, no. 35. New Haven, 1988.

Kupperman, Karen Ordahl. *Settling with the Indians: The Meeting of English and Indian Cultures in America, 1580–1640*. London, 1980.

Lyman, Christopher. *The Vanishing Race and Other Illusions: Photographs of Indians by Edward S. Curtis*. New York, 1982.

Lyng v. Northwest Indian Cemetery (1987). Brief of *amici curiae* (no. 86–1013) submitted in support of respondents by the National Congress of American Indians, Association on American Indian Affairs, The Karuk Tribe of California, The Tolowa Nation, The Hoopa Tribe of California, The Confederated Salish and Kootenai Tribes of Montana, the Kootenai Tribe of Idaho, and the Tunica-Biloxi Tribe of Louisiana for the case of Richard E. Lyng, Secretary of Agriculture, et al., Petitioners, *versus* Northwest Indian Cemetery Protective Association, et al., Respondents, heard in the Supreme Court of the United States during its October term, 1987. On writ of *certiorari* to the United States Court of Appeals for the Ninth Circuit. Obtainable from Steven C. Moore, Esq, Counsel of Record for Amici Curiae, Native American Rights Fund, 1506 Broadway, Boulder, Colorado 80302.

Martin, Calvin, ed. *The American Indian and the Problem of History*. New York, 1987.

Momaday, N. Scott. *House Made of Dawn*. New York, 1969.

————. *The Way to Rainy Mountain*. Albuquerque, 1969.

Morrison, Kenneth M. *The Embattled Northeast: The Elusive Ideal of Alliance in Abenaki-Euramerican Relations*. Berkeley, 1984.

Nabokov, Peter. "Unto These Mountains: Toward the Study of Sacred Geography," in Gordon Brotherston, ed., *Voices of the First America: Text and Context in the New World*. Special issue of *New Scholar* 10. 1–2 (1986): 479–489.

Nabokov, Peter, and Robert Easton. *Dwellings at the Source: Native American Architecture*. New York, 1989.

Philip, Kenneth R., ed. *Indian Self-Rule: First-Hand Accounts of Indian-White Relations from Roosevelt to Reagan*. Current Issues in the American West, vol. 4. Salt Lake City, 1986.

Powers, Marla N. *Oglala Women: Myth, Ritual, and Reality*. Chicago, 1986.

Ridington, Robin. *Trail to Heaven: Knowledge and Narrative in a Northern Native Community*. Iowa City, 1988.

Schlegel, Alice, ed. *Sexual Stratification: A Cross-Cultural View*. New York, 1979.

————. "Hopi Gender Ideology of Female Superiority," *Quarterly Journal of Ideology* 8.4 (1984): 44–52.

Sullivan, Lawrence E. *Icanchu's Drum: An Orientation to Meaning in South American Religions*. New York, 1988.

Talamantez, Inés. *Apache Women's Initiation* (forthcoming).

Vaughn, Alden T. *New England Frontier: Puritans and Indians, 1620–1675*. Boston, 1965.

Vizenor, Gerald. "Socioacupuncture: Mythic Reversals and the Striptease in Four Scenes," pp. 180–192 in Martin, 1987.

Walker, Deward E., Jr. "Protection of American Indian Sacred Geography: Toward a Functional Understanding of Indian Religion Focusing on a Protective Standard of Integrity." Appendix A to *Lyng v. Northwest Indian Cemetery* (1987).

Whiteman, Henrietta. "White Buffalo Woman," pp. 162–170 in Martin, 1987.

Wilbert, Johannes. *Tobacco and Shamanism in South America*. New Haven, 1987.

Wright, Robin M., and José Barreiro, eds. *Native Peoples in Struggle: Russell Tribunal and Other International Forums*. Boston, 1982.

Zolla, Elémire. *I letterati e lo sciamano: l'Indiano nella letteratura americana dalle origini al 1988*. 2d ed. Venice, 1989.

MARCH 1989   LAWRENCE E. SULLIVAN

ONE

THE RELIGIOUS LIFE OF
NATIVE NORTH AMERICA

1

THE RELIGIOUS LIFE OF NATIVE NORTH AMERICANS

Åke Hultkrantz

Because of the isolation of the New World from the high civilizations of Europe, Asia, and Africa and from the communicative network between them, North America had preserved, until the end of the last century, cultures and religions of archaic types. Local historical traditions, intertribal diffusion, social structure and environmental pressure combined to form among the North American Indian tribes a series of religions that were only secondarily influenced by elements from outside the continent. North American religions have become known as varied, colorful, and spiritual. In the religio-scientific debate among anthropologists and historians of religion, such concepts as power and supreme being, guardian spirits and totems, fasting visions and shamanism, myth telling and ritualism, have drawn on North American ideas and religious experiences.

Soon after the arrival of the white man in the 1500s the first information concerning Indian religious worship reached the Europeans. Through Jesuit documents and other reports the religious development of the Iroquoian and eastern Algonquian groups can be followed continuously from 1613 onward. Spanish sources from the same time illuminate at least some aspects of Southwest Indian religious history. In the eighteenth century travel records and other documents throw light on the Indians of the Southeast Woodlands, of the mid-Atlantic region, and of the Prairies and on their religions. It was, however, only at the end of the eighteenth century and in the course of the nineteenth century that knowledge spread of the Plains, Basin, California, Plateau, Northwest Coast, western Canadian, and Alaskan Indian religions.

Main Religious Features

North America is a continent with many diverse cultures, and it is therefore meaningless to speak about North American religion as a unified aggregate of beliefs, myths, and rituals. Still, there are several religious traits that are basically common to all the Indians but variously formalized and interpreted among different peoples. These traits are also found in the religions of other continents and areas, particularly among the so-called primitive or primal peoples. Two characteristics are, however, typically Amerindian: the dependence on visions and dreams, which can modify old traditional rituals, and an intricate and time-consuming ceremonialism that some-times almost conceals the cognitive message of rituals.

SPIRIT WORLD

To these common elements belongs the idea of another dimension of existence that permeates life and yet is different from normal, everyday existence. Concepts such as the Lakota *wakan* and the Algonquian *manitou* refer to this consciousness of another world, the world of spirits, gods, and wonders. This supernatural or supra-normal world is sometimes manifest in nature, which then receives a sacred import. Often the campsite or the village is arranged in a pattern that establishes a ritual identity with the supernatural world. In twentieth-century pan-Indian religion the connection between terrestrial phenomena and the other world is extremely impor-tant.

Supreme Being. The supernatural world is primarily expressed through the spiri-tual powers residing in a host of gods, spirits, and ghosts. In many American tribes prayers are directed to a collectivity of divine or spiritual beings, as in the pipe ceremony. Foremost among these divinities is, in most tribes, a sky god who repre-sents all other supernatural beings or stands as their superior and the ruler of the universe. The Pawnee Indians in Nebraska, for instance, know a hierarchy of star gods and spirits, all of them subservient to the high god in the sky, Tirawa. It could be argued that their idea of a high god is formed after Mexican conceptual patterns, since the Caddoan-speaking peoples to whom the Pawnee belong were much in-spired by the Mexican-derived prehistoric Mississippian culture. However, there are clear examples of a supreme being among many North American peoples, and scholarly attempts to trace these figures to Christian influence have so far failed. In most cases the supreme being is vaguely conceived as the ulterior religious force in situations of need and frustration.

The supreme being is closely associated with the *axis mundi,* or world pillar. The Delaware Indians say that he grasps the pole that holds up the sky and is the center of the world. In ceremonial life the world pole, or world tree, is the central cultic symbol in the great annual rites of peoples of the Eastern Woodlands, the Plains, the Basin, and the Plateau. At this annual celebration the Indians thank the supreme being for the year that has been (the ceremony takes place in the spring in most cases) and dance in order to secure the support of the Great Spirit and all the powers for the year to come: the Plains Sun Dance is a good example. In California, a region of frequent earthquakes, similar world renewal rituals have as their main aim the stabilizing of the universe. In the east, the Delaware Big House ceremony is an adaptation of the hunters' annual ceremony to the cultural world of more settled maize-growing peoples: the sacred pillar is here built into a ceremonial house. In many places throughout North America myths testify that the annual ceremony is a repetition or commemoration of the cosmic creation at the beginning of time. This connection is, however, not present everywhere, and many Sun Dance rituals have origin myths of quite a different character.

The Culture Hero. The connection of the supreme being with creation is often concealed by the fact that in mythology another supernatural being, the culture hero, is invested with creative powers. His true mission is to deliver cultural institutions,

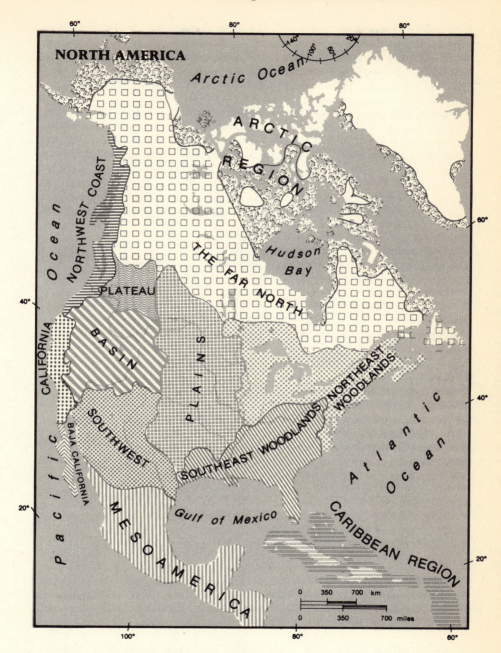

NORTH AMERICA

including religious ceremonies, to the first human beings, but he is sometimes an assistant creator as well. In this quality he competes with the Great Spirit and appears as a ludicrous figure, a trickster, or an antagonist of the Great Spirit, an emergent "devil." (It should be observed that all this takes place only on a mythological level, for the culture hero disappears after his work has been completed and in many quarters becomes a star.)

Trickster tales occupy a major part of American Indian mythologies and have attracted all kinds of comic folk-tale motifs. The tales usually portray the culture hero/trickster as a zoomorphic being: a white hare in the Northeast; a coyote on the western Plains, in the Basin, the Plateau, and California; and a raven in the Northwest.

Spirits and Ghosts. The other beings of the supernatural world—and they are innumerable, varying from tribe to tribe—may be partly distinguished according to their physical location.

1. *Sky beings,* including star gods, Sun (usually a manifestation of the supreme being), and Moon (who sometimes represents the vegetation goddess). The Milky Way is thought of as the road of the dead in some places, and the northern lights as the dead at play.
2. *Atmospheric spirits,* which usually comprise the Four Winds (they emanate from caves situated in the four cardinal directions), Whirlwind (often thought of as a ghost), the rain spirits, and Thunderbird. This last spirit, of which a parallel conception is also found in Siberia, is a giant eaglelike bird; according to many informants his blinking eyes make the lightning, while his flapping wings cause the thunder.
3. *Spirits of the biosphere,* many of them rulers, or owners, of animal species or plant species (Buffalo Spirit, Caribou Spirit, Maize Spirit), others connected with natural places like mountains, stones, deserts, swamps, waters, and so on. Human beings (medicinemen, for example) may also manifest supernatural powers.
4. *Powers of the underworld,* such as Mother Earth, underwater monsters (snakes or panthers), and the ruler of the underground dead, who is usually identical with the first ancestor or is a brother of the culture hero.

However, there are powers that do not fit into this scheme. Such powers are the dead, who operate in different places in different types of cultures. Hunters believe the dead are in the sky or somewhere beyond the horizon—beyond the western mountains, beyond the sea where the sun sets. Horticulturists may believe that the dead are in the ground, returning to Our Mother's bosom, or at the place of emergence of mankind; and in stratified agricultural societies like those of the Mississippian culture there are different abodes for different social categories of dead. At the same time there is everywhere a belief in ghosts on earth, who are often heard whistling in the night. Independent of these beliefs is a ubiquitous idea of reincarnation or transmigration into animals.

Guardian Spirits and Vision Quests. Other spirits are the guardian spirits acquired in fasting visions by youths of the Plateau and the Northeast Woodlands and by both boys and men of the Plains and the Basin. These spirits are mostly zoomorphic. They may be animal spirits or spirits that show themselves in animal disguise. Everywhere except among the pueblo-dwelling peoples of the Southwest it has been the individual hunter's ambition to acquire one or several of these guardian spirits. They usually appear to the person after a vision quest during which he has spent several days and nights in fasting and isolation at some lonely spot in the wilderness. The spirit endows his client with a particular "medicine," that is, supernatural power (to hunt, to run, to make love, to cure), gives him a sacred song, and instructs him to make a pouch or medicine bag in which he is to keep the sacred paraphernalia associated with his vision. The vision quest is basic to most American Indian hunting religions.

In some places special societies were established for young spirit seekers who expected to meet the same spirit. This was, for instance, the case among the Kwakiutl of Vancouver Island and vicinity. The vision itself was no longer central here, the neophyte being abducted by masked men to the woods and told there the secrets of his patron, Cannibal Spirit, whose frenzied behavior he imitates in a ceremony on his return.

There seems to be a direct relationship between the individual's guardian spirit and the complex of totemism. If totemism is defined as the mysterious relationship between a segment of a tribe, usually a clan or other unilineal kinship group, and a particular animal species that is its congener and patron, then totemism exists in many places where unilineal societies exist. Several American cases suggest that the totem is the original guardian spirit of an individual that has then been inherited by this person's descendants as their common supernatural partner.

In some more complex societies the medicine bags, or sacred bundles, have become inherited treasures within the vision seekers' families; in other societies they can even be purchased. Where a powerful object has been handed down in a family it is often made a symbol for a larger community, and its uncovering is surrounded by rituals and recitations of its origin myth. A typical example is the sacred bundle of the Arapaho, which contains a flatpipe.

Medicine Men and Medicine Societies. The medicine man is a visionary who has succeeded in receiving power to cure people. However, visionaries with other extraordinary powers, such as the capacity to find lost things or divine the future, have also been labeled "medicine men." In very many cases a bear spirit is the medicine man's patron, so he dresses in a bearskin and mimics a bear's movements and sounds when doctoring people. Diseases may be ascribed to any of several causes, such as witchcraft or the breaking of a taboo. They manifest themselves mainly in two ways: a spirit or disease object is supposed to have intruded into the body (or even, on the Northwest Coast, to possess the person in a psychological sense); or the sick man's soul—in some cases, his power—has been stolen. In the former case it is the medicine man's task to frighten the spirit away or to remove it from the body by sucking, fanning, or drawing it out; in the latter case he has to catch the lost soul, which can be done in an imitative séance. Alternatively, the medicine man may sink into a trance, release his own soul, and send it out after the runaway or stolen soul. The medicine man who becomes entranced in this way may be characterized as a shaman.

In cultures with more complicated social organizations, medicine men may join together, exchanging experiences and working out a common, secret ideology, or they may form medicine societies into which persons are accepted after passing through a series of ritual events. An example of this is the Midewiwin, or Great Medicine society, of the Ojibwa, which is organized like a secret order society and has four or eight hierarchical grades.

In some cultures in the Southwest where collectivism is part of the cultural pattern—as, for instance, among the agricultural Pueblo—the medicine man is replaced by an organization of professional healers, and rituals are performed to aid individuals. Among the Navajo, the old medicine man lives on as a diagnostician ("hand trembler") whereas the curing itself is performed by a ritually skilled singer. The regaining of the patient's health means that harmony has been restored between man and the world of the gods and spirits.

RITUAL ACTS

Harmony or spiritual balance is what North American Indians want to achieve in their relations with the supernatural powers. A harmonious balance can be reached through prayers and offerings or through imitative representation of supernatural events.

Prayers and Offerings. Prayers range from a few words at meal offerings to detailed ritual prayers, from casual petitions of blessing to deeply emotional cries for help and sustenance. Indeed, Navajo prayer has been characterized by one researcher as "compulsive words," by another as "creative words." There is often beauty in Indian prayers, the usual eloquence of the Indians giving moving expression to their religious experience.

There are many kinds of offerings. A simple form is throwing tobacco or food into the fire or onto the ground at mealtimes. Another example is the placing of tobacco pouches on the ground at the beginning of dangerous passages, such as crossing a lake or walking over a mountain ridge.

Tobacco has been intimately related to American Indian religious practice. Even today no Indian conventions or powwows are undertaken without a preliminary pipe ceremony, an invocation of the powers that grant harmony between men and between gods or spirits and men. [*See* Tobacco.]

When hunters killed game they usually performed rites over the body. For instance, after the animal was eaten, the bones might be given a ritual burial; they were reassembled in anatomical order, and the skull of the animal was elevated on a pole or a tree. These rituals were especially important in the case of the bear. This so-called animal ceremonialism was often intended to appease a particular spirit, the master of the game, but the primary purpose of such burials was to ensure the return of the game by showing proper respect for the animals. True sacrifices were not common, but did occur in the Northeast Woodlands, where white dogs were sacrificed to the powers. In many places the skins of animals (and, later, pieces of cloth as well) served as offerings. There was religious cannibalism in the East, even endocannibalism (the eating of one's family dead) in ancient times. Mutilations of fingers and other cases of self-mutilation as offerings occurred in the Sun Dance of the Lakota and in the closely related Mandan Okipa ceremony.

Ritual Representations. Harmonious relations with the supernatural world could be restored by the dramatic imitation of the creation, often in an annual rite, as, for instance, the Sun Dance. The performance of such rituals often had the character of dancing, and most observers have therefore described American Indian ceremonies as dances. In the enactment of mythical drama, performers assumed the roles of supernatural beings, as in the representation of the *kachina,* cloud and rain spirits, and spirits of the dead in the Pueblo Indian Kachina Dances. In the Pawnee sacrifice to Morning Star, a young captive girl was tied to a frame and shot with arrows; she was supposed to represent Evening Star, a personification of the vegetation whose death promotes the growth of plants. Even today a Navajo patient is cured through a process of ritual identification with the universe and its powers: the patient sits in the middle of a sand painting symbolizing the cosmos and its powers while the practitioner pours colored sand over him.

Historical Survey

Most North American religions express the worldview typical of hunters and gatherers. This is natural, since the first immigrants who arrived perhaps forty to sixty thousands years ago were Paleolithic hunters who came by way of the Bering Strait. At that time the sound between Asia and North America was dry, due to the absorption of oceanic waters into the glaciers of the Great Ice Age. A narrow corridor stretched between the ice fields, allowing the migration of North Asiatic proto-Mongoloid groups into Alaska. The migration probably involved small groups who traveled independently, perhaps at a rate of four miles a year. Since ecological conditions were similar on both sides of the Bering Sea, the migration did not entail any break in historical and cultural traditions.

THE ARCTIC SUBSTRATUM

This origin in northern Asia explains why so much of American Indian religion bears an Arctic or sub-Arctic stamp, and why so many features even in more temperate areas seem to be derived from northern cultures. Of course, particularly in the extreme north, we find native religions that are direct counterparts to the circumpolar religions of northern Eurasia. Both ecological and historical factors account for this uniformity. We may pinpoint such common religious elements as belief in a high god, Thunderbird, and Mother Earth; practices such as the bear ritual, hunting taboos, the sweat bath for ritual cleaning, and shamanic rituals; and a good many myths and tales. All these circumpolar traits represent Arctic or sub-Arctic forms of the ancient Paleolithic hunting culture in Eurasia.

There are some problems in establishing American connections with the Old World circumpolar culture, however. The weaker cultural links in eastern Siberia may be correlated with the influx into this area of Tunguz and Turkic tribes from the south during the last millennia. Perhaps under the influence of Lamaism and other forms of Buddhism, there evolved in Siberia an intense form of shamanism, with emphasis on deep ecstasy and possession by spirits. This specialized form of shamanism, so typical of parts of Siberia, finally spread to North America, where it influenced the Northwest Coast Indians and the Inuit (Eskimo). Other shamanic rituals in North America, such as the so-called Shaking Tent (the tent is shaking when spirits enter at the request of the shaman, who is fettered in the dark), found among Inuit groups, and Algonquian- and Salish-speaking tribes of the Plateau, also have their close counterparts in Siberia. But these other rituals derive from a more general form of shamanism that is also present in South America and Southeast Asia and is certainly a heritage from very ancient times.

The languages of the North American Indians are enormously diverse, and with the exception of the relatively lately arrived Athapascan groups none seem related to known Old World languages. The common factor joining them all is their polysynthetic structure, whereby many sentence elements are included in a single word by compounding and adding prefixes and suffixes. Paul Radin suggested many years ago that there may be a genetic relationship between most of these languages, except those of the Aleut and Inuit, who differ from the mainstream of American aborigines in race, culture, and religion.

DEVELOPMENT OF HUNTING RELIGIONS

The early hunters brought with them a legacy of ideas and rituals developed in the Old World. These were adapted to the changing habitats in the New World. We can follow the major trends in cultural differentiation after about 10,000 BCE, and we can draw some conclusions also about probable religious orientations.

Thus, the Paleo-Indians of eastern North America were big-game hunters, concentrating on animals like the mammoth, the giant bison, the three-toed horse, and the camel. In all likelihood the inherited concepts of animal ceremonialism and the master of the animals were applied to these animals. The big game died out, because of climatic changes or human overkilling, during the period from 8000 to 4000 BCE. Only one big animal—the bear—survived and continued to be the focus of special rites. The ritual around the slaying of the bear, distributed from the Saami (Lapps) of Scandinavia to the Ainu of northern Japan, and, in North America, from the Inuit and Athapascans in the north and west to the Delaware in the east and the Pueblo Indians in the south, seem to be a leftover from these Paleolithic and Mesolithic days.

It is difficult to say whether Asian ideas still streamed into North America at this time, but it seems probable. We know that many myths disseminated from Asia are mostly found south of the sub-Arctic area in North America. To this category belongs the myth of the earth diver, a primeval divine hero who fetches mud from the bottom of the sea, thereby creating the ground on which men live. [*See* Cosmogony.] It is important because it includes not only the flood myth, or the myth of the primeval sea, but also the idea of twin creators, one good and one less good or even bad, or one the main creator and the other his assistant (the culture hero). Another important myth that scholars have traced to Asia is the Orpheus myth, but proofs of its dissemination are inconclusive. Several mythic motifs have, however, definitely spread from the Old World, such as the magical flight and the Symplegades (clashing rocks), or the motif of the celestial vault that moves up and down.

The old hunting culture slowly disintegrated into a series of more specialized regional cultures about 7000–5000 BCE, and there are reasons to presume that the religious structures changed accordingly. In fact, it seems that the native hunting, fishing, and gathering cultures and religions that persisted into the historical period began to take form at this time, the changes stimulated to a major extent by ecological and climatic shifts.

An exceptional development took place in the south. In the increasingly arid regions of the Great Basin, the Southwest, and parts of California a so-called desert tradition was established, with heavy dependence on wild plants, seeds, and nuts.

The corresponding religious system survived in late Great Basin religions, and part of it was also preserved in many Californian Indian religions. In the Southwest, the Basket Making culture, while an example of the desert tradition, also served as a link to horticultural development.

There is some evidence that psychotropic or hallucinogenic drugs were used primarily in plant-collecting areas. Within the region covered by the desert tradition jimsonweed, peyote (in northern Mexico), pulque, and, of course, tobacco were all employed.

GROWTH OF AGRICULTURAL RELIGIONS

It seems fairly certain that the cultivation of tobacco spread from Mexico into North America with maize, for maize and tobacco cultivation share the same general distribution within the eastern regions of North America. In the Southwest, however, while maize was cultivated, tobacco was gathered wild.

The introduction of maize, or Indian corn, had basic consequences for aboriginal religions, for it changed the whole outlook on life, the religious pattern, and the character of supernatural powers. There were many incentives for this change: the concentration of the population in more or less settled villages; the preoccupation with sowing, planting, and harvesting; the enhanced position of women (from that of seed collectors to that of seed producers); and the new forms of social organization (matrilineage, or, among the Iroquois, even some sort of matriarchy). Typical of these agricultural religions were concern for crops and fertility, the rise of priestly organizations, the creation of temples and shrines, and the appearance of deities, often of the female sex (or even androgynes), who impersonate the plants or lend fertility. Rituals, in turn, grew more complex, incorporating greater numbers of discrete actions, and sacrifices of a bloody kind (including human sacrifice) became more widespread. Nowhere, however, did agriculture entirely supplant hunting, particularly not in the east, where the rituals for encouraging the growth of maize, beans, and squash are basically the same as the rituals for slain animals. Of course, the death-and-revival pattern is fundamental to both animal and vegetational ceremonialism.

Appearance of Maize Religion in the Southwest. The introduction of maize into North America occurred in two places, the Southwest and the Southeast. From all appearances it was known earlier in the Southwest, where it is recorded from 3000 to 2000 BCE in the wooded highland valleys of New Mexico. Village agriculture was firmly established about the time of the birth of Christ, and was effective after 500 CE.

Some of the religious innovations surrounding the maize complex and accompanying it on its diffusion from Mexico have been revealed through archaeology. The best illustrations are provided by the so-called Hohokam culture in southern Arizona. It was deeply influenced by Mesoamerica from about 500 to 1200 CE, when it suddenly declined, probably as a consequence of the fall of its model, the Toltec empire in Mexico. The most important evidence of the cultural influence from the south is the architectural planning of the towns: irrigation canals, oval ball courts for ritual games, and platform mounds of earth or adobe serving as substructures for temples with hearths and altars.

The Mexican influence on religion can also be seen in the neighboring Anasazi or Pueblo cultures down to our own time. Mesoamerican symbols appear in the bird designs that decorate Hopi pottery. Some of the religious fraternities that meet in the semisubterranean ceremonial chambers probably have Mexican prototypes, for instance, the *kachina* societies that are reminiscent of the cult organizations that surrounded the Mexican rain god Tlaloc.

Appearance of Maize Religion in the Southeast. The maize complex entered the Southeast slightly later than the Southwest, perhaps sometime after 1000 BCE; there is, however, no certain proof of agriculture there until the birth of Christ. It seems that influences from Mesoamerica were responsible for the so-called Burial Mound cultures, 1000 BCE to 700 CE, with their earthworks, including mortuary mounds, and for their ceramic figurines. At least the latest of these cultures, the Hopewell, was acquainted with maize ceremonialism.

A major change took place with the introduction of the so-called Mississippian tradition about 700 CE. Large rectangular and flat-topped mounds of unprecedented size were arranged around rectangular plazas. The mounds served as foundations of temples, whence the name Temple Mound, also used to designate these cultures. Intensive agriculture belonged to this new tradition, which flourished in the lower and middle Mississippi Valley but was particularly anchored in the Southeast. Its last representatives were the historical Natchez Indians of the lower Mississippi, known for their hierarchical class system with a sacred king, called the Great Sun, at its apex, for their sacred center, including temple and burial mounds, and for an elaborate ceremonial complex.

The agricultural religions rarely reached such an advanced stage of development in eastern North America, but they spread from the Southeastern hearth in different directions. Mississippian traits mingled with older Woodland traits in the Iroquois culture in the north and, after 1000 CE, with Plains hunting religions in the river valleys to the west.

A Regional Survey

The religions of the indigenous peoples in North America have developed on the foundations that have just been described. However, factors other than historical have contributed to the differentiation in religious profiles that occurs in every region, and especially in the Pacific Northwest, the Southwest, and the Plains. Such factors include local geographic conditions and the ecological adaptations of individual cultures. Religious differentiation is closely related to cultural diversity, for geographical and ecological factors act first of all on a group's cultural and social structure, and then through these structures on religion.

Roughly speaking, North America can be divided geographically into two main parts, the mountainous regions in the west, or the Rocky Mountains system, and the large plain and woodland country to the east. We find a relatively greater number of tribes and tribelets, often in great isolation from each other, in the mountainous West. The cultural variation there is therefore considerable. The vast eastern country, on the other hand, is populated by widely dispersed, large tribes in close contact with each other. Culturally, it can be seen as one large, relatively uniform area, in which the regional variants are relatively undifferentiated.

As Clark Wissler and others have noted, the geographic regions and the cultural areas correspond closely to each other. Since geographical and ecological factors have influenced religious forms, each region reveals unique features.

ARCTIC

The barren country around the Arctic coasts is sparsely inhabited by the Inuit and, on the Aleutian Islands, their kinsmen the Aleut. Inuit religion carries all marks of a hunting religion, concentrating on beliefs and rituals related to animals and on shamanism. The hunting rituals are rather intricate, in particular in Alaska where they focus on the whale (whale feasts are also found among the Nootka of the Northwest Coast and the Chukchi and Koriak of Siberia). A great role is played by the mistress of the sea animals, called Sedna among the Central Inuit. She figures in shamanic rites: when taboos have been transgressed her hair gets filthy, and in rage she holds back the animals; it is the shaman's task in a séance to descend to her home at the bottom of the sea and clean her hair so that she will free the animals again. [*See* Inuit Religion *and* Sedna.]

SUB-ARCTIC

A vast region of the coniferous forests, lakes, and swamps in interior Alaska and Canada, the sub-Arctic is sparsely inhabited by Athapascan-speaking Indians in its western half and Algonquian-speaking Indians in its eastern half. The Athapascans are latecomers from Siberia, arriving perhaps around 9000 BCE; their linguistic affiliations are with the Sino-Tibetan tongues. The Algonquian tribes conserve religious traits that associate them closely with the circumpolar culture.

The region is inhabited by hunting cultures, with inland game, in particular the caribou and the moose, as food resources. People are organized in loose bands or, since the introduction by Europeans of the hunting of fur-bearing animals, in family groups who have hunting grounds reserved for their exclusive use.

Religion is dominated by hunting ceremonialism and, to a certain extent, by shamanism. Bear ceremonialism is widespread, and hunting taboos are very common. Sweat baths grant their practitioners ritual purity before hunting or important ceremonies. The vision and guardian-spirit quest is fairly common. Shamanism is characterized by shaking tent ceremonies, usually performed for divination, and by scapulimancy (foretelling the future by inspecting the shoulder blades of animals). Athapascan and Algonquian groups show separate development: the former hold girls' puberty rites and fear their dead; the latter are known for a strong high-god belief, a consistent system of masters of the animals (in which each species has its own master), and an intense dread of cannibal monsters, which are called *windigo*.

NORTHEAST WOODLANDS

Formerly covered by mixed coniferous and deciduous trees, the Northeast Woodlands held a large population of Algonquian-, Iroquoian-, and Siouan-speaking tribes. In historical and protohistorical times both agriculture and hunting were practiced, particularly by the Iroquoian groups; the Algonquian tribes were hunters with only limited horticulture. The social systems of these groups were often complicated, with unilineal kinship groups, clan organization, and chieftaincy.

The double economic heritage is to some extent mirrored in the religious pattern. The hunters concentrate on hunting rituals and vision quests, the planters on rituals and beliefs surrounding the crops. The Iroquois, for instance, have a series of calendar rites celebrating the planting, ripening, and harvesting of the "three sisters": maize, squash, and beans. The Midwinter ceremony, formerly a new year ceremony with the kindling of new fire and the sacrifice of a white dog, is the main ritual event. As in many other rituals of agricultural peoples, great attention is paid to the dead, in whose honor feasts are arranged.

SOUTHEAST WOODLANDS

In the southern deciduous forests, with their savannas and swamps, the tribes of Muskogean stock, interspersed with Siouan groups and the Iroquoian-speaking Cherokee, kept up a peripheral high culture, the last vestiges of the prehistoric Mississippian culture. The Southeastern Indians were, at least at the beginning of the historical era, predominantly engaged in agriculture, and their sociopolitical organization was adjusted to this fact. Thus, the Creek had a maternal clan system, with clans subordinated to both phratries and moieties. The latter had ceremonial functions, often carried out in ball games.

Characteristic of Creek religion is the emphasis laid on ceremonialism and priestly functions. The priests, who were instructed in secrecy in the woods, along lines reminiscent of the vision quest, were divided into several classes: one was in charge of the sacred cult objects, another divined hidden things (such as the causes of diseases), and still another cured people from diseases. Even today, a major part of the curing ceremonies is the recitation of sacred formulas.

The main religious ceremony is the maize harvest ceremony, called the Busk. It is also a New Year ritual, in which old fires are extinguished and a new fire is kindled and people ritually cleanse themselves through washing and the drinking of an emetic.

PRAIRIES AND PLAINS

The tall-grass area (with some parkland and river-bottom woodland) between the woodlands in the east and the high Plains in the west is known as the Prairies. The Plains are the short-grass steppe country, too dry for agriculture, that stretches toward the mountains and semideserts in the far West. (In Canada, the Great Plains are sometimes referred to as the Prairies.)

The historical cultures were formed during the seventeenth and eighteenth centuries when the acquisition of horses made the wide-open spaces easily accessible to surrounding tribes and white expansion forced woodland Indians to leave their home country for the dry, treeless areas. Algonquian and Siouan tribes immigrated from the east and northeast, Caddoan tribes from the south. Several groups ceased practicing horticulture (the Crow and Cheyenne) and turned into buffalo hunters, but they kept parts of their old social and political organization. In the west, Shoshonean groups held the ground they had traditionally occupied, and groups of Athapascans—for example, the Apache—forced their way to the southern parts of the region.

Whereas the Prairies could be regarded as a periphery of the Eastern Woodlands, the Plains region offers a late cultural and religious complex of its own. The religion is a mixture of derived agricultural ceremonialism and hunters' belief systems. The major New Year ceremony is the Sun Dance, during which asceticism, dancing, praying, and curing take place. Other forms of ritualism center around tribal and clan bundles, and the sacred ritual known as the Calumet Dance, or Pipe Dance. There is much cosmological speculation and an advanced concept of the godhead. The vision and guardian spirit complex is well developed. The Plains religious pattern has become among modern Indians the model for a pan-Indian religion, transcending old tribal and cultural boundaries.

NORTHWEST COAST

The broken coastline, high mountains, and deep fjords of the Northwest Coast were the home of the Tlingit, Haida, Tsimshian, and Wakashan tribes and some Coast Salish and Chinookan groups in the south. With their totem poles, their plank houses and canoes, and their headgear reminiscent of East Asian conic hats, these Indians make an un-American impression, an impression that is strengthened by their social organization with its give-away feasts (potlatches) intended to "shame" invited guests and thus increase the host's prestige. There have apparently been contacts with both northern and eastern Asian cultures, although the nature of this exchange is little understood. The basic substratum seems to be a fishing culture that developed on both sides of the North Pacific and gave rise to both Inuit and Northwest Coast cultures. The abundant animal and fish life along the coast, together with the rich herbal and animal life of the dense woods, provided a living standard that sometimes excelled that of the agriculturists. It is perhaps not surprising that rank differentiation, based partly on wealth, and slavery appeared here.

The religion is characterized partly by its association with the activities of hunters and fishermen, partly by its secret societies adapted to the complicated social structure. The animal ceremonialism is focused on the sea fauna, and there are many sea spirits in animal forms. The dead have their realm, or one of their realms, at the bottom of the sea. The secret societies recruited individuals who had an inherited right to make contact with a certain kind of guardian spirit. Famous societies are the Wolf society of the Nootka and the Cannibal society of the Kwakiutl. Possession by spirits also occurred in shamanism, which here reached a high point of development in America.

PLATEAU

The Intermountain area, which includes both the Columbia and the Fraser river drainages, is known as the Plateau; it was inhabited by Salish and Shahaptin tribes that lived on fish and, secondarily, on land animals and roots. The area is partly wooded, partly a bunchgrass steppe. The culture area is an offshoot of the sub-Arctic hunting culture, tempered by influences from the Northwest Coast and the Plains. The sociopolitical group consisted of the village, under the formal control of a hereditary chief.

In their religion the Plateau Indians stressed the visionary complex and food ceremonies. The vision quests were undertaken at puberty by both sexes. The relation between the guardian spirit and his client was displayed in the Winter Dance, or Spirit Dance, a ceremony, under the supervision of a medicine man, in which the spirit was impersonated. Important celebrations were firstling rites, first-fruits rites, and the First-Salmon rite. In this last rite, which was guided by a so-called salmon chief (who had the salmon as one of his guardian spirits), the first salmon was greeted and its "leader" hailed with special ceremonies.

GREAT BASIN

A dry region of sands and semideserts, the Great Basin was inhabited by Shoshonean (Numic) groups, some of them, like the Gosiute, the most impoverished of North American groups. Seeds, nuts, and rodents provided the principal food. The social organization was often atomistic. The cultural profile represented a remnant of the old desert tradition.

The religious pattern was closely adapted to a life-style based on the bare necessities. Hunters had to be blessed by spirits in visions in order to be successful, but there was little elaboration of guardian-spirit beliefs. Medicine men had specialized powers; for instance, the antelope medicine man attracted the antelopes by singing. Harvest ceremonies were round dances at which thanks were given to the supreme being.

CALIFORNIA

Whereas the northern, eastern, and southern parts of California were peripheral to the Northwest Coast, Great Basin, and Southwest cultural areas, respectively, the central valleys and coastland constituted a separate cultural area, known as the California region, densely populated by Penutian, Hokan, and Numic groups. These natives, living in a mild climate, dedicated themselves to collecting, hunting, and fishing. Their staple food consisted of wild plants and their fruits, in particular acorns, all of which were found in abundance. The political unit was usually the village (under the leadership of a headman), but was sometimes a lineage.

In this diversified culture area religious expressions were most varied. North-central California is known for its lofty concept of a supreme being and for its initiation of youths into religious societies, such as the Kuksu, Ghost, and Hesi societies. Guardian spirit quests were rare, and medicine men received unsought visions. In the southern part of the area, initiation ceremonies were accompanied by the drinking of drugs prepared from jimsonweed and by various symbolic acts referring to death and rebirth. In some places there were great commemorative ceremonies for the dead.

THE SOUTHWEST

A magnificent desert country with some oases, particularly along the Rio Grande, the Southwest was populated by hunting and farming groups of Piman and Yuman descent, by former hunters like the Athapascan Apache and Navajo—who did not arrive here until about 1500 CE—and by the Pueblo peoples, intensive agriculturists mostly belonging to the Tanoan and Keresan linguistic families. I shall here concentrate on the Pueblo groups, the descendants of the prehistoric Anasazi culture. Their culture is famous for its big community houses on the mesas, its intensive horticulture (with irrigation in the Rio Grande region), and its complex and beautiful ceremonialism. Each Pueblo town is an independent unit governed by the heads of the religious societies.

Religion penetrates all aspects of Pueblo life. A rich set of ceremonies that mark the divisions of the year are conducted by different religious societies. Their overall aim is to create harmony with the powers of rain and fertility, symbolized by the ancestors, the rain and cloud spirits, and the Sun. Each society has its priesthood, its attendants, its sacred bundles, and its ceremonial cycle. There are also medicine societies for the curing of diseases—the inspired, visionary medicine man has no place in this collectivistic, priestly culture.

No other American Indian societies lay so much stress on ceremonialism as do the Pueblo. Their supernatural beings are almost unthinkable without the rituals through which they are manifested.

BIBLIOGRAPHY

For discussion of sources and research the reader is referred to my work *The Study of American Indian Religions* (Chico, Calif., 1983) and Harold W. Turner's *North America,* vol. 2 of his *Bibliography of New Religious Movements in Primal Societies* (Boston, 1978).

On the topic of North American Indian religions, several surveys and introductions are available. In chronological order there is first Werner Müller's "Die Religionen der Indianervölker Nordamerikas," in *Die Religionen des alten Amerika,* edited by Walter Krickeberg (Stuttgart, 1961), a thoughtful presentation of native religious structures. Ruth M. Underhill's *Red Man's Religion* (Chicago, 1965) describes religious beliefs and practices in their cultural interaction. Two later syntheses are my *The Religions of the American Indians* (Berkeley, 1979), which concentrates on religious ideas in historical perspectives, and Sam D. Gill's *Native American Religions* (Belmont, Calif., 1982), which emphasizes some major features of Indian religious life. A detailed, provocative investigation of the religions east of the Rocky Mountains will be found in Werner Müller's *Die Religionen der Waldlandindianer Nordamerikas* (Berlin, 1956).

A number of scholars in the field have issued collections of their articles on North American native religions. Here could be mentioned Müller's *Neue Sonne—Neues Licht,* edited by Rolf Gehlen and Bernd Wolf (Berlin, 1981), a representative selection of this author's most engaging articles; my *Belief and Worship in Native North America* (Syracuse, N.Y., 1981), which among other things discusses belief patterns, ecology, and religious change; and Joseph Epes Brown's *The Spiritual Legacy of the American Indian* (New York, 1982), a book that beautifully outlines the deeper meaning of Indian philosophy and ceremonialism. An older publication in the same genre is the philosopher Hartley Burr Alexander's posthumous work, *The World's Rim: Great Mysteries of the North American Indians* (Lincoln, Nebr., 1953). Anthologies by several authors are *Seeing with a Native Eye,* edited by Walter Holden Capps (New York, 1976), and *Teachings from the American Earth,* edited by Dennis Tedlock and Barbara Tedlock (New York, 1975). The former contains articles by scholars of religion; the latter, articles by anthropologists.

Among general comparative works, a classic in the field is Ruth Fulton Benedict's *The Concept of the Guardian Spirit in North America* (Menasha, Wis., 1923). Shamanism in North America is the object of a study by Marcelle Bouteiller, *Chamanisme et guérison magique* (Paris, 1950). The patterns of soul and spirit beliefs are analyzed in my work *Conceptions of the Soul among North American Indians* (Stockholm, 1953). The corpus of American Indian myths and legends is carefully annotated in *Tales of the North American Indians,* edited by Stith Thompson (Cambridge, Mass., 1929). My study *The North American Indian Orpheus Tradition* (Stockholm, 1957) is an extensive treatment of the Orpheus myth and its religious prerequisites. One mythological character, the culture hero and trickster, is the subject of Arie van Deursen's detailed research work *Der Heilbringer* (Groningen, 1931). Secret societies and men's societies are penetratingly discussed in Wolfgang Lindig's *Geheimbünde und Männerbünde der Prärie- und der Waldlandindianer Nordamerikas* (Wiesbaden, 1970). Among comparative works on rituals and ritualism three interesting studies are Ruth Underhill's well-known *Ceremonial Patterns in the Greater Southwest* (New York, 1948), John Witthoft's illuminating *Green Corn Ceremonialism in the Eastern Woodlands* (Ann Arbor, 1949), and William N. Fenton's detailed ethnohistorical study *The Iroquois Eagle Dance: An Offshoot of the Calumet Dance* (Washington, D.C., 1953).

An Indian's own view of native American religions in their relations to Christianity and to whites is presented, somewhat polemically, in Vine Deloria, Jr.'s *God Is Red* (New York, 1973).

2

THE PLAINS

William K. Powers

Plains Indian religion is as varied and complex as the various peoples who inhabit the Plains region, an area delineated by the Rocky Mountains on the west; the Canadian provinces of Alberta, Saskatchewan, and Manitoba on the north; the Mississippi River on the east; and the Gulf of Mexico on the south. The Great Plains measure 1,125,000 square miles, an area roughly equal to one-third the land mass of the United States, and serve as the home for more than thirty American Indian ethnic groups, conventionally known as bands, tribes, nations, and confederacies. The Plains present linguistic as well as ethnic complexity; seven distinct language families are found. In historical times, these language groups have been identified in the following way:

1. *Algonquian,* represented by the Northern Arapaho of Wyoming and the Southern Arapaho of Oklahoma; the Atsina, or Gros Ventre of the Prairies; the Blackfeet Confederacy comprising the Siksika, the Kainah (or Blood), and the Piegan; the Northern Cheyenne of Montana and the Southern Cheyenne of Oklahoma; the Plains Cree; and the Plains Ojibwa (also known as Chippewa, or Bungi).
2. *Athapascan,* represented by the Lipan Apache and the Kiowa Apache of Oklahoma, and the Sarsi of Alberta. The Sarsi are counted with the Blackfeet Confederacy despite the difference in languages.
3. *Caddoan,* represented by the Arikara, or Ree; the Caddo; the Kichai; the Pawnee; and the Wichita. These tribes ranged from Texas to North Dakota but now reside in North Dakota (Arikara) and Oklahoma (all others).
4. *Kiowa-Tanoan,* represented on the Plains by only one tribe, the Kiowa, who now live in Oklahoma.
5. *Siouan,* by far the largest on the Plains, represented by the Assiniboin, also known in Canada as the Stoney; the Crow, or Absoroka, of Montana; a subdivision of the Siouan family known as Deghiha, comprising the Kansa (or Kaw), the Omaha, the Osage, the Ponca, and the Quapaw, all of whom live in Oklahoma; the Hidatsa, or Gros Ventre of the River; the Iowa, Oto, and Missouri, who form a linguistic subdivision called Chiwere and who reside in Oklahoma; the Mandan, who share a reservation with the Arikara and Hidatsa in North Dakota; the Dakota, or Santee; the Lakota, or Teton; and the Nakota, or Yankton. The Mandan, the

19

Arikara, and the Hidatsa are currently referred to as the Three Affiliated Tribes. The Dakota, the Lakota, and the Nakota are conventionally designated as the "Sioux," a term that, despite its pejorative origin, continues to be employed by scholars as the only one available under which to group these three closely related tribes and their numerous subdivisions. [*For further discussion, see* Lakota Religion.]

6. *Tonkawan,* represented exclusively by the Tonkawa of Oklahoma.
7. *Uto-Aztecan,* represented by one tribe, the Comanche of Oklahoma.

Although archaeologists conclude that the Plains area has been inhabited by humans continuously for the past twelve thousand years, Plains Indian culture is a historical phenomenon coalescing after the introduction and diffusion of the horse in the seventeenth century, which led to the development of nomadic, equestrian bands whose economy was based on buffalo hunting, though some groups conserved aspects of an older horticultural way of life. Sedentary villages continued to flourish among the Mandan, Hidatsa, and Arikara on the northern high Plains, and among the Pawnee and Deghiha speakers on the southern Plains. These people lived part of the year in earth lodges and tilled the soil near their homes. The more nomadic tribes lived most of the year in tipis, and transportation was by horse and dog travois over land and by round-shaped bullboats over water.

There was extensive trade among Plains tribes, facilitated by an invention unique to the Plains, sign language, which permitted traders speaking diverse languages to communicate for the purpose of exchange. Although cultural similarities existed between tribes during the historical period, individual ethnic groups displayed an unusual amount of cultural variation. There was, however, a progressive homogenization, partly a response to European contact and resultant disease, warfare, and, ultimately, conquest. Although population figures are difficult to ascertain, there are currently 225,000 Indians on the Plains, and most authorities believe that, following a dangerous population decline at the turn of the twentieth century, the present-day Indian population equals or surpasses precontact figures.

The Plains culture essentially comprises a potpourri of religious ideas from other parts of the United States and Canada, and it is useful to see the Plains as a point of synthesis of various customs, beliefs, and rituals that amalgamate as a result of emigration and, ultimately, diffusion. Nearly all the basic religious ideas found in other parts of native North America are found on the Plains. If the focus is on the historical period, these basic religious ideas can be seen to fall into three major categories.

The first category may be regarded as tribal religion, idiosyncratic beliefs and rituals that are perceived by their adepts to be unique to their own tribe. In practice, idiosyncratic rituals may in fact have diffused, unbeknownst to the adepts, to other tribes, as in the case of the Pawnee Hako and the Lakota Hunka, which are ritual variants that are believed by each tribe to be unique to itself.

The second category is made up of pantribal religion, beliefs and rituals acknowledged to have been diffused usually from a known single source. Frequently there is a conscious effort made to learn a new religion from a foreign ethnic group. Examples of pantribal religion are the hallmark of Plains religion and include the Sun Dance, the Ghost Dance, and the Native American Church (in order of historical occurrence), although not all of these religions are limited to the Plains area.

A third category falls somewhere between the first two and consists mainly of two ubiquitous religious institutions, the vision quest and the Sweat Lodge ceremony, as well as a number of other beliefs and practices that, although present in all Plains tribes, are still considered by their followers to be unique to each.

VISION QUEST AND SWEAT LODGE

The ideas behind the vision quest and the Sweat Lodge ceremony and their associated ritual paraphernalia are essentially the same among all Plains tribes, but there is some variation found even within any single tribe. During the vision quest, a person, usually a male, embarks upon an ordeal in which he will isolate himself from the remainder of the tribe. Under the direction of a medicine man, he is led to a hill or other secluded spot, where he stays for an agreed-upon number of days and fasts until he receives a vision that will later be interpreted for him by the medicine man. The vision usually takes the form of a communication between the supplicant and an animal, bird, or inanimate object such as a stone. The supplicant may also envision a ghost, but in all cases, he will receive instructions that will affect his future. He may also be instructed to obtain the skin of an animal or bird or another object that will serve as a personal fetish or good-luck charm. He may learn a song, acquire a name, or even receive a calling to become a medicine man.

Guardians or tutelary spirits sometimes are acquired in the vision quest, at other times obtained in a ritual from a shaman. Guardian spirits may be represented by animals, birds, inanimate objects, or the ghosts of humans. Frequently, the guardian spirit is manifested in the form of a bundle, fetish, or other object that an individual wears or carries during ordeals or dangerous encounters, such as those met on the warpath. Along with the object, a quester may acquire special prayers or songs learned in the vision and may employ these incantations in times of need.

In the Sweat Lodge ceremony, a small number of (usually) males join together with a medicine man in a small dome-shaped lodge constructed of saplings and covered with hides and blankets to make it airtight and dark. In the center of the lodge a hole is dug and stones heated outside are handed in by means of ladles by the fire tender and placed into the center hole. The hides are secured firmly over the lodge and the medicine man sprinkles water over the heated stones, causing a great rush of hot air to fill the lodge. The participants perspire profusely and slap their bodies with switches made from pine boughs or with buffalo tails in order to increase their blood circulation. At the same time they sing and pray together, asking for special favors from the spirits who come into the lodge, and also praying for the general welfare of the people. During the course of the ceremony, the lodge is opened occasionally so that the adepts may breathe fresh air, and at that time the ceremonial pipe is smoked.

Frequently, the Sweat Lodge ceremony is conducted as a prefatory ritual before going on the warpath or before undertaking the vision quest or some other religious ceremony. The Sweat Lodge is regarded as a means of purifying individuals both physically and spiritually.

RITUAL PRACTITIONERS

The most important figure in Plains religion is the ritual leader, who is known by a variety of names depending on his or her specialization. Normally, a shaman cures people of symbolic illness by ritual means, such as singing, dancing, or praying, while a medicine man or woman is a specialist in herbal curing. In most cases both types of ritual leaders employ the knowledge of the other, and frequently the medicine man or woman relies on supernatural aid in the selection of the proper herb, just as the shaman occasionally uses herbal teas and other concoctions in the course of a shamanic ceremony. Although *shaman* is a preferred term among scholars who study ritual behavior that is highly individualistic and informal, most Plains Indians refer, in English, to both ritual curers and herbalists as "medicine men." In the native languages, however, discrete terms are used.

Each ritual practitioner is well known in a tribal community and achieves high status by performing cures for his patients and by conducting the important ceremonies. He is often a conjurer or magician capable of amazing his adepts with his mystical abilities. With a modicum of skill in sleight of hand he can give the appearance of sucking a foreign object out of his patient's body through a bone tube, later spitting out for all to see a bird or rock or other substance that allegedly caused the illness or the pain. The ritual practitioner is usually well paid for his services, previously in horses, buffalo robes, or blankets, now in food and money, although most shamans admit that payment is not required. Part of the popularity of the ritual practitioner is predicated on his success rate with patients and the particular way he conducts the important public ceremonies. Frequently the greatest difference in technique between shamans is stylistic: there are many variants of public and private ceremonies since they are conducted and performed according to instructions received in visions by individual shamans. In many cases, the popular shaman is simply the one who can put on the most interesting performance, but showmanship is not seen as a detraction from the sincerity of the performances.

In former times the shaman was also called upon for consultation in matters of war, hunting, moving camp, finding buffalo, naming children, conducting the great public ceremonies, and analyzing visions. In formal ceremonies such as the Sun Dance, the shaman continues to serve as an intermediary between the common people and the supernaturals who control the universe. Some may serve as directors of the Sun Dance because of their exclusive knowledge of the cosmological mysteries. Often this knowledge is discussed among medicine men in a special argot, a sacred language believed to be understood only by the supernaturals and other medicine men. Because of their supernatural abilities shamans are often feared by the common people and in some instances by other shamans who believe that some ritual practitioners are capable of performing magic and witchcraft.

Although witchcraft and sorcery are not common on the Plains, several tribes have such beliefs. The Plains Cree and Plains Ojibwa brought from their Great Lakes homeland a number of ceremonies, and although they quickly learned the Sun Dance from the Assiniboin, they continued to bury their dead in the ground and conduct an annual Feast of the Dead. They were particularly frightened of witchcraft and sorcery and had one ceremony, probably related to the ceremonies of the Midewiwin, or Great Medicine society, in the Great Lakes, in which a shaman was bound hand and foot and placed in a lone tipi. It was believed that spirits entered thetipi, untied the shaman, and taught him how to cure the sick and find lost articles. Sometimes to the amazement of the devotees, the tent began to shake while the shaman was being untied and frequently he was found in a ridiculous position, sometimes wedged in between the tipi poles. For this reason, this particular ceremony (called a "shamanic cult institution" in the anthropological literature) is referred to as the Shaking Tent rite. Modified forms of this ceremony are still popular on the northern Plains among the Arapaho, Cheyenne, Lakota, and others. The Lakota call the ritual Yuwipi, a term referring to the act of rolling up into a ball the rope with which the shaman is tied.

THE SUPERNATURAL

The notions of sacredness and taboo are common to Plains religion. Both designate states, desirable or not, that may be changed through the mediation of prayer, song, dance, or general propitiation of the proper spirits. The idea of the holy is most often expressed by native terms such as the Lakota *wakan;* the Algonquian variants of *manitu;* the Ponca *xube;* and Comanche *puha.* All animate and inanimate objects are capable of serving as a receptacle for this sacred state. The rituals employed to transform persons or objects from a profane state to a sacred one have frequently but erroneously been called in English "medicine," or "making medicine." Frequently the source of a medicine man's personal power is kept in a "medicine bundle." *Medicine* is here a misnomer for *sacred power.*

All Plains people distinguish in their respective languages between power and sacredness. *Great Mystery* and *Great Spirit* are also English terms associated with the Plains belief in a creator god or prime mover, a belief that led to the Christian interpretation that Plains Indians believed in a monotheistic god prior to European contact. There is no empirical evidence for this, however, and today the term *supreme being* usually designates the total of all supernatural beings and powers in the tribal universe. Thus the Lakota word *wakantanka,* most often translated as "Great Mystery" or "Great Spirit," more accurately means "most sacred" and symbolizes sixteen separate entities in the Lakota belief system.

Most often the symbols used to designate the important gods of the tribal pantheons are analogized or personified by references to astral phenomena, and the chief god of many tribal religions is addressed as "the Sun," while the terrestrial counterpart is always "Mother Earth," but there is no evidence to support the idea that these references are anything but metaphorical.

The Plains culture hero or trickster who figures importantly as the mediator between the supernaturals and humankind goes by a number of names—Inktomi ("spider") among the Lakota; Great White Hare among the Algonquian speakers; and Old Man or Coyote among the Crow. In the creation myths this being teaches humans about culture after the establishment of the earth. He also plays another important role in the mythology of the Plains people: he is the principal character in a cycle of morality stories in which positive values of the Indian people are taught through negative examples, that is, the hero always makes mistakes and demonstrates poor judgment. Children are told not to behave as the trickster.

Taboos associated with sexual intercourse, menstruation, and food are as prominent on the Plains as they are elsewhere in American Indian culture, although recent evidence shows that menstrual taboos are positive, in their reinforcement of the female biological role, as well as negative, in their reinforcement of the male fear of "pollution."

THE HEREAFTER

A belief that each person had more than a single "soul"—one that inheres in the living until death, another that corresponds to the common notion of ghost—was common among the Plains tribes.

The hereafter was described as a hazy duplicate of the living world. There people dwelled in tipi camps, hunted buffalo, sang, feasted, danced, and were reunited with their kin. Enemies also abounded, and one had to beware of vengeance from the spirit of a slain enemy. It is alleged that the practice of scalping prevented the enemy spirit from going to the spirit camp after death.

The Milky Way figures prominently as the route over which the souls of the departed travel toward their final destination, the myriad of stars representing the campfires of the deceased. At a fork in the celestial road, judgment is pronounced over the soul, usually by a woman who instructs some of the souls to continue to the hereafter, while others are remanded back to earth to live as ghosts.

The most common forms of burial on the Plains were scaffold and tree burials. The deceased was dressed in fine clothing and wrapped in a buffalo hide. Then the body was placed in the scaffold or tree and secured tightly; it remained there until it decomposed. Most Indians were generally fearful that the spirit of the deceased haunted the place of its burial, so burial grounds were usually avoided. At the time of the burial, however, close relatives of the deceased would come and linger near the corpse. They prepared foods for the spirit's journey to the hereafter and placed new hunting and fighting implements near the scaffold. Frequently a favorite horse was killed and placed at the foot of the scaffold so that the spirit of the deceased could ride that of the horse in the other world.

Mourners might stay near a close relative's body for several days. To show their grief women would often cut their hair short, gash their arms and legs, and blacken their faces. It was also customary for the relatives of the deceased to give away all their belongings to the needy.

The Lakota mourned their dead for one year. They had a special ceremony called Ghost Keeping in which a close relative would keep a lock of hair of the deceased in a special bundle for one year. Each day the ghost was ritually fed by the keeper, and at the end of the year elaborate ceremonies were held on its behalf. At this time all the people in the camp assembled to watch the ghost being fed for the last time, and the soul of the deceased was finally freed.

It was also commonly believed that when a person died, its ghost would attempt to entice a close relative to join it in death. These ghosts heralded their presence in numerous ways and some believed that if they heard a baby crying outside in the night or a wolf howl or a rooster crow, it was some boundless spirit calling someone to die. When this occurred members of the family would fire guns to frighten away the spirit. Shamans would burn incense with an aroma that was displeasing to these angry ghosts. Belief in ghosts was common, and it was accepted that ghosts were capable of advising humans about the welfare of the tribe. Shamans were believed to commune with ghosts at night. The shamans freely asked the advice of ghosts about how to cure people, and the ghosts predicted certain events in the lives of the living. Ghosts were also capable of finding lost or stolen articles and in some cases were capable of taking another life.

MAJOR SYMBOLS

Perhaps there is no more universal a symbol of Plains Indian religion than the long-stemmed pipe, sometimes called the "peace pipe." The pipe is essentially a medium of prayer, and when people pray with the pipe it is believed that the smoke rising from the pipe will carry the message of the supplicants to the spirits above. Pipe smoking is a necessary prelude to every important religious ceremony. In the past a pipe was also frequently smoked when deliberations had to be made over hunting or warfare. Normally, each man owned his own pipe and carried it in an elaborate bag or bundle.

The prized pipe is one made with a bowl fashioned from catlinite, a red stone that is found in Pipestone, Minnesota, and that is distributed widely throughout the Plains through trade. The bowl is made separately from the pipe stem, which is wood, or in some cases pipestone. It is considered unlucky by some tribes to store the pipe with the bowl attached to the stem, and consequently the two parts are disjoined when not in use. Because the pipe is powerful in communicating with the supernaturals, it is treated with a great deal of respect by everyone. Children are not allowed to touch the pipe or even approach it for fear that they will abuse it. Showing disrespect to the pipe by stepping over it or dropping it might cause a great disaster or even death to someone in the offender's family.

Several types of Indian tobacco are smoked in the pipe, and it too is considered to have certain sacred powers. It is often wrapped in pouches and hung in trees as offerings to the supernaturals. Prior to the Indians' confinement to the reservation, there were various types of commercial tobacco traded between traders and Indians, as well as indigenous types cultivated by tribes such as the Crow.

Among the Crow, tobacco was considered to be so important to the general welfare of the tribe that they instituted a Tobacco society whose members were given the task of overseeing the planting and harvesting of the crops. Both men and women belonged. The society had its own songs, dances, and ceremonies, most of which were of a secret nature. To the Crow, tobacco was synonymous with medicine, and they believed that it was bestowed upon their tribe by supernatural forces. [*See also* Tobacco.]

The eagle was regarded by most tribes as the chief of all birds because of its perceived ability to fly higher than any other bird. It was believed that the bird was the paramount messenger of the Great Spirit, and thus its feathers were highly prized for ceremonial purposes and to indicate prestige, as in the famous Plains headdress, the warbonnet.

The Hidatsa are the best known of the Plains tribes for their ability to trap eagles. Eagle trapping was regarded as both a sacred and a dangerous event. Late in the fall the eagle trappers would build a camp a mile or so from the village. High atop hills each trapper dug a pit about three feet deep that he covered with grass and twigs to form a blind. Using a rabbit or small fox for bait, the man climbed into the pit and waited for an eagle to soar overhead and spot the bait. When the eagle landed on top of the pit, the man thrust his handsupward and grabbed the eagle by its legs, pulling it down into the pit, and strangling it. After the feathers were secured there was sometimes a ceremony in which the eagle's body was buried and offerings made to its spirit.

CREATION MYTHS

The sedentary tribes that lived in permanent villages devoted much time to elaborate rituals and accompanying belief systems. The Pawnee seemed to have been great religious innovators, having established one of the most comprehensive philosophies of all the Plains Indians.

The Pawnee elaborated a series of myths that described the creation of the world, the origin of humans, and the power of the gods. The Pawnee believed that Tirawa, the supreme being, was married to the Vault of Heaven, and both reigned somewhere in the heavens in a place beyond the clouds. Yet they were purely spiritual beings and took no earthly shape. Tirawa sent his commands to humans through a number of lesser gods and messengers who manifested themselves to the Pawnee.

Next in importance to Tirawa and his wife was Tcuperika ("evening star"), who was personified as a young maiden. Evening Star was keeper of a garden in the west that was the source of all food. She had four assistants, Wind, Cloud, Lightning, and Thunder. She married Oprikata ("morning star"), and from them was born the first human being on earth. Morning Star was perceived as a strong warrior who drove the rest of the stars before him. In some Pawnee ceremonies, the sacrifice of a young captive girl was offered to him, suggesting some relationship between Pawnee religion and the religions of central Mexico where human sacrifice was also known.

Of lesser status were the gods of the four directions, the northeast, southeast, southwest, and northwest, and next in rank to the four directions were the three gods of the north: North Star, chief of all the stars; North Wind, who gave the buffalo to humans; and Hikus ("breath"), who gave life itself to the people. Next in line came Sun and Moon, who were married and produced an offspring, the second person on earth, whose marriage to the offspring of Morning Star and Evening Star gave rise to the first humans.

There were lesser gods who also figured in Pawnee mythology. Star of the South, for example, stood at the southern end of the Milky Way, which comprised the campfires of the departed, and received the spirits of the dead. It is also believed that another star called Skiritiuhuts ("fool wolf") became offended at one of the councils of the star people and in revenge introduced death to mankind.

MAJOR CORPORATE RITUALS

Not only were the philosophy and mythology of the Pawnee rich, but their ceremonies were many and varied. There were ceremonies to Thunder, to Morning Star and Evening Star, for the planting and harvesting of Mother Corn, as well as lesser ceremonies for the general welfare of the people.

The Hako. One of the best documented rituals of the Plains, the Hako was performed so that the tribe might increase and be strong, and so that the people would enjoy long life, happiness, and peace. The ceremony was conducted by a man called the *kurahus* ("man of years") who was venerated for his knowledge and experience. To him was entrusted the supervision of the songs and prayers, which had to be performed precisely in the same order each time. The Hako was usually performed in the spring when birds were nesting, or in the fall when they were flocking because it was believed that when prayers were offered for life, strength, and growth of the people it must be done when all life was stirring.

Those taking part in the ceremony were divided into two groups, the fathers who sponsored the ceremony and the children who received the intentions, prayers, and gifts from the fathers. The head of the fathers' group, called Father, was responsible for employing the *kurahus*. The head of the children's group, called Son, also played an important part in the ceremony, acting on behalf of the other children.

The most important paraphernalia used in the Hako were the sacred feathered wands resembling pipe stems without the bowls attached. The ceremony took three days and three nights during which time twenty-seven rituals were performed, each ritual and song unveiling Pawnee sacred lore. At the end of the ceremony, the wands were waved over the children, thus sealing the bond between fathers and children. At the end of theceremony most of the ritual paraphernalia was discarded except for the feathered wands, which were given to one of the children for his keeping. At a later date the children might take the part of the fathers and offer the prayers to another group of children, thus perpetuating the ceremony and the continued solidarity of the Pawnee. It was also believed that the children could take the wands to other tribes as an offering of peace. This latter custom undoubtedly led to the diffusion of the Hako to the Lakota, who at one time were at war with the Pawnee.

The Sun Dance. The most characteristic religious ceremony of the Plains was the well-known Sun Dance, usually performed in the early summer in conjunction with the annual communal buffalo hunt. It owes its name to the fact that certain men who had taken vows to participate danced for several days gazing at the sun, or more precisely, in the direction of the sun. It is useful to note that the Sun Dance was held also in cloudy and even rainy weather, and there is some speculation that the progenitor of the dance may actually have been performed at night during the time of a full moon. There is some linguistic evidence to support this idea. For example, in Lakota there is no distinction between sun and moon; both are called *wi,* the only distinction being made by a qualifier: day *wi* and night *wi.* Thus "to gaze at the sun" is not linguistically differentiated from "to gaze at the moon," although conventionally the current translation signifies the sun.

There is some agreement that the oldest form of the Sun Dance originated among the Mandan. Unlike the sun dances of other tribes, the Mandan Sun Dance, called Okipa, was held indoors in the tribe's medicine lodge. The ceremony lasted for four days, during which time the dancers were actually suspended by skewers through their chest from the lodge rafters and the bodies spun around by helpers below. The dance was usually done in advance of warriors going out on a war party.

In other tribes, dancers had skewers of wood placed through the fleshy part of their chest; the skewers were attached to rawhide thong ropes that were tied to a center pole. The dancers pulled backward as they bobbed in time with drum beats until they tore the flesh, thus releasing themselves from the thongs. The Lakota philosophized that the only thing that one could offer to the Great Spirit was one's own body since it was the only thing that a human being really owned. The Sun Dance was one form of making such an offering, the skewering of the dancer also being equated with being in a state of ignorance, and the breaking free as symbolic of attaining knowledge.

The Blackfeet form of the Sun Dance was unlike that of other tribes inasmuch as it centered around a woman known for her industry who vowed to lead the dancers and who bore the title "medicine woman." While she did not go through tortures like her male counterparts in other tribes, she did participate in a number of elaborate ceremonies that preceded the actual dance. Two important ceremonies over which she presided were the Buffalo Tongues and the Sweat Lodge ceremonies. Before the Sun Dance, people in the camp were asked to bring buffalo tongues to a certain lodge erected for that purpose. In the lodge the tongues were ceremoniously skinned, cleaned, and boiled and then distributed to the remainder of the people in camp. Later a special sweat lodge was constructed from one hundred willow saplings, which were placed in the ground and tied together at the tops like those of an ordinary sweat lodge. The dancers then fasted and joined in the Sweat Lodge ceremony before dancing.

Because of the self-mortification practiced by some of the tribes, and a general belief that native religious practice was primitive, the United States government banned the Sun Dance during the 1880s. It was never renewed on the southern Plains; however, on the northern Plains the Sun Dance went underground, emerging publicly again in 1934. By 1959 the Lakota and Plains Ojibwa had again incorporated self-mortification, which continues today. [*For further discussion, see* Sun Dance.]

Sacred Arrow Renewal. In addition to the Sun Dance there were other public ceremonies that Plains tribes participated in. One of the most important for the Cheyenne was the Sacred Arrow Renewal.

The Cheyenne believe that long ago their supreme being, Maiyun, gave four sacred arrows to the mythological hero Sweet Medicine in a cave in what are now called the Black Hills of South Dakota. Maiyun taught Sweet Medicine that two of the arrows had supernatural powers over the buffalo and the other two over human beings. Maiyun instructed the young man in the proper care of the arrows and the sacred ceremonies associated with them and charged Sweet Medicine with the responsibility of teaching the Cheyenne about their mysterious powers.

Sweet Medicine taught the Cheyenne that if the two arrows associated with hunting were simply pointed at the buffalo herds, they would be easy to kill. He also taught that if the other two arrows were pointed at enemies before battle it would cause them to be blinded, confused, and vulnerable to defeat by the Cheyenne warriors.

The Cheyenne say that from the time Sweet Medicine taught them about the ritual of the sacred arrows, the arrows have been kept in a fox-skin bundle, which has been handed down from one generation to another and guarded by a person known as the sacred-arrow keeper. In alternate years an individual pledges to sponsor aSacred Arrow Renewal ceremony and the arrows are unwrapped and displayed to all the male members of the tribe. The man making the pledge does so in order to fulfill a vow, such as is the case with the Sun Dance. The vow was originally made when a warrior was threatened during a fight, or someone became sick and was fearful of dying. Although only one person makes the pledge, the ceremony is given on behalf of all Cheyenne, so that they will be ensured of a long and prosperous life.

The Sacred Arrow Renewal ceremony traditionally took four days to perform. A special lodge was prepared on the first day. Warriors held in high esteem were selected to choose the site on which the lodge was to be erected. New poles were cut and the lodge covering borrowed from families of good reputation. Inside the lodge the priests of the tribe sat on beds of sage. As part of the preparation each Cheyenne family gave a special counting stick to the conductor of the ceremony. Symbolically, the sticks represented each member of the tribe.

On the second day the sacred arrows were obtained from the keeper and the bundle was opened and examined. If the flight feathers of the arrows were in any way damaged, a man known for his bravery was chosen to replace the feathers. On the third day the arrows were renewed and each of the counting sticks was passed over incense to bless all the families in the tribe. On the last day the arrows were exhibited to the male members of the tribe. The Cheyenne said that it was difficult to look directly at the arrows because they gave off a blinding light. To conclude the ceremony, the priests made predictions about the future of the Cheyenne people. With the conclusion of a Sweat Lodge ceremony the Sacred Arrow Renewal ceremony was officially over, and the Cheyenne symbolically began life anew.

The Ghost Dance. Although missionaries provided Christianity as a viable option to native Indian religions, Plains Indian traditional religions persist in most parts of the Plains. After missions had been established for only a few years, there was one last attempt to rebel against white domination in a pacifistic movement called the Ghost Dance. It began in the state of Nevada when a Paiute Indian named Wovoka had a vision that the white man would disappear from the face of the earth in a cataclysmic event: the earth would turn over, taking all the white men with it. All the old Indians who had died, as well as the buffalo, now all but extinct, would return to live the old way of life. Wovoka claimed that in his vision he visited with these spirits of the deceased Indians and they taught him a dance that would bring about the destruction of the whites. Wovoka preached to other tribes that it was useless to fight with the white man anymore, for soon this cataclysm would be upon them and they would disappear.

After the teachings of this Indian messiah, who had been raised by a Bible-reading white family, the Ghost Dance spread rapidly throughout the Plains, spilling over occasionally into bordering culture areas. All but the Comanche, who preferred their own, more individualistic form of religion, participated.

During the dance the dancers performed for long periods of time until they went into trances. When they awoke they sang of great meetings with their dead kin and of how glad they were that the old way of life would soon return.

But the cataclysm did not come. Instead, the federal government, fearing that the Ghost Dance would serve to engender hostilities among the Indians, ordered all dancing stopped. On 29 December 1890 a band of Ghost Dancers under the leadership of Chief Big Foot was halted on Wounded Knee Creek on the present-day location of the Pine Ridge Indian reservation. Shots rang out, and 260 men, women, and children were massacred, thus ending the short-lived movement. [*For further discussion, see* Ghost Dance *and the biography of Wovoka.*]

THE NATIVE AMERICAN CHURCH

A pantribal religion that has become popular since the turn of the twentieth century is the Native American Church, better known in the anthropological literature as the peyote cult. Long before Columbus arrived in the New World the native peoples of Mexico were using a sacred plant of the cactus family in their religious rituals. The Aztecs called it *peyotl,* a term that refers to a number of plants with elements that produce hallucinatory sensations when ingested in a green or dry state or in a tea. Because of its effects, peyote *(Lophophora williamsii LeMaire),* as it is known in the United States and Canada, has been regarded by the Indians as a sacred plant, a gift of the Great Spirit that may be consumed for the welfare of the people during prayer meetings.

Since peyote is classified as a controlled substance, there has been a great deal of controversy over Indians' use of the plant in their religious meetings. But neither the legal issue nor the implied immorality, in the white man's eyes, of peyote's use has prevented peyotism, or, as its members prefer, the Native American Church, from becoming an important religious movement in the United States and Canada.

The majority of peyotists are found among the southern Plains tribes, though members of almost all tribes on the Plains as well as other culture areas belong.

The peyote plant, whose "buttons" contain the hallucinogenic agent mescaline, is found in Mexico and Texas on both banks of the Rio Grande. From the tribes of Mexico, the plant itself and certain ceremonies associated with it diffused northward to the Apache, Tonkawa, Kiowa, Comanche, Cheyenne, and Arapaho, and ultimately to surrounding tribes.

Peyotism is strongly influenced by Christianity and individual tribal beliefs; thus there are minor differences in the ceremonies from one tribe to the next. There are two major divisions, analogous to denominations: the Half Moon, by far the most popular, and the Cross Fire. The rituals of the two divisions differ somewhat, the greatest ideological difference being that the Cross Fire uses the Bible in its ceremonies. Peyote ceremonies are likely to vary also from one tribe to the next, or even from one practitioner to the next. If all members attending a meeting are from the same tribe, it is likely that the native language will be used. If members from several tribes congregate, English is used as the religious lingua franca. Despite the many variations of peyotism, however, there are some customs, rituals, and paraphernalia that are common to all.

Peyote meetings are held on Saturday nights, usually from sundown to sunup on Sunday. The ceremony takes place in a traditionally shaped tipi made from canvas. It is especially erected for the occasion and dismantled after the meeting is concluded. The doorway of the tipi faces east, and inside an altar is built containing a fireplace in the center of the lodge behind which is a crescent-shaped earthen altar. On top of the altar is placed a large peyote button called Father, or Chief Peyote. Between the fire and the altar is another crescent made from ashes. Between the fireplace and the doorway of the lodge are placed food and water that later will be ceremonially consumed.

The principal leaders of the meeting are assigned special seats inside the tipi. The peyote chief, also known as the "roadman" or "road chief," sits directly opposite the doorway, in what is for most Plains tribes the traditional seat of honor. On his right sits the drum chief, the keeper of the special drum used in the ceremony. To his left sits the cedar chief. Next to the doorway sits the fire boy. The remainder of the congregation are interspersed between the ritual leaders around the perimeter of the tipi. If a Bible is used it is placed between the earth altar and the peyote chief.

Each member has his own ritual paraphernalia that are stored in a "feather box," usually rectangular and made of wood and often decorated with inlaid silver or with painted designs including representations of the crescent moon, the tipi, a stylized version of a water turkey *(Anhinga anhinga),* a star, and utensils used in the ceremony. The box usually contains a "loose fan," so called because the feathers are not set rigidly into the handle; a large Chief Peyote; a staff, constructed from three sections of a rare wood such as ebony and joined together when in use by means of inserted ferrules (in the Christian-influenced rituals it is called the "staff of life," but in the Indian interpretation it is a bow with no bowstring, hence a symbol of peace); and a gourd rattle and an arrow with a blunt head, also symbols of peace. Most peyotists wear a blanket made of red and blue material, usually an expensive copy of old-time wool cloth received from traders. The red is symbolic of day, the blue of night.

The drum chief is entrusted with keeping a commercially made three-legged brass kettle over which he stretches a hide. The kettle is partially filled with water to regulate the tone, and the hide is tied to the kettle by a rope in such a manner that when the tying is completed the rope forms an outline of a six-pointed star, called the "morning star," on the underside of the drum. Each person has his own drumstick, usually carved out of the same wood as the staff and the gourd handle.

Peyote meetings may be held for special purposes such as curing ceremonies, birthday celebrations, funerals, memorial services, or on occasions when persons leave the Indian community to travel great distances or return from the armed services. Some are simply prayer meetings conducted on a regular schedule similar to Christian services. Persons wishing to participate in the ceremony arrive at the home of the sponsor, who provides all the peyote buttons for consumption during the meeting as well as the food that will be shared by the participants at the conclusion. At dusk the roadman asks all who wish to pray to follow him into the tipi. He leads the line of members around the tipi first before entering the doorway. Once inside all take their seats, and put their paraphernalia in place.

The roadman places the Chief Peyote upon the altar and the cedar chief sprinkles needles on the fire. Instead of using the traditional long-stemmed pipe, cigarettes made from corn husk and tobacco are rolled and passed around the circle of participants. When the ritual smoking has ended, the ashes of the cigarettes are collected and placed near the altar. Sage is passed around and each member rubs some of the sage on his hands, arms, and face, or chews pieces of it. Next the peyote buttons are passed around and each member takes four of them. At this point the singing begins.

The peyote chief takes some sage, the staff, and the gourd rattle and tells the drum chief to begin. As the drum resounds, the peyote chief sings the opening song of the ceremony. This is a rather standardized song at all peyote meetings, no matter what tribe. He sings it four times, the sacred number for most Plains tribes. When he finishes, each member in turn eats some of the peyote buttons and sings four songs. The man on the right of the singer plays the drum while the singer shakes the gourd rattle. In this manner the ritual of eating and singing progresses around the tipi clockwise. The particularly fast drumming on the water drum and the rapid phrasing of the peyote songs may have a great deal to do with creating the hallucinatory effects experienced in peyote meetings.

Concurrent with the visionary experience is the feeling of a closeness with God. Because peyotism is now greatly influenced by Christianity, the members pray to Jesus Christ, equate the consumption of the peyote button with Holy Communion, and espouse the basic tenets of the Christian churches in their prayers and songs.

The praying, eating of peyote, and singing continue until midnight, when there is a special ceremony. The fire boy informs the peyote chief that it is midnight and then leaves the tipi to get a bucket of water. He returns with the water and presents it to the peyote chief, who dips a feather into the bucket and splashes water on the people in the tipi. After smoking and praying, the water is passed around to the members so that each may drink. During this part of the ceremony another standard song is sung. After the water drinking at midnight, the bucket is removed and it is time to resume the peyote eating and singing.

Before each major segment of the ritual, the cedar chief burns incense and the members purify themselves and their paraphernalia in the smoke. The ceremony lasts until dawn, when a woman is called into the lodge bearing another bucket of water. She is called the morning-water woman and is usually a relative of the peyote chief, who now sings the dawn song. After praying and smoking again, the water is passed around the tipi. The peyote chief smokes and prays and may doctor those who are ill or simply pray for the welfare of the people. After the ceremonial water drinking, the woman retrieves the bucket and leaves the tipi. The peyote chief then sings the "quittin' song" while the morning-water woman prepares the traditional breakfast consisting of water, corn, fruit, and meat.

Despite its Christian aspects, peyotism is frowned on by many missionaries. Yet the Native American Church thrives. It has already become increasingly popular among tribes who were once adherents of their native religions or outright Christians. In the early years peyotism was extremely popular with adjacent communities of black Americans, and today many other nonIndians are joining the Native American Church.

[*For discussion of the religious systems of two Plains tribes that have been the subjects of much ethnographic study, see* Blackfeet Religion *and* Lakota Religion.]

BIBLIOGRAPHY

Bowers, Alfred W. *Mandan Social and Ceremonial Organization.* Chicago, 1950. This book, written by a gifted ethnographer, includes a detailed description of the Okipa, the Mandan Sun Dance.

Catlin, George. *O-kee-pa: A Religious Ceremony and Other Customs of the Mandan* (1867). Edited and with preface by John C. Ewers. New Haven, 1967. This edition contains the controversial "Folium Reservatum," not included in the original edition, which discusses sexual symbolism in the ceremony.

Fletcher, Alice C., and Francis LaFlesche. *The Omaha Tribe* (1911). Reprint, Lincoln, Nebr., 1972. Includes important information on Omaha religion by one of the earliest female ethnographers in collaboration with a member of the Omaha tribe.

Grinnell, George Bird. *Blackfoot Lodge Tales* (1892). Reprint, Lincoln, Nebr., 1962. This book is particularly rich in the cosmology of the Blackfeet, written by a pioneer in Plains studies.

Grinnell, George Bird. *The Cheyenne Indians* (1923). 2 vols. Reprint, Lincoln, Nebr., 1972. Volume 2 contains important information on the medicine lodge, Sweet Medicine, and the Massaum ceremony, and is a classic cultural history of the Cheyenne.

Hultkrantz, Åke. *Religions of the American Indians.* Los Angeles, 1979. By a leading historian of comparative religions who specializes in American Indian religion. It contains a great deal of comparative material on Plains Indians.

La Barre, Weston. *The Peyote Cult*. Hamden, Conn., 1964. The best source by the leading expert on the Native American Church.

Lowie, Robert H. "Plains Indian Age-Societies: Historical and Comparative Summary." *Anthropological Papers of the American Museum of Natural History* 11 (1916): 881–984. A summary of research conducted on Plains Indian societies at the turn of the century that includes basic information on ceremonial associations of the Plains Indians.

Lowie, Robert H. *The Crow Indians* (1935). Reprint, New York, 1956. The religious life of the Crow Indians is neatly related to their workaday world in one of the classics of anthropology, by one of the founders of the field in America.

Mooney, James. *The Ghost Dance Religion and the Sioux Outbreak of 1890* (1896). Abridged, with an introduction by Anthony F. C. Wallace. Chicago, 1965. Mooney interviewed participants of the Ghost Dance at the time it was being performed. The book provides comparative materials on the Arapaho, Caddo, Cheyenne, Comanche, Kiowa, Kiowa Apache, Lakota, and some non-Plains tribes.

Powers, William K. *Indians of the Northern Plains*. New York, 1969. A survey of the principal tribes of the northern Plains with a separate chapter on religion.

Powers, William K. *Indians of the Southern Plains*. New York, 1971. A survey of the principal tribes of the southern Plains with separate chapters on traditional religion and on the Native American Church.

Powers, William K. *Oglala Religion*. Lincoln, Nebr., 1977. A structural analysis of the religion of a major subdivision of the Lakota that emphasizes the current persistence of Plains Indian religion despite encounters with Christianity.

Powers, William K. *Yuwipi: Vision and Experience in Oglala Ritual*. Lincoln, Nebr., 1982. A translation of an entire shamanic curing ceremony conducted on the Pine Ridge reservation in 1966, showing the relationship among Yuwipi, the vision quest, and the Sweat Lodge ceremony.

Spier, Leslie. "The Sun Dance of the Plains Indians: Its Development and Diffusion." *Anthropological Papers of the American Museum of Natural History* 16 (1921): 451–527. This is a comparative analysis of the research done on the Sun Dance at the turn of the century by leading anthropologists.

Underhill, Ruth M. *Red Man's Religion*. Chicago, 1965. A classic survey of American Indian religions by the grand dame of ethnology. The language is somewhat dated but there is a wealth of information on the Plains.

Wood, W. Raymond, and Margot Liberty, eds. *Anthropology on the Great Plains*. Lincoln, Nebr., 1980. A state-of-the-art review of anthropological research on the Plains Indians with separate chapters on the Sun Dance, the Ghost Dance, and the Native American Church, compiled by some of the foremost experts on Plains Indian culture.

3 BLACKFEET

Howard L. Harrod

The Blackfeet Indians are a people of Algonquian linguistic stock. Their historic territory was bounded on the north by the Saskatchewan River in the present province of Alberta, Canada; on the south by the Missouri River in the present state of Montana; on the west by the Rocky Mountains; and on the east by a line running through Saskatchewan and eastern Montana at approximately 105° west longitude.

The Blackfeet are a confederacy of closely related peoples: the Siksika, or Blackfeet proper; the Kainah, or Blood; and the Piegan. Before conquest, the Blackfeet proper occupied the northern part of their traditional homeland, while the Blood were located in the middle and the Piegan in the south. Today, these divisions live in roughly the same geographical configuration on three reserves in Alberta and one in northwestern Montana.

Population figures for the three divisions of the Blackfeet may be viewed in historical perspective. In 1780, for example, the total population was estimated at 15,000. By 1909, as a consequence of wars and disease, that population had dropped to 4,635, of whom 2,440 were in Canada and 2,195 were in the United States. By 1978, the population had risen to a total of 21,466, of whom 9,879 were in Canada and 11,587 were in the United States. As of June 1982, official population figures for Blackfeet in the United States were 12,298; figures for the Canadian reserves were not available.

Before their migration onto the Great Plains, the Blackfeet probably lived in the woodlands to the east. But by the time they were met by Europeans, the Blackfeet had become typical Plains dwellers, living in conical tipis and depending upon buffalo for their livelihood. Blackfeet culture, like that of other Plains tribes, was marked by periods of rapid social change associated with new economic conditions, such as the acquisition of the horse and the gun in the mid-eighteenth century.

The Blackfeet believed in a sacred power pervading all things. This power was symbolically represented by the nourishing radiance of the sun. Sun power manifested itself to humans in a variety of ways, being especially visible through the activities of important sky, earth, and water beings. Sun, Moon, and Morning Star were powerful sky beings, as were Thunder and Eagle. Potent earth beings included Buffalo and Bear; water beings included Otter and Beaver.

35

VISION EXPERIENCES

A central theme in traditional Blackfeet religious life was the experience of vision. Such experiences might overtake individuals in the midst of their waking lives, but more commonly they irrupted in dreams. So important were these experiences that they were actively sought, especially by young men, although their occurrence was not limited by age or sex. Young men sought visions by retiring to lonely places, there to fast and pray until the vision world opened up to them.

Typically, vision experiences involved the transfer of sacred power to a person. Beings that appeared in dreams or waking visions might include significant animals or powerful natural forces, such as thunder. The form of these dream beings was not always fixed: animals might change into persons, becoming animals again at the conclusion of the dream or vision. The moment when these beings spoke was especially powerful, and through such communication sacred power was transferred to the dreamer or visionary.

MEDICINE BUNDLES

In the vision, the dream being instructed the visionary to acquire certain special objects, such as skins of animals, which would be gathered together in a personal medicine bundle. Instructions concerning appropriate songs, dances, body paints, and other ritual acts might also be communicated in the dream. The bundle was the symbolic representation of sacred power, but it was the ritual that was of central importance. The material objects contained in the bundle might be lost or destroyed, but as long as the person preserved the ritual, the bundle could be reconstructed.

A person who experienced an important communication of power might transfer this power to another person. The transfer ceremony required a gift of property, as well as instruction by the owner in the ritual associated with the bundle. Once the bundle was transferred, the former owner could no longer call upon its sacred power for assistance.

In addition to such personal bundles, there were among the Blackfeet other more important bundles. These bundles derived from a special relationship that had been established with the people by powerful sky and water beings. A variety of oral traditions preserved the origin myths of such bundles, and, although they were individually owned, they had significance for the welfare of the entire tribe. Like personal bundles, the power of these larger bundles could also be transferred.

Perhaps the most ancient of these bundles was believed to have been given to the Blackfeet by Beaver, a powerful water being. The ritual of the Beaver bundle was complex, and the songs associated with its opening ran into the hundreds. Years were required to learn the details of the ritual. Among the important powers of this bundle, which its owner was called upon to exercise in times of scarcity, was the ritual for calling the buffalo. Beaver bundle owners also kept track of tribal time by means of special counting sticks, and in their bundles were kept the seeds used for planting sacred tobacco. It is probable that the Sun Dance bundle was originally a part of the Beaver bundle. Another important bundle was transferred to the Blackfeet by Thunder, who gave the people a sacred pipe. The medicine pipe bundle was traditionally opened at the sound of the first thunder in the spring. Among other things, it was believed to be efficacious in the healing of illnesses.

Persons who owned such a complex bundle as the medicine pipe or the Beaver bundle were required to become knowledgeable in all aspects of its care and in the details of its rituals. In some cases, the owner might obtain the services of a more experienced person to assist in opening the bundle. Owners of bundles were highly respected among the people, and there were several of these sacred objects distributed among the Blackfeet confederacy. At the turn of the century, for example, there were at least seventeen medicine pipe bundles.

MAJOR CEREMONIES

Most important ceremonies, such as the opening or transfer of bundles, were accompanied by ritual purification of the individuals principally involved. Purification ceremonies took place in a sweat lodge, normally constructed of willow branches and covered with skins or blankets. Heated stones were passed into the lodge. Water was sprinkled upon the stones, producing steam and intense heat. Individuals participating in this ritual engaged in a variety of symbolic acts and sang a number of songs. Typically, songs were addressed to Sun, Moon, Morning Star, or important constellations. Through such ritual acts, individuals were removed from the profane world and prepared to enter into relations with sacred powers.

The great tribal ceremony among the Blackfeet was the Sun Dance. Widely distributed among the Plains tribes, this complex religious ceremony was essentially a ritual of individual, social, and world renewal. Each year the Sun Dance was sponsored by a woman of impeccable character. In times of illness or other social crisis, such a virtuous woman would come forward, vowing to sponsor the dance. The vow constituted a public pledge to acquire by transfer a Sun Dance bundle and to bear, along with relatives, the significant expenses and personal sacrifices required by the performance of the ceremony.

The entire tribe participated in the construction of the Sun's lodge, which was built in the form of a circle, perhaps symbolizing the world or the universe itself. Especially sacred was the center pole that symbolically linked the earth with the sacred powers of the sky, principal among which was the Sun. Through the medium of the center pole, sacred power that nurtured all of life flowed into the world. Through the complex ritual of the Sun Dance, individuals, the social world, and nature were renewed.

The Sun Dance ritual formed a rich symbolic universe. There were transfers of important bundles, shamanistic activities, and the performance of dances before the Sun's pole. Upon occasion, sacrifices of flesh were offered by both men and women. In one important male sacrifice, skewers were inserted under the flesh of both sides of a man's chest; ropes were attached to the skewers and then tied to the center pole. The man would dance, leaning against the ropes until the flesh was torn. Persons who performed flesh sacrifices were considered especially sacred and possessed of more than ordinary powers. [*For further discussion, see* Sun Dance.]

Blackfeet religious life was suffused with a rich symbolism that permeated all major phases of ritual activity—sweat lodge ceremonies, bundle openings, and the Sun Dance. Symbolic dances, such as those that traced the cardinal directions, were prominent, as were dances that imitated powerful animals, such as the beaver and the bear. Color symbolism was pervasive, both in the form of body painting and in the decoration of tipis and other objects. The colors red and black were much used, often symbolizing the sun and the moon, respectively. Shapes that symbolized sacred powers were also numerous, such as the circle and representations of the sun, the moon, and the morning star. Sacred objects, both large and small, were commonly depicted. Among these was the buffalo skull, symbolizing the great animal upon which the people were dependent for life and for sacred power.

Despite well over a century of Christian missionary activity, survivals of traditional religious forms can still be observed among some modern Blackfeet. Sacred objects such as the medicine pipe bundle are still owned and opened, and the Sun Dance is still performed, although not always every year. This evidence suggests that a core of traditional religious meaning still persists in the experience of some Blackfeet.

BIBLIOGRAPHY

The best general work on the Blackfeet is John C. Ewers's *The Blackfeet: Raiders on the Northwestern Plains* (Norman, Okla., 1958). For works on Blackfeet mythology, consult Clark Wissler and D. C. Duvall's "Mythology of the Blackfoot Indians," *Anthropological Papers of the American Museum of Natural History* 2 (1908): 1–63, and George Bird Grinnell's *Blackfoot Lodge Tales* (Lincoln, Nebr., 1962). Detailed descriptions of Blackfeet bundles and of the Sun Dance can be found in Wissler's "Ceremonial Bundles of the Blackfoot Indians," *Anthropological Papers of the American Museum of Natural History* 7 (1912): 65–269, and "The Sun Dance of the Blackfoot Indians," *Anthropological Papers of the American Museum of Natural History* 16 (1918): 223–270. For a discussion of the impact of Christian missions upon Blackfeet religion and culture, see my *Mission among the Blackfeet* (Norman, Okla., 1971).

LAKOTA

WILLIAM K. POWERS

Lakota is the native term for those Plains Indians conventionally known as the Teton or the Western Sioux, the latter of which is a pejorative name, meaning "snakes," applied to them by their Algonquian-speaking enemies, the Ojibwa. *Lakota,* the preferred term, also designates the language spoken by the seven divisions of the Teton: Oglala, Sicangu (or Brulé), Mnikowoju, Hunkpapa, Itazipco (or Sans Arcs), Oohenupa, and Sihasapa. These Lakota speakers, who occupied a number of semisedentary villages in Minnesota before moving onto the Great Plains in the early eighteenth century, represented the largest division of the political body known as the Oceti Šakowin ("seven fireplaces"). Their migration to the Great Plains coincided with the dissolution of the Seven Fireplaces.

Regarded as the "typical" Indians of the Plains, the Lakota were an equestrian, nomadic people who lived in tipis and hunted buffalo in what is now Montana, Wyoming, North and South Dakota, Nebraska, and parts of adjacent states. They participated in the great wars of the West under such leaders as Red Cloud, Crazy Horse, Sitting Bull, Gall, and Rain in the Face, and they were notably responsible for the annihilation of George Armstrong Custer's forces at the Battle of the Little Bighorn on 25 June 1876. The Lakota, along with other Plains tribes, signed a treaty with the federal government at Fort Laramie, Wyoming, in 1868, after which they were placed on reservations. As a result of their participation in the famous Ghost Dance movement of 1888–1890, several hundred Lakota men, women, and children were massacred at Wounded Knee, South Dakota, located on the Pine Ridge reservation. As of 1984, approximately one hundred thousand Lakota resided on reservations in South Dakota, North Dakota, Montana, and Saskatchewan.

THE RELIGIOUS SYSTEM

The emigration from the Great Lakes to the Great Plains and the dissolution of the Seven Fireplaces resulted in a number of changes in Lakota religion. A cosmology that exhibited the characteristics of a village-dwelling, lacustrine culture remained integral to the religion of the eastern division of Dakota speakers (*Lakota* and *Dakota* are dialect markers), but the Lakota abandoned many of their earlier beliefs to accommodate a new nomadic way of life that often subjected them to long periods of starvation. The focal points of the new religion involved the propitiation of super-naturals in order to ensure success in buffalo hunting and protection from an unpredictable and often hostile environment.

Cosmology. The published works of James R. Walker, a physician at Pine Ridge, South Dakota, between 1896 and 1914, provide most of the information on Lakota cosmology, although some of his interpretations are specious. His reconstruction outlines a cosmological system in which prior to the creation of earth, gods resided in an undifferentiated celestial domain and humans lived in an indescribably subterranean world devoid of culture. Chief among the gods are the following: Takuškan-škan ("something that moves"); the Sun, who is married to the Moon, with whom he has one daughter, Wohpe ("falling star"); Old Man and Old Woman, whose daughter Ite ("face") is married to Wind, with whom she has four sons, the Four Winds. Among numerous other named spirits, both benevolent and malevolent, the most important is Inktomi ("spider"), the devious trickster. Inktomi conspires with Old Man and Old Woman to increase their daughter's status by arranging an affair between the Sun and Ite. The discovery of the affair by the Sun's wife leads to a number of punishments by Takuškanškan, who gives the Moon her own domain and, in the process of separating her from the Sun, initiates the creation of time. Old Man, Old Woman, and Ite are sent to earth, but the latter is separated from Wind, who, along with the Four Winds and a fifth wind presumed to be the child of the adulterous affair, establishes space. The daughter of the Sun and the Moon, Wohpe, also falls to earth and later resides with South Wind, the paragon of Lakota maleness, and the two adopt the fifth wind, called Wamniomni ("whirlwind").

The Emergence. Alone on the newly formed earth, some of the gods become bored, and Ite prevails upon Inktomi to find her people, the Buffalo Nation. In the form of a wolf, Inktomi travels beneath the earth and discovers a village of humans. Inktomi tells them about the wonders of the earth and convinces one man, Tokahe ("the first"), to accompany him to the surface. Tokahe does so and upon reaching the surface through a cave, now presumed to be Wind Cave in the Black Hills of South Dakota, marvels at the green grass and blue sky. Inktomi and Ite introduce Tokahe to buffalo meat and soup and show him tipis, clothing, and hunting utensils. Tokahe returns to the subterranean village and appeals to six other men and their families to travel with him to the earth's surface. When they arrive, they discover that Inktomi has deceived them: buffalo are scarce, the weather has turned bad, and they find themselves starving. Unable to return to their home, but armed with a new knowledge about the world, they survive to become the founders of the Seven Fireplaces.

THE SEVEN SACRED RITES

Falling Star appears to the Lakota as a real woman during a period of starvation. She is discovered by two hunters, one of whom lusts for her. He is immediately covered by a mist and reduced to bones. The other hunter is instructed to return to his camp and tell the chief and people that she, Ptehincalaskawin ("white buffalo calf woman"), will appear to them the next day. He obeys, and a great council tipi is constructed. White Buffalo Calf Woman presents to the people a bundle containing the sacred pipe, and she tells them that in time of need they should smoke the pipe and pray to Wakantanka for help. The smoke from the pipe will carry their prayers upward. She then instructs them in the great Wicoh'an Wakan Šakowin ("seven sacred rites"), most of which continue to form the basis of Lakota religion.

1. *The Sweat Lodge*. Called Inikagapi ("to renew life"), the Sweat Lodge ceremony is held in a domical structure made of saplings, which is symbolic of the shape of the Lakota universe. Heated stones are placed in a central hole and water poured over them by a medicine man to create steam. The purpose of the ceremony is to revivify persons spiritually and physically, and during the ceremony benevolent spirits enter the darkened sweat lodge and instruct the medicine man about curing his patients.

2. *The Vision Quest*. Hanbleceya ("crying for a vision") is an ordeal undergone by an individual under the supervision of a medicine man. A person elects to go on a vision quest for personal reasons and pledges to stay on an isolated hill, usually lying in a shallow hole for one to four days without food or water. With only a blanket and a pipe, the individual prays for a vision, which usually comes toward the end of his ordeal. The significance of the vision is then later interpreted by the medicine man.

3. *Ghost Keeping*. It is believed that when a person dies his soul lingers for a year. Wanagi Wicagluha ("ghost keeping") is a ceremony performed by a mourner, especially one grieving for a favorite child. The spirit is ritually fed every day and after one year is finally freed in an elaborate ceremony.

4. *The Sun Dance*. The most important annual religious ritual, Wiwanyang Wacipi ("gaze-at-the-sun dance"), was held immediately before the communal buffalo hunt each summer. Principal dancers pledged to hang suspended from a sacred pole by skewers of wood inserted into their chests or to drag buffalo skulls skewered to the flesh over their scapulae. This was also a time when women offered bits of flesh from their arms, and medicine men pierced the ears of children. [*For further discussion, see* Sun Dance.]

5. *Making Relatives*. Hunka, the ritual for "making relatives," created an adoptive tie between two unrelated persons, one that was stronger than a kin tie. It was usually performed to unite an older and a younger person as ritual "father" and "son."

6. *Puberty Ceremony*. At the onset of a girl's first menses, the ritual called Išnati Awicalowanpi ("they sing over her menses") was performed to ensure that the girl would grow up to have all the virtues of a Lakota woman.

7. *Throwing the Ball*. Tapa Wankayeyapi ("throwing the ball upward") was a game in which a young girl threw a ball upward and several people vied to catch it. The winner was considered more fortunate than the others, for the ball was symbolically equated with knowledge.

ESSENTIAL BELIEFS

Lakota religion is reincarnative. Life is seen as a series of recurrent travels. People live through four generations: childhood, adolescence, maturity, and old age. When a person dies, one of his four "souls" travels along the Wanagi Tacanku ("spirit path," i.e., the Milky Way) southward, where it meets with an old woman who adjudicates its earthly virtues, directing it either to the spirit world, a hazy analog of earthly life where there is an unending supply of buffalo and where people rejoin their kin, or back to earth where they live as ghosts to haunt others and entice the living to join them. Other aspects of these four souls are invested into unborn fetuses, thus giving them life. Twins are particularly auspicious and are considered intellectually mature at birth.

The sacred lore is the domain of *wicaša wakan* ("sacred men"), locally known as medicine men, who conduct all the religious ceremonies. The most important symbol is the sacred pipe that is smoked to Wakantanka (sometimes translated as "Great Spirit" or "Great Mystery," but better left untranslated), a single name representing sixteen important supernatural beings and powers, half of which existed prior to the creation of the earth, half as a result of it. Wakantanka is metaphorically called Tobtob ("four times four") in the sacred language of the medicine men, underscoring the belief that all sacred things come in fours. The root *wakan* ("sacred") is a dynamic concept indicating the potentiality of anything to become transformed from a secular to a sacred state.

Inktomi, the trickster, named all things, taught culture to humans, and remains on the earth to continually deceive them. A set of Inktomi tales called *ohunkankan* ("myth"), in which Inktomi's pranks are ultimately turned against himself, serve as lessons in morality for young children.

CONTEMPORARY RELIGION

All of the Seven Sacred Rites are still performed, with the exception of Tapa Wankayeyapi. A more vital religious practice known as Yuwipi has become popular in the twentieth century. Based on a number of cultural concepts related to a buffalo-hunting way of life combined with problems confronting contemporary Indians on reservations, this ritual is performed in a darkened room under the supervision of a "Yuwipi man." The object of the ritual is to cure persons and at the same time to pray for the general welfare of all Indian people and for long life for the kinship group to which the adepts belong.

BIBLIOGRAPHY

Brown, Joseph Epes, ed. *The Sacred Pipe*. Norman, Okla., 1953. An interview with the Lakota medicine man Nickolas Black Elk on the Seven Sacred Rites, inspired by earlier interviews by John G. Neihardt.

Deloria, Ella C., ed. *Dakota Texts*. New York, 1932. The best bilingual compilation of Lakota mythological texts by an author who was both a Lakota and an anthropologist.

Densmore, Frances. *Teton Sioux Music*. Washington, D.C., 1918. Contains a number of interviews with Hunkpapa medicine men, transcriptions and translations of sacred songs, and vivid ethnographic accounts of most of the sacred ceremonies.

Hassrick, Royal B. *The Sioux: Life and Customs of a Warrior Society*. Norman, Okla., 1964. A comprehensive account of Lakota culture prior to the reservation period.

Neihardt, John G. *Black Elk Speaks* (1932). Reprint, Lincoln, Nebr., 1979. Although only a few chapters relate to Lakota religion, this interview between Nickolas Black Elk and the poet Neihardt has become an increasingly popular reference to American Indian spirituality in general. The problem lies in the reader's inability to distinguish between what is Neihardt's and what is Black Elk's. Brown's interview with Black Elk is much more authentically Lakota, but both Brown and Neihardt neglect to point out that Black Elk was a Catholic lay catechist at the time of the interviews.

Powers, William K. *Oglala Religion*. Lincoln, Nebr., 1977. A structural analysis of Oglala myth and ritual and their relationships to other aspects of Lakota culture such as kinship and political organization.

Powers, William K. *Yuwipi: Vision and Experience in Oglala Ritual*. Lincoln, Nebr., 1982. A translation of an entire Yuwipi ritual showing the relationship between Yuwipi and the Sweat Lodge ceremony and the vision quest. It also contains a chapter on the history of the development of Yuwipi at Pine Ridge.

Riggs, Stephen Return. *Tah-koo Wah-kan: The Gospel among the Dakotas*. Boston, 1869. Written by a missionary who spoke Dakota fluently, this account gives some indication of the early Dakota foundations of Lakota religion. Paternalistic, but insightful.

Walker, James R. *The Sun Dance and Other Ceremonies of the Oglala Division of the Teton Dakota*. New York, 1917. A seminal publication on the cosmology and rituals of the Oglala. Some of the myths should be read judiciously as some of them are obvious romantic reconstructions of Lakota myth from a classical Greco-Roman perspective.

Walker, James R. *Lakota Belief and Ritual*. Edited by Raymond J. DeMallie and Elaine Jahner. Lincoln, Nebr., 1980. Previously unpublished papers of J. R. Walker. Mainly interviews with Oglala men, some of whom were medicine men.

Wissler, Clark. *Societies and Ceremonial Associations in the Oglala Division of Teton Dakota*. New York, 1912. One of a number of monographs by the former curator of the American Museum of Natural History on Lakota religion. In particular, this monograph addresses the nature and function of "dream cults," and harbingers of the modern Yuwipi.

5 THE SOUTHWEST

Peter M. Whiteley

From the southern end of the Rocky Mountains in Colorado, the Southwest culture area extends southward through the mountains, high sandstone mesas, and deep canyons of northern New Mexico and Arizona, and dips over the Mogollon Rim— the southern edge of the Colorado Plateau—into the arid, flat, and sparsely vegetated, low-lying deserts of southern New Mexico and Arizona and northwestern Mexico, to the warm shores of the Gulf of California. It is interspersed throughout with mountain ranges, some bearing dense forests and large game animals. Major rivers are few: the Colorado, its tributaries, and the Rio Grande are the primary sources of water for large sectors of the southwestern ecosystem.

Given the variegation in topography, vegetation, and climate, it is not surprising that the Southwest should contain an equal cultural variety. Four major language families (Uto-Aztecan, Hokan, Athapascan, Tanoan) are represented by a large number of peoples, and two other languages (Zuni and Keres) comprise language isolates. But it should not be thought that language boundaries are a guide to cultural boundaries. The thirty-one pueblos of New Mexico and Arizona include speakers of six mutually unintelligible languages from four language groups. Yet they share numerous cultural, and specifically religious, features. On the other hand, among the groups speaking Uto-Aztecan languages are found sociocultural forms as disparate as the hunter-gatherer bands of Shoshoneans in the north and the great Aztec state to the south of the Southwest culture area.

ECONOMIC PATTERNS

General typologies of Southwest cultures inevitably simplify such diversity. Despite such shortcomings, they may provide a framework within which to make some systematic generalizations. Edward Spicer (1962) has suggested four major divisions according to distinctive economic types at the time of European contact: rancheria peoples, village peoples, band peoples, and nonagricultural bands. The rancheria peoples all traditionally practiced agriculture based on the North American crop triumvirate of maize, beans, and squash. They lived in scattered settlements with households, or "small ranches," separated by some distance from each other. This general economic pattern was followed by groups as disparate as the Tarahumara and Concho in the Sierra Madre of Chihuahua, the Pima and Papago of southern Arizona, the Yaqui and the Mayo concentrated in the river deltas along the Sonoran coast of the Gulf of California, and the riverine and upland Yuman groups. Considerable differences of settlement pattern, including greater population concentrations among Pimans and seasonal movements from ridges into valleys for the Tarahumara and Concho, obtain from people to people. Still, the designation *rancheria* is helpful as a general characterization of Southwest agricultural economies that do not support densely populated, permanently sedentary communities.

The village peoples of Spicer's classification are, by contrast, sedentary communities with tightly integrated populations in permanent villages of stone and adobe construction. These are the Pueblo peoples, who have come to be regarded as the archetypical indigenous agriculturalists of the Southwest. The Tanoan Pueblos include the Tiwa, Tewa, and Towa, whose villages stretch up and down the upper portion of the Rio Grande in New Mexico. Also living for the most part along the Rio Grande or its tributaries are several Keresan Pueblos, with linguistically close Laguna and Acoma a little farther west, on the San Jose River. Moving west across the Continental Divide lies the pueblo of Zuni on a tributary of the Little Colorado River. At the western edge of Pueblo country, on the fingerlike mesas that extend southwestward from Black Mesa of the Colorado Plateau, are the eleven Hopi villages, whose inhabitants speak Hopi, a Uto-Aztecan language. Also located in this vicinity is one Tewa village, Hano, settled by refugees from the Rio Grande valley after the Great Pueblo Revolt of 1680.

The Pueblos are intensive agriculturalists. Among the Eastern Pueblos (those occupying the Rio Grande area) and in Acoma, Laguna, and Zuni (which with the Hopi constitute the Western Pueblos), agriculture is based on a variety of irrigation techniques. Hopi country has no permanent watercourses, and agriculture there is practiced by dry farming. Their sedentariness is a striking feature of the village peoples: Acoma and the Hopi village of Oraibi vie for the status of oldest continuously inhabited community in North America, with ceramic and tree-ring dates suggesting occupation from at least as far back as the twelfth century CE.

Spicer's third subtype is that of the band peoples, all Athapascan speakers. These consist of the Navajo and the several Apache peoples. These Athapascans migrated into the Southwest, probably via the Plains, from northwestern Canada not long before the arrival of Spanish colonists at the turn of the sixteenth century. They variously modified a traditional hunting and gathering economy with the addition of agriculture from the Pueblos (Navajo and Western Apache) and of sheep (Navajo) and horses (all groups) from the Spanish. The means of acquisition of these economic increments— through raiding of the pueblos and Spanish settlements— points up another important feature of Apache economies.

The fourth economic subtype Spicer refers to as nonagricultural bands. The Seri of the northwestern coastline of the Mexican State of Sonora are the primary representatives of this subtype. Traditionally, they hunted small game, fished and caught sea turtles, and gathered wild plant resources along the desert coast of the Gulf of California.

Variations in economy do not, of course, suggest variations in religious structure and orientation *tout court*. Still, modes of environmental adaptation do, within certain bounds, constrain the possibilities of social complexity. Southwest Indian religious patterns frequently do reflect forms of environmental adaptation because of a prevailing notion of social rootedness within a local environmental setting. Since many of the religious concerns of Southwest peoples pertain toman's relationship with environmental forces, the interplay between economic and religious spheres is fundamental.

RELIGIOUS PATTERNS

Among the panoply of indigenous Southwestern cultures, two general patterns of religious action are evident: that focusing on the curing of sickness and that celebrating, re-affirming, and sanctifying man's relationship with the cyclical forces of nature. Religious actions of the former type are usually shamanic performances whose participants include an individual patient and an individual ritual specialist (or a small group of specialists). The latter type includes communal rituals involving large groups of participants under the direction of cadres of hereditary priests. These two general forms are present in the Southwest in a variety of combinations and permutations. Among the Yumans, the Tarahumara, and the Apache, shamanistic curing is the prevalent religious form, and little emphasis is placed on communal agricultural rituals. (The Havasupai, who until the turn of the century held masked ceremonial performances at stages of the agricultural cycle—a practice probably borrowed from their near neighbors, the Hopi—provide a partial exception.) Historically the Pima and Papago peoples held communal agricultural rituals as well as shamanic performances, but with sociocultural change the former have passed from existence while the latter, by themselves, have come to represent traditional religion. At the other end of the continuum, the Pueblos devote most religious attention to the calendrical cycle and have even communalized their curing ceremonies by creating medicine societies to fill the role played in less communally oriented societies by the individual shaman. (The Hopi are an exception, in that they still recognize individual medicine men and women.)

In general, the religious activities oriented around shamanic curing and the acquisition of personal power through individual control over supernatural resources occur in those societies with less (or no) emphasis on agriculture and without concentrated settlement patterns. Communal ceremonies interwoven with the seasonal cycle predominate in agriculture-dependent societies, which have developed highly elaborate and complex ritual systems; as Åke Hultkranz states, "No other Amerindian societies lay so much stress on ceremonialism" as do the Pueblos.

SEVERAL CAVEATS TO STUDENTS OF SOUTHWEST RELIGIONS

A key problem facing the student of Southwest Indian religions is sociocultural change. The Spanish conquest and colonization of the sixteenth and seventeenth centuries affected all Southwest cultures, though individual peoples were treated differently. Our knowledge of indigenous religious beliefs and practices is in some cases (for example, the Seri) severely limited by the wholesale abandonment of indigenous beliefs and their replacement with Christian concepts. Syncretism of traditional and introduced forms is, as among the Yaqui and Mayo, so historically entrenched that it is impossible to isolate the threads of precontact religious life. The traditional Yaqui and Mayo system of three religious sodalities fused in the seventeenth century with Jesuit beliefs and came to embody largely Christian notions, but these peoples' version of Christian ceremonies, such as the rituals recapitulating the

Passion of Christ, incorporate traditional figures with clear similarities to the *kachinas* and clowns of the Pueblos. Since such syncretic processes began long before careful ethnographic records were made of indigenous belief and practice, the "pure forms" are simply irretrievable.

The Pueblos, the Navajo, and the Apache have maintained more of their traditional religious systems intact than other Southwest peoples. Of these groups, the Pueblos have the most complex religious systems, which in many instances preserve indigenous forms intact and distinct from religious elements introduced by Europeans. Hence I shall focus upon the Pueblos in this essay. The persistence of Pueblo religious patterns, despite almost four hundred years of colonial domination, is remarkable. The presence of Puebloan peoples in the Southwest, and of the earlier so-called Basket Makers, with whom there is a clear cultural continuity in the archaeological record, reaches far back into antiquity. The remains found in New Mexico's Chaco Canyon and Colorado's Mesa Verde of the civilization of the Anasazi are simply the better-known evidences of this socially complex and culturally sophisticated people, the direct ancestors of the historical Pueblos. The height of Anasazi culture (twelfth and thirteenth centuries CE) is represented by monumental architecture and elaborately constellated settlement patterns that suggest extensive social networks over large regions. For reasons we can only guess at—perhaps drought, war, disease, population pressure, internal social strife, or all of these in concert— the larger Anasazi pueblos had given way to the smaller pueblos by the time of the earliest historical records (c. 1540).

How much change and persistence have occurred in religion is an unfathomable problem. Nevertheless, the religious conservatism of the modern Pueblos, as well as archaeological indications (such as certain petroglyphs) suggest that more than a few Pueblo religious practices have persisted for a very long time. These two factors—the conservatism and antiquity of Pueblo religious practices—reflect another prominent characteristic: that the more important Pueblo beliefs and ritual practices are deliberately and rigorously preserved by an all-encompassing cloak of secrecy. The Pueblos have been and remain today extremely reluctant to reveal anything beyond the superficial aspects of their religious life. No anthropologists, apart from native Pueblo individuals, have been allowed to conduct extended resident field research by any of the Eastern Pueblos. Questions about religion meet with evasion or a purposive silence. Often information obtained by outsiders has been gathered in unusual ways, such as by interviewing individuals in hotel rooms distant from their pueblos. Only limited aspects of Pueblo religious performances are public; no non-Indian outsider has been permitted to witness a *kachina* performance in any of the Rio Grande pueblos since the seventeenth century.

Secrecy is pervasive not simply to preserve the integrity of traditional religion from the corrupting influences of the outside world, but also to protect the religious practices' integrity within the pueblos themselves. Initiates into religious societies are inculcated with the idea that their disclosure of secret, ritually imparted knowledge will have dire supernatural (their own or their relatives' deaths) and social (their ostracism from the pueblo) consequences. The result is that knowledge of Pueblo religion is fragmentary, flimsy, and in some cases inaccurate. We do know something of the surface contours of Pueblo religion, and these are discussed below. In deference to the Pueblos' rights to maintain their religions as they see fit, perhaps this surface level is as far as we may consciably prosecute our inquiries.

THE PUEBLO COSMOS

In Pueblo thought generally, there is no absolute origin of life or of human beings. Although there have been a number of transformations since the earliest times, the earth and the people have always existed. Accordingly, there is less concern with primordial origins than with the process through which human beings were transformed into their present state of being from previous states.

Southwest peoples in general envision a multilayered cosmos whose structure is basically tripartite: "below," "this level," and "above." Each level has subdivisions, but the number and character of the subdivisions vary from culture to culture. All the Pueblos believe themselves to have originated beneath the present earth's surface. The layer below is characterized as a previous world, or as several previous worlds (or "wombs") stacked one atop another. The Zuni and the Keresans conceive of four previous worlds, the Hopi of three, and the Tewa only one. The last world "below" lies under a lake or under the earth's surface. At the beginning of the present age, the people were impelled—by supernatural signs in some versions of the Emergence story, by the need to flee evil in other versions—to seek a new life in the world above. By methods that vary from story to story (in some versions by climbing a tree, in others a giant reed), the people ascended to this level. The earth's condition was soft, and it required hardening. This was accomplished with the supernatural aid of the War Twins, who are found among all the Pueblo groups, or it was done by a human being with special powers—for example by the Winter Chief, who in the Tewa story hardened the ground with cold.

Accounts differ with regard to the creation of the Sun, Moon, and stars and to the origin of cultigens. For the Eastern Pueblos, the Sun was a beckoning force encouraging the people's ascent into this world. In Hopi tradition, by contrast, the ritual leaders had to create the Sun and Moon by flinging disks of buckskin or cotton into the sky. After the Emergence, the Hopi met with a quasi-anthropomorphous supernatural, Maasawu, who introduced them to maize, beans, and squash. The stars were formed, the Hopi recount, by Coyote's negligence. Coyote had been instructed to carry a sealed pot toward the eastern house of the Sun, but before he reached his destination he grew weary and decided, against instructions, to lift the lid off the pot. All the stars flew out and formed the Milky Way. In Zuni tradition, a supernatural slayer of monsters cut up one monster's body parts and threw them into the sky, where they became the stars.

The timing and methods of the creation of natural phenomena vary, but the trajectory of human progress is the same throughout the various Pueblo traditions. After their emergence onto the earth's surface through an opening referred to as an "earth navel," the people migrated over the earth, stopping at locations that are identified by oral tradition with the numerous ruins throughout the Southwest, before reaching their final destination in the present-day villages. Variant migration patterns reflect differing forms of social organization: the matrilineal clans of the Hopi migrated independently and arrived at the present Hopi towns as separate units, whereas the two moieties of the Tewa—Winter and Summer—migrated down opposite banks of the Rio Grande from their Emergence point in the north.

Hence Pueblo origin myths emphasize the process of becoming the Pueblo peoples of the present. Each pueblo is highly independent, and, but for exceptional occasions requiring dire responses (such as in the Pueblo Revolt of 1680 or during severe famines), there is no political unity among pueblos whatsoever. Such independence is reflected in Pueblo worldview: each pueblo regards itself as the center of the bounded universe. Forces radiate both centripetally from the outer limits and centrifugally from a shrine at the pueblo's center, which is represented as the heart of the cosmos. Thus the Zuni are "the people of the middle place," the Hopi of Second Mesa live at the universe center, and each of the various Tewa villages lies about its "earth-mother earth-navel middle place" (Ortiz, 1969, p. 21). The outer limits of the world are marked variously. Among the Eastern Pueblos and the Acoma and Laguna, the world is a rectangular flat surface (although of course broken by topography) bounded by sacred mountains in the cardinal directions. For the Zuni, the surface is circular and is surrounded by oceans that are connected by underworld rivers. The Hopi world is more abstractly bounded, although sacred mountains and rivers act as circumscribing features.

All Pueblo worlds are rigorously aligned by six cardinal directions, four of which correspond to our north, west, south, and east (or, in the Hopi case, sunrise and sunset points on the horizon at the solstices—roughly northwest, southwest, southeast, and northeast) and the zenith and nadir. From the viewpoint of its inhabitants, each pueblo lies at the center formed by the intersection of the axes of opposed directions. The directions are symbolized by numerous devices: colors, mammals, birds, snakes, trees, shells, sacred lakes, deity houses, and so forth.

The Zuni and the Tewa seem to have elaborated the axial schema to the greatest extent. For the Zuni, the six directions serve as a multipurpose organizational model for society—in terms of matrilineal clan groupings, priesthood sodalities, *kiva* (ceremonial chamber) groupings—and for nature, in that the taxonomy of species is directionally framed. The fourfold plan (i.e., excluding the vertical axis) of the earth's surface is represented by the Tewa as a series of concentric tetrads, which are marked by four mountains at their extremities and by four flat-topped hills, four directional shrines, and four village plazas as the center is approached. Neither is this a static abstraction in Tewa belief: ritual dancers in the plazas must face the four directions; songs have four parts; and so forth. Each of the physical features marking the corners of the concentric boundaries (the four mountains, hills, shrines, and plazas) is a place of power. Each contains an "earth navel" that connects the three levels of the cosmos and that is presided over by particular supernaturals.

THE PUEBLO PANTHEON

Associated with the levels and sectors of the Pueblo world is a panoply of supernatural beings. Elsie C. Parsons (1939) divides these beings into collective and individualized categories.

Collective Supernaturals. The collective category signally includes clouds, the dead, and the *kachina*s. Clouds and the dead have an explicit association: the specific destiny of the deceased person depends upon the role he played during life, but in general the dead become clouds. The cloud beings are classified according to the directions and, accordingly, associated with colors. *Kachina* is a fluid spiritual concept that refers both to supernatural beings and to their masked impersonators at Pueblo ceremonies. *Kachina*s appear in numerous guises and represent many features of the natural and supernatural worlds. They are dramatized in masked impersonation and in stories, where they appear in the forms of animals, plants, birds, the sun, and stars and as spirits such as the War Twins, sky deities, culture heroes, and so on. Some *kachina*s also represent game animals, and *kachina*s associated with the directions are also linked with hunting. *Kachina*s dwell in locations on the edges of the bounded world: in mountains, for instance, or in lakes or other sites associated with the powers of moisture. The three concepts of the dead, the clouds, and the *kachina*s overlap: the dead may become *kachina*s, and *kachina*s may manifest themselves as clouds. The interrelation among clouds, the dead, and *kachina*s points up a significant concern of Pueblo beliefs and ritual practices: the importance of rainfall in this largely arid environment is paramount, and the *kachina*s, as rain spirits, have the power to bring rain to nourish the crops—the central link in the Pueblo chain of being.

Individualized Supernaturals. In some respects, individualized supernaturals reflect the arrangement of the cosmos into levels. Thus among the Hopi, Sootukwnangw ("star–cumulus cloud"), the zenith deity, is associated with lightning and powerful rain; Muyingwu, an earth deity associated with the nadir, is the spirit of maize, germination, and vegetation; and Maasawu is the guardian of this level, the surface of the earth. But each of these figures has multiple aspects and cannot be neatly slotted into an abstract cosmic layer. Through his power to shoot lightning like arrows, Sootukwnangw is also an important war deity, and Maasawu, especially, has a cluster of characteristics. He is associated with fire, war, death, and the night, and he looks and behaves in a more manlike fashion than do the deities of above and below. Supernaturals associated with cosmic features also embody moral principles (Maasawu represents humility, conservatism, lack of avarice, serious commitment to the duties of life, and the terrifying consequences of excessive individualism) and biological principles (Sootukwnangw's lightning arrows are associated with male fertilization). Further, there is a plethora of other supernaturals who are not arranged hierarchically but who crystallize a number of religious concerns. The Pueblo pantheon lacks systematization: supernaturals often overlap in meaning and function, and this is further evident in the pattern of religious organization. Discrete segments of Pueblo society often focus exclusively upon the sets of supernaturals under their control; individuals not in a particular social segment do not have rights of appeal to its set of deities, and they risk severe social repercussions for unauthorized attempts at intercourse with such deities.

The sun, regarded everywhere as male, is a powerful fertilizing force, the father in relation to the earth, who is the mother. Traditionally, every individual was expected to offer cornmeal and to say a prayer to the sun at dawn, when the sun leaves his house (or *kiva*) at the eastern edge of the world and begins his journey to his western house. Prayers to the sun refer to the desire for a long and untroubled path of life for each individual. After a period of seclusion in darkness, the newborn Pueblo infant is taken out and shown to the sun to request a long and happy life and the sun's beneficent attention. As Father, the sun is equated with the care and spiritual nurturance of his children. Songs are addressed to him to ask for his life-giving powers of light and warmth, kept in balance so as not to burn the crops or dry them out. Sun is also a deity of hunting and war; the Keresans, Tiwa, and Hopi seek his assistance in these endeavors.

Other Celestial Deities. Less significant by comparison, other celestial deities include, first, the moon, who is variously female (Zuni, where Moonlight-Giving

Mother is the sun's wife) and male (Tewa, Towa, Tiwa). Moon is rarely addressed in prayer or song. In association with the sun and some constellations, however, the moon's movements and phases are utilized to plan the calendrical cycle of ceremonies. The antiquity of such practices is suggested by the numerous lunar and solar marking devices found in prehistoric Puebloan sites, such as the well-known Sun-Dagger petroglyphs in Chaco Canyon.

The morning star and the constellations Orion and the Pleiades have associations with war and with the timing of ceremonies. The movement of celestial phenomena is critically linked to the seasonal passage of the year. The ceremonial moiety division of the Tewa into Winter and Summer people, each of which has ritual and political charge of half the year, is an indication of the thoroughgoing nature of seasonal principles. The Hopi and Zuni divide their seasons by the solstices, the Tewa by the equinoxes, but the pattern of opposed dual principles is pervasive.

Dawn is deified in the form of Dawn Youths (Tewa), Dawn Mothers (Zuni), and Dawn Woman (Hopi). At Hopi, Dawn Woman is linked with another female deity, Huruingwuuti ("hard substances woman"), who has a formative role in the cosmogonic process. In the Keresan pueblos, she seems to have a counterpart in Thought Woman, whose every thought became manifest into substance. Thought Woman mythologically precedes Iyatiku, a chthonic being who is the mother of people, *kachina*s, game, and maize and who occupies the most prominent role in the Keresan pantheon. Iyatiku is in some respects parallel to Muyingwu, the Hopi maize and germination deity of the below. The principle of human and animal fertility is represented at Hopi by Tiikuywuuti ("child-water woman"), who is Muyingwu's sister.

Other Common Supernaturals. This group includes the War Twins, who are war gods, culture heroes, and patrons of gamblers; the maternal spirit animating the earth (whose body parts may be represented by vegetation, hills, and canyons); the Feathered and Horned Serpent, who lives in the water forms of the earth—springs, pools, rivers, the oceans—and who is a dangerous, powerful water deity responsible for floods and earthquakes; Spider Grandmother, a cosmogonic creator whom the Hopi consider grandmother of the War Twins; Salt Woman or Salt Man, deities of salt lakes and other salt sources; Fire Old Woman, Ash Man, and Ash Boy, with obvious associations; a giant eagle, or Knife Wing (Zuni), one of several war deities; Poseyemu, generally father of the curing societies, a miracle worker, and a possible syncretic counterpart of Christ; the master spirits of particular animals, such as Bear, Badger, Mountain Lion, Wolf, and Coyote, who are patrons of specific curing societies; the sun's children, patrons of the clown societies; and many others.

Each of these supernatural entities embodies a different form of power. They are, however, discrete forms and not subsumable under a concept of pervasive supernatural power such as *mana* or *orenda*. [*See* Power.] They may be harnessed by human beings and used to transform events and states in the world. Access to power is, however, strictly limited in these societies and is based upon initiation into a religious sodality and, especially, a priestly office. There is no vision quest whereby power (at least for males) is democratically accessible.

RELIGIOUS ORGANIZATION AND RITUAL PRACTICE

The basic form of religious organization in the pueblos consists of ritual societies, which serve a variety of purposes. Pueblo religion focuses on a number of issues: agricultural fertility and productivity, human fertility, fertility and productivity of game animals, war, and curing. These major issues are further divisible into aspects. Thus agricultural concerns are trained on the attainment of adequate—but not excessive—moisture, adequate heat and light, and the effective prevention of many crop pests and of excessive wind and cold. Rituals concerning game animals and hunting may be divided according to the species pursued. War society rituals are prophylactic, ensuring strength and success, as well as being celebrations of victory and rituals of purifying and sacralizing scalps taken in battle. Curing societies are organized according to the types of sicknesses they cure. "Bear medicine," "Badger medicine," and so forth are sympathetically and contagiously associated with particular ailments and are used by societies of the same names to produce cures. Typically, societies are composed of small numbers of priests and some lay members, and each society follows an annual cycle of ritual undertakings. In their most spectacular forms, such undertakings climax in dramatic public performances at specified times of the calendrical cycle.

Hopi Religious Societies. An examination of Hopi religious societies provides insight into the structure of such societies in Pueblo cultures generally. In Hopi thought, the religious societies have different degrees of importance and confer different degrees of power on the initiated. A ranking of the societies into three orders of ascending importance may be constructed as follows (translations are given where Hopi names are translatable): Kachina and Powamuy are third-order societies; Blue Flute, Gray Flute, Snake, Antelope, Lakon, and Owaqöl are second-order societies; and Wuwtsim, One Horn, Two Horn, Singers, Soyalangw, and Maraw are first-order societies.

Each of these societies focuses upon a different set of supernatural beings and a different set of specific concerns. The ranking into three orders parallels the age requirements for initiation into particular societies. All children aged six to ten (male and female) are initiated into either (the choice is their parents') the Kachina or the Powamuy society. After this initiation, they are eligible to join second-order societies, although not all individuals will actually join. (Second-order societies are distinguished by sex: Lakon and Owaqöl are female; the rest male.) At about age sixteen, all males (traditionally) are initiated into one of the four manhood societies (Wuwtsim, One-Horn, Two-Horn, Singers) and females into the Maraw (womanhood) society. Initiation into one of the manhood societies, together with birthright, is prerequisite to participation in the Soyalangw society; since this society carries no formal initiation, it can be regarded as a more exclusive extension of the manhood societies.

The Ceremonial Cycle. The public dimension of each society's activities is concentrated at particular points in an annual liturgy. The beginning of the year, which is reckoned in lunar months, falls from late October to late November and is marked by the manhood society ceremonies. Following an eight-day retreat in the *kivas* (semisubterranean ceremonial chambers), which involves private rituals, two of the societies (the Wuwtsim and the Singers) process slowly around the village in two facing columns. (Members of both societies are in each column.) The columns are "guarded" at both ends by some members of the Two-Horn society. The Wuwtsim and Singers sing songs composed for the occasion, some of which poke fun at the sexual proclivities of the Maraw society (the women's counterpart to the Wuwtsim society). The remaining members of the Two-Horn society and all the One-Horns are meanwhile continuing with private rituals in their respective *kivas*. After the final circuit of the Wuwtsim and Singers, all the Two-Horn and One-Horn members, in two separate processions (which are dramatic although unaccompanied by song) visit a series of shrines around the village and deposit offerings. Each manhood society is regarded as complementary to the other three, and each is associated with a particular religious concern: the Wuwtsim and Singers with fertility, the Two-Horns with hunting and game animals, and the One-Horns with the dead and with supernatural protection of the village.

A month later, at the time of the winter solstice, the Soyalangw ceremony occurs. This is one of the most complex Hopi ceremonies and involves the participation of the most important priests in the village. They ritually plan the events of the coming year and perform a variety of ritual activities concerned with reversing the northward movement of the sun and with the regeneration of human, floral (both wild and cultivated), faunal (wild and domestic), and meteorological harmony. Several key themes of Hopi religious concern are sounded in this winter solstice ceremony, which renews and reorients the world and man's position within it. After Soyalangw, game animal dances are held (nowadays particularly Buffalo Dances). These are regarded as "social" dances, as are a group of dances performed in September, which include, among others, Butterfly Dances and "Navajo Dances." The distinction between social dances and sacred performances is not completely clear; songs sung at social dances frequently express desires for beneficial climatic conditions, and in general the social dances evince continuity with the religious concerns of the sacred performances. Clearly, however, the social dances are regarded with less solemnity, and there are only minor religious proscriptions on the performers.

The Soyalangw ceremony opens the *kachina* "season." *Kachina*s are impersonated in repeated public performances from January to July. As has been noted, the *kachina* concept is multiple. The *kachina* costume worn by impersonator-performers includes a mask (there are more than three hundred kinds) and specific garments and body paints. The Hopi regard the masked representations of *kachina*s to be fully efficacious manifestations of the *kachina* spirits; when speaking English, they avoid the term *mask* because of the implication that "masking" is somehow less than real. Many *kachina*s have distinct emblematic calls and stylized body movements. *Kachina* performers represent a great variety of spirits, including those of plant and animal species, deities, and mythological figures of both benign (e.g., the "mudheads") and severe (e.g., the cannibal ogres) countenance. Positive and negative social values are sometimes fused in the same *kachina*. Often a *kachina* represents many elements and practices simultaneously and contains a thick condensation of symbolic devices. Some *kachina*s ("chief *kachina*s") are more important than others and are "owned" by particular clans and regarded as significant clan deities. Usually from January through March *kachina*s appear in groups to dance at night in the *kivas*; for the remainder of the *kachina* season, they appear during the day to dance in the village plaza. During daytime performances, the *kachina*s may be accompanied by a group of unmasked sacred clowns, who conduct a ceremony in parallel to the *kachina* performance. Clowns are given broad license and are social commentators *par excellence*. They expose numerous social aberrancies on the part of village members and poke fun at everything from sacred ceremonial actions to current events. [*See also* Clowns.]

The two most important *kachina* ceremonies occur in February (Powamuy, "the bean dance") and in July (Niman, "the home dance"). At Powamuy, children may be initiated into either the Kachina or Powamuy society in an evening ceremony inside a *kiva*. During the day a large and multifarious assemblage of *kachina*s proceeds in ceremonial circuits around the village. This facinating and beautiful pageant features a series of minipageants occurring in different parts of the village simultaneously. Powamuy purifies the earth and also prefigures the planting season. Beans are germinated in soil boxes in the *kiva*s by the artificial warmth of constant fires. During the day of the public pageant, the bean plants are distributed by *kachina*s to each household, where they are cooked in a stew. At the same time the *kachina*s distribute painted wooden *kachina* dolls and basketry plaques to girls and painted bows and arrows to boys, ensuring their futures as fertile mothers and brave warrior-hunters.

The Niman ("homegoing") ceremony, marks the last *kachina* performance of the year. At the close of Niman, the *kachina*s are formally "sent" by several priests back to their mountainous homes in the San Francisco Peaks and elsewhere. They are requested to take the prayers of the people back with them and to present them to the community of *kachina* spirits.

The *kachina* season is followed by the season of "unmasked" ceremonies. In August occur the Snake-Antelope ceremonies or the Flute ceremonies, the performance of which alternates from year to year. In either case, the two societies from which the ceremonies take their names come together at this time to perform complex rituals that last nine days. The Snake-Antelope rites include a public performance in which the Snake men slowly dance in pairs around the plaza while the Antelope men form a horseshoe-shaped line around them and intone chants. The Snake-Antelope and the Flute ceremonies are densely expressive. Both include a magical attempt to bring clouds over the fields to give rain to the crops; both mark the sun's passage; and both dramatize the mythological entrance of particular clans into the village.

Following these ceremonies in the annual liturgy come the ceremonies of the women's societies. The Lakon and Owaqöl, both referred to in English as Basket Dances, feature a circular dance in the plaza. Selected society members run in and out of the circle throwing gifts to the men, who throng the edges of the circle and dispute over the gifts. Both Lakon and Owaqöl women hold basketry plaques in front of them while they sing. The Maraw society's ceremony features a similar circle in which women hold long prayer-sticks. A number of other rites occur during the nine-day Maraw, including burlesques of male ceremonial activities. Maraw rites relate to war and fertility; Lakon and Owaqöl rites stress fertility and the celebration of the harvest.

This bare outline of the Hopi ceremonial cycle reveals some basic concerns of Pueblo religion. The timing of ceremonies is intimately connected with the annual progress of nature. The *kachina* performances are especially related to the life cycle of cultivated plants, and they occur at critical points in this cycle. The first ceremonies of the year prefigure the planting and successful fruition of crops; they are designed to bring snow and rain to saturate the earth with moisture, which will remain there until planting occurs in April. The daytime *kachina* performances likewise seek rainfall to help the crops grow. Niman, the Homegoing, signals the end of the early phases of crop maturation; the *kachinas*' departure suggests that the spirits of the crops are sufficiently mature no longer to require the *kachinas*' nurturance. The Snake-Antelope and Flute ceremonies complete the course of metaphysical encouragement and nourishment of the crops. Coming at the hottest, driest time of the year, they invoke powerful forces to bring one last bout of rain to ensure the full maturing of the crops and to prevent the sun's fierce gaze from withering them. The women's society Basket Dances celebrate the success of the harvest by the joyful distribution of basketry plaques and household goods.

Private Rituals. All ceremonies include private rituals in *kivas* prior to the public performance. Typically such private rituals include the construction of an altar, which consists of a rectangular sand painting in front of a vertical assemblage of painted and carved wooden pieces that incorporate symbolic designs of birds, animals, and supernaturals. The sand painting also incorporates many symbolic elements. Long songs are incanted over the altar, and tobacco is ceremonially smoked and blown to portray clouds. (Smoking binds together the hearts of the priests as they pass the pipe around a circle and gives them a collective power to express their prayers more forcefully.) The *kiva* itself is a multiplex symbol: it is axially oriented by the directions, and at its center is a hole representing the *sipapu,* the place of emergence from the world below. The *kiva*'s four levels, from the underfloor to the roof, are identified with the worlds through which man has ascended; the passage into this world is portrayed by the *sipapu* and the *kiva* ladder that leads to the roof.

MAIZE SYMBOLISM AND RITUAL

Maize is the dominant, pervasive symbol of Hopi religious life. Maize is regarded as the mother of people, since it is the primary sustainer of human life. "Corn *is* life," the Hopi say. Two perfect ears of white maize are given to a newborn child as its "mothers"; when a person dies, ears of blue maize similarly accompany him on his journey beyond life. Maize seeds, ears, tassels, milk, pollen, and meal all serve as sacramental elements in differing contexts. Moreover, other important symbols are related to the maize cycle. Clouds, rains, lightning, feathered serpents, and various species associated with water, such as frogs, ducks, reeds, and so forth, all underline a paramount interest in securing water for maize.

Two devices, above all others, serve as mechanisms for establishing holiness or for communicating with supernatural forces: cornmeal and prayer feathers. Cornmeal is an all-purpose sanctifying substance; it is sprinkled on *kachina* dancers, used to form spiritual paths for *kachinas* and the dead, offered to the sun and to one's own field of growing maize plants, and accompanies all forms of private and public prayer. The act of making a prayer to various supernatural forms with the sprinkled offering of cornmeal may be considered the most fundamental religious act for the Hopi as for all the Pueblos.

Feathers of many different bird species are used in innumerable ways in Hopi ritual; they are worn in the hair and around arms and ankles, and they decorate *kachina* masks, altars, and religious society emblems. Prayer sticks and prayer feathers are the two basic forms of feather offerings. Prayer sticks, carved in human or supernatural forms, are living manifestations of prayer and are simultaneously petitions for aid. Feathers are regarded as particularly effective vehicles for conveying messages to supernaturals: they "carry" the prayers of people with them.

COMPARISONS

It is evident from the Hopi situation that religious action is multiple. There is no single set of activities we can demarcate as "Hopi religion" as distinct from Hopi agriculture or even Hopi politics, since political activity goes on even within the context of private ceremonial gatherings. Also, the exclusiveness of religious societies above the third order suggests a socially fragmented pattern of religious belief and practice. Religious knowledge is highly valued and tightly guarded, and it serves as the primary means of making status distinctions in Hopi society. Hopi explanations of the diversity of their religious activities point to historical circumstances: each cult is identified with a particular clan that introduced it when the clan negotiated admission to the village in the distant past. Although lay cult members may be from any clan, the chief priests should always be of the clan which "owns" the ceremony. In part, then, ceremonial performances celebrate separate clan identities and mark off particular ritual activities as the exclusive prerogative of particular clans. This pattern of closed ceremonial societies with exclusive rights in certain forms of religious action is a fundamental characteristic of Pueblo religion.

The Zuni Cult System. Other Pueblo groups depart significantly from the Hopi scheme yet still exhibit similarities that suggest some common patterns of belief and practice. Ethnologists have identified six major types of Zuni cults or societies.

1. *The Sun cult.* Responsibility for the important religiopolitical officer called the *pekwin* (Sun priest) belongs to the Sun cult. Membership is restricted to males, and the sodality conducts its ceremonies at the solstices.
2. *The Uwanami ("rainmakers") cult.* This cult is composed of twelve distinct priesthoods of from two to six members each. Membership is hereditary within certain matrilineal families. Each priesthood holds retreats (but no public ceremonies) during the summer months from July through September.
3. *The Kachina cult.* Unlike the Hopi Kachina society, membership in the Zuni Kachina society is not open to females. The cult has six divisions, which are associated with the six directions and are accordingly headquartered in six *kivas*. Each *kiva* group dances at least three times per year: in summer, in winter following the solstice, and following the Shalako ceremony in late November or early December.
4. *The cult of the kachina priests.* Whereas the Kachina society is primarily concerned with rain and moisture, the cult of the *kachina* priests focuses on fecundity—of human beings and game animals. The *kachina* priests are responsible for the six Shalako *kachinas*, the ten-foot-tall, birdlike figures whose appearance marks the most spectacular of Zuni religious dramas, and for the *koyemsi* ("mudhead") *kachinas*, who are at once dangerously powerful beings and foolish clowns. Other *kachinas* under the charge of the *kachina* priests appear at solstice ceremonies, at the Shalako ceremonies, and every fourth year at the time when newcomers are initiated into the general Kachina cult.

5. *The War Gods cult.* The Bow priesthood, which is exclusively male, controls the War Gods cult. Traditionally, initiation required the taking of an enemy's scalp. The Bow priests are leaders in war and protectors of the village, and they serve as the executive arm of the religiopolitical hierarchy, in which role they prosecute witches. (The extinct Momtsit society may have been the Hopi counterpart of the Bow priests.)

6. *The Beast Gods cult.* The cult is overseen by twelve curing societies, and membership is open to both men and women. Each society focuses on a particular source of supernatural power, which is embodied in the bear, mountain lion, or another predatory animal. The individual societies practice general medicine, but each also specializes in healing specific afflictions. The collective ceremonies of the societies are held in the fall and winter.

The division of Zuni religious practice into cults is underpinned by an extremely complex ceremonial calendar that coordinates and interrelates ritual activities throughout the year. Each cult has a cycle that includes private and public ritual actions and that begins and ends with the winter solstice. As among the Hopi, the year is divided by the solstices. From winter to summer solstice, the main focuses of ceremonial action are medicine, war, and human and game-animal fertility. Throughout the summer, ceremonial emphasis is upon rain and the maturation of the crops. At the solstices, all major religious interests converge. Thus at Zuni, religious organization shows significant differences of emphasis, formally and functionally, though these appear as nuances rather than radical divergences. Overall, there appears to be greater emphasis on curing and less on agriculture than at Hopi, a difference of emphasis that intensifies as one moves on to Pueblo groups further east.

Keresan Pueblo Religious Practice. Among the Keresan Pueblos—Acoma and Laguna to the west, Santo Domingo, Cochiti, San Felipe, Santa Ana, and Zia to the east on the Rio Grande and its tributaries—the chief religious organizations are referred to as "medicine societies." With variations from pueblo to pueblo, the basic pattern consists of four major medicine societies—Flint, Cikame (an untranslatable Keresan word), Giant, and Fire—and a number of minor societies, including Ant, Bear, Eagle, and Lizard. The medicine societies conduct a communal curing ceremony in the spring, echoing a theme of the Hopi Bean Dance, and they hold performances throughout the year to effect the cure of individual patients. The societies also have rainmaking functions, which they fulfill at private ritual retreats during the summer months. Reportedly, these societies erect altars and construct sand paintings similar to those described for the Hopi and the Zuni. The same major sacramental elements—prayer sticks and cornmeal—are central vehicles for religious action, and extensive songs and prayers designed to make unseen power manifest in the world are a key part of ceremonial content. The medicine societies also have important roles in solstitial ceremonies aimed at reversing the course of the sun.

Other important Keresan societies include a paired group: the Koshare, which is a clown society parallel in many ways to Hopi clown societies, and the Kwirena, which is primarily associated with weather control. A Hunters society, with a permanently installed "hunt chief," and a Warriors society, composed of scalp-takers, are other important societies that traditionally held ceremonies during the winter. A village-wide Kachina society is divided into two ceremonial moieties, Turquoise and

Squash, associated with the two *kiva*s in the village. *Kachina* performances by both moieties occur during fall and winter, but especially during the summer immediately following the rainmaking retreats of the medicine societies. These retreats include a supernatural journey to the *sipapu,* from which the *kachina*s are brought back to the village. As among other Pueblo groups, ritual activities among the Keresans are dominated by males; although both sexes may join medicine societies, women serve as secondary assistants, and only men may perform as *kachina*s.

The climatic and ecological situation of the Keresan Pueblos is of much greater reliability than that of the Hopi. The Keresans' religious concern with the agricultural cycle is evident, but, since the Keresans have irrigation and more plentiful precipitation, they put less emphasis on the agricultural and more on the curing functions of religious societies. A primary function of the more important medicine societies is to combat witchcraft by evil-hearted human beings and evil supernaturals, which is believed to be the cause of illness. Witchcraft is, and has been historically, a profound concern of Hopi and Zuni also, although at Hopi the concern receives less concerted attention from the major religious societies.

The theme of dualism, which appears at Hopi and Zuni in the form of the solstitial switching of ritual emphases, is manifested at the Keresan Pueblos with the division of the ceremonial organization into moieties centered in two *kiva*s.

Tewa, Tiwa, and Towa Religious Systems. The theme of dualism in Southwest religion achieves perhaps its maximum expression in the religious life of the six Tewa pueblos: San Juan, Santa Clara, San Ildefonso, Tesuque, Nambe, and Pojoaque. The division of people into Winter and Summer ceremonial moieties is part of a thoroughgoing dual scheme phrased in terms of seasonal opposition. The division of significance among the Tewa is by equinoxes; the seasonal transfer ceremony that is held (roughly) at each equinox places one or the other of the ceremonial moieties in charge of the village for the following season. Hence there are two overarching religious leaders, or caciques, each the head of a moiety. The calendar of religious activities is planned in accordance with the division into summer (agricultural activities) and winter (nonagricultural activities).

Typically, each Tewa pueblo has two *kiva*s in which the ceremonial moieties are headquartered. There are eight religious societies in all: the Winter and Summer moiety societies, each headed by a moiety priest; the Bear Medicine society; the Kwirena ("cold clowns") and Kossa ("warm clowns") societies; the Hunt society; the Scalp society; and the Women's society. The most intensive ritual activity occurs between the autumnal and vernal equinoxes. This contrasts with the Hopi model, in which the most active part of the cycle occurs from the winter to the summer solstice (and just thereafter). Parallel elements are otherwise clear: religious-society organization among the Tewa is reminiscent of the nearby Keresans. Religious concerns, too, are similar between the Tewa and Keresan Pueblos, though the Tewa Pueblos place less emphasis on curing. The main sacraments are the same; the *kachina* performance is a fundamental religious practice, though more restricted here than among the Hopi, Zuni, and western Keresans.

The traditional religious practices of the Tiwa pueblos—Taos and Picuris in the north and Sandia and Isleta in the south—are the least well known. Taos, in particular, has been most effective in protecting matters it regards as not appropriate for public consumption. At Taos, each of the six *kiva*s (which are divided into three on the "north side" and three on the "south side" of the pueblo) houses a religious society. *Kiva* society initiation involves a set of rituals prolonged over a number of years and is restricted by inheritance to a select group. The *kiva* organization at Taos seems to serve the same purpose as religious societies at other pueblos. At Taos, there is greater ritual emphasis upon game animals and hunting, in line with the pueblo's close cultural ties with Plains peoples, than there is upon the agricultural cycle. Taos may be the only pueblo in which *kachina*s are not represented in masked performances. Picuris seems traditionally to have done so, and it otherwise exhibits more religious similarity with the Tewa pueblos than it does with Taos, its close linguistic neighbor. *Kachina*s do occur, however, in Taos myths.

The southern Tiwa in Isleta pueblo have a system of ceremonial moieties divided into Winter (Black Eyes) and Summer (Red Eyes), each with its "moiety house" (which is equivalent to a *kiva*). In addition, Isleta Pueblo's five Corn groups, associated with directions and colors, seem to parallel *kiva* organizations at Taos. The moieties conduct seasonal transfer ceremonies similar to those at Tewa pueblos, and likewise each moiety controls the ritual activities for the season over which it presides. The ceremonial cycle is attenuated in comparison with that at other pueblos; there is a Land Turtle Dance in the spring and a Water Turtle Dance in the fall. Although unverified, it has been reported that *kachina* performances are conducted by a colony of Laguna Pueblo people who have lived in Isleta since the late nineteenth century.

Jemez, the only modern representative of the Towa Pueblos, exhibits an extraordinarily complex ceremonial organization, with twenty-three religious societies and two *kiva* moieties. Every Jemez male is initiated into either the Eagle society or the Arrow society; other societies are more exclusive. Societies can be classified according to function: curing, rainmaking and weather control, fertility, war and protection, and hunting. The Jemez ceremonial cycle includes a series of retreats by the different religious societies. In the summer, these celebrate agricultural growth; in the fall the ripening of crops; in the winter war, rain, ice, snow, and game animals; and in the spring the renewal of the forces of life. The two ceremonial *kiva* moieties are Turquoise and Squash, the same as among the eastern Keresans, and although the principle of dualism is in evidence it is not so pronounced as among the Tewa.

LIFE, DEATH, AND BEYOND

The Pueblos hold that an individual's life follows a path, or plan, that is present in his fate from birth. A long, good life and a peaceful death in old age are the main requests contained in prayers delivered at the birth of a new person. Through the course of maturation, the person becomes increasingly incorporated, in a ritual sense, into the world. So the Tewa, for example, perform a series of childhood baptismal rites—"name giving," "water giving," "water pouring," and "finishing"—that progressively fix and identify the individual in relation to the forces of society and the cosmos. Religious society initiations and marriage mark further passages in the individual's path of life.

Beliefs about and rituals surrounding death reveal some of the most essential features of Pueblo conceptions of the nature of existence. I have noted above the association between the dead, clouds, and *kachina* spirits. In general, Pueblos believe that when a person dies, the spirit, or breath, returns to the place of the Emergence and becomes transformed into cloud. Cloud spirits have myriad conceptual associations, and the dead (or certain of them) may likewise be given special associations. So, although clouds are generally regarded as the spirits of all the ancestral dead, distinctions are also made between different afterlife destinations, which vary according to the status the deceased person held while alive.

All the Pueblos distinguish between two kinds of people: those who hold important religious offices (or who are initiated members of religious societies) and everyone else. The former are regarded as supernaturally and socially powerful, ritually significant people; the latter are commoners. For the Tewa, the distinction is between "made," or "completed," people and "dry food" people; for the Zuni, the distinction is between valuable and ceremonially poor, or unvaluable, people; among the Keresans the term *sishti* ("commoners") denotes those without ceremonial affiliation; and for the Hopi, the distinction is between *pavansinom* ("powerful" or "completed" people) and *sukavungsinom* (common people).

The afterlife fate of these different categories may vary from one Pueblo group to another. Deceased members of the Hopi Two-Horn and One-Horn societies judge the newly dead at the house of the dead. Witches, suffering a different fate from that enjoyed by the righteous, may be transformed into stinkbugs! Zuni rain priests join the *uwanami* spirits who live in the waters, whereas Zuni Bow priests join their spiritual counterparts in the world above as makers of lightning. Other religious society members return to the place of the Emergence, but Zuni commoners go to "*kachina* village," the home of the *kachina*s, which is at a distance of two days' walk to the west of Zuni. In short, the social and religious organization in life is replicated in the organization of the dead.

SYNCRETISM AND CHANGE

The Pueblos were first exposed to Christian practices through the Franciscan friars who accompanied Francisco Vasquez de Coronado during his exploration of the Southwest (1540– 1542). When the Province of New Mexico was made a colony of Spain in 1598, the Franciscan order was given special jurisdiction over the souls of the Indians. Missions were built in most of the pueblos; tributes were exacted; strenuous discipline was enforced; and extremely brutal punishments were levied for infractions of the total ban on indigenous religious practices. In reaction to this colonial domination, and especially to the religious oppression, all the pueblos united in an uprising in 1680, under the leadership of Popé, a Tewa priest. Many Spanish priests and colonists were killed, and the rest were forced to withdraw from New Mexico. Most of the pueblos immediately dismantled their missions. The Oraibi Hopi record that in the Great Pueblo Revolt the Roman Catholic priests were actually killed by warrior *kachina*s, symbolically demonstrating the spiritual rectitude of the action and the greater power of the indigenous religion.

Removed from the mainstream of Spanish settlements, the Hopi never allowed Spanish missions to be built among them again, and their religious practices remained free of Franciscan influence. The other Pueblos all suffered the reestablishment of missions after the Spanish reconquest of the 1690s. The influence of the missions depended upon the regularity and zeal with which they were staffed. At Zuni, a desultory missionary presence seems to have had little impact on traditional religious forms. The Rio Grande pueblos, on the other hand, came under a great deal of Franciscan influence. These pueblos are all nominally Catholic and observe many ceremonies of the Christian calendar. Each town has a patron saint and holds a large dance—called a Corn Dance or Tablita Dance—to celebrate the saint's day. The dance is thoroughly indigenous in character; however, a Christian shrine honoring the saint stands at one side of the plaza during the dance. At the conclusion of the dance, all the participants enter the church and offer prayers and thanks in a Christian fashion. Thus the two traditions coexist in a "compartmentalized" fashion. In some areas, such as rites of passage, Christian practices have supplanted indigenous Pueblo forms, especially in those pueblos that have become increasingly acculturated during the twentieth century (Pojoaque, Isleta, Picuris, and Laguna are examples). Many Eastern Pueblos have also taken over Spanish and Mexican religious dramas, such as the Matachine performances, which are also practiced among the Yaqui, Mayo, and Tarahumara.

Protestant churches have been attempting to proselytize the Pueblos since the latter nineteenth century, though in general without much success. Despite sustained long-term efforts by the Mennonites, Baptists, Methodists, Roman Catholics, Mormons, and Jehovah's Witnesses among the Hopi, their rate of conversion to Christianity has remained below 10 percent. On the other hand, major Christian holidays such as Christmas and Easter are popular occasions and may be having some impact on traditional religion. A *kachina* dance is regularly scheduled for Easter weekend nowadays, and among the array of presents they bring the *kachina*s include baskets of colored eggs. Regarding other nontraditional religions, only at Taos has peyotism to some extent been adopted, and even there its practice is evidently kept compartmentalized and apart from both indigenous religious practice and Catholicism.

CONCLUSION

The religious traditions of other Indians of the Southwest contain their own conceptual and historical complexities. I have chosen to focus upon the Pueblos here because of the richness of their extant religious practices and because of the separate treatment that the Apache and the Navajo receive in this encyclopedia. [*For treatment of the religious practices of some Yuman groups, see* North American Indians, *article on* Indians of California and the Intermountain Region, *above.*] This does not imply that Pueblo religions are somehow representative of the religions of other native Southwest peoples, though certain Pueblo themes are echoed in different ways among non-Pueblo peoples. Sodalities and clown societies exist among the Yaqui and Mayo; sand painting is practiced by the Navajo, Pima, and Papago; and masked impersonators of supernatural beings perform rainmaking dances among the Havasupai, Yavapai, Pima, and Papago: but these common threads occur in cloths of quite different weaves. Let me emphasize at the last that the indigenous Southwest is enormously diverse. The sheer complexity of its religious practices belies any attempt to standardize these into a meaningful common pattern.

[*For discussion of non-Pueblo peoples of the Southwest, see* Apache Religion *and* Navajo Religion.]

BIBLIOGRAPHY

On account of their richness and complexity, Southwest Indian religions have proven irresistible to generations of scholars. As the cradle of American anthropology, the indigenous

Southwest has produced perhaps a greater volume of ethnographic studies than any other comparably populated area in the world. W. David Laird's *Hopi Bibliography: Comprehensive and Annotated* (Tucson, 1977), for example, contains listings for about three thousand items on this people alone. The contemporary *sine qua non* of Southwest ethnographic material is the *Handbook of North American Indians,* vols. 9 and 10, *The Southwest,* edited by Alfonso Ortiz (Washington, D.C., 1979, 1983). Encyclopedic in scope, these volumes treat Pueblo (vol. 9) and non-Pueblo (vol. 10) cultures; particularly pertinent synthetic articles include Dennis Tedlock's "Zuni Religion andWorld-View" (vol. 9, pp. 499–508), Arlette Frigout's "Hopi Ceremonial Organization" (vol. 9, pp. 564–576), Louis A. Hieb's "Hopi World View" (vol. 9, pp. 577–580), and Louise Lamphere's "Southwestern Ceremonialism" (vol. 10, pp. 743–763). Complex and detailed statements on specific religious practices may be found in the numerous writings of Jesse Walter Fewkes, H. R. Voth, and A. M. Stephen for the Hopi (see the Laird bibliography mentioned above); Frank H. Cushing for the Zuni; Matilda Coxe Stevenson for the Zuni and Zia; Leslie White for the individual Keresan pueblos; and Elsie C. Parsons for many Pueblo groups (the bibliography in volume 9 of the *Handbook* should be used for specific references).

I recommend a number of works (presented here in order of publication) that either focus specifically on religious practice or devote significant attention to it. H. K. Haeberlin's *The Idea of Fertilization in the Culture of the Pueblo Indians* (Lancaster, Pa., 1916) is an early synthesis that has yet to be superseded. Ruth L. Bunzel's "Introduction to Zuni Ceremonialism," in the *Forty-seventh Annual Report of the Bureau of American Ethnology* (Washington, D.C., 1932), and her other articles in the same volume are excellent windows not only into Zuni religion but into Pueblo religion more generally. The classic, comprehensive (albeit fragmentary) source is Elsie C. Parsons's *Pueblo Indian Religion,* 2 vols. (Chicago, 1939). Mischa Titiev's *Old Oraibi: A Study of the Hopi Indians of the Third Mesa* (Cambridge, Mass., 1944) is perhaps the best single account of the Hopi, although the second volume of R. Maitland Bradfield's *A Natural History of Associations: A Study in the Meaning of Community,* 2 vols. (London, 1973), brings together an enormous amount of earlier material on Hopi religion for a novel synthesis. Alfonso Ortiz's *The Tewa World* (Chicago, 1969) is the most sophisticated and best-written account of any of the Pueblos, and it stands as the single most essential monograph on one Pueblo people. Edward P. Dozier's *The Pueblo Indians of North America* (New York, 1970) is a complete, concise summary concerning all the Pueblos. *New Perspectives on the Pueblos,* edited by Alfonso Ortiz (Albuquerque, 1972), contains several articles on religious practices and beliefs. Although somewhat difficult of access for readers of English, two exceptionally good interpretations of Pueblo ritual and myth have appeared in French: Jean Cazeneuve's *Les dieux dansent à Cibola* (Paris, 1957) and Lucien Sebag's *L'invention du monde chez les Indiens pueblos* (Paris, 1971).

Beyond the Pueblos, and excluding the Navajo and the Apache, little of comparable depth exists. Ruth M. Underhill's *Papago Indian Religion* (New York, 1946) and *Singing for Power* (Berkeley, 1938) are notable exceptions, and her *Ceremonial Patterns in the Greater Southwest* (New York, 1948) is another historic synthesis. For sources on other Southwestern cultures, volume 10 of the *Handbook* is the best guide. Edward H. Spicer's *Cycles of Conquest: The Impact of Spain, Mexico, and the United States on the Indians of the Southwest, 1533–1960* (Tucson, 1962), cited above, is a thorough historical study of all indigenous Southwestern peoples.

6 APACHE

MORRIS EDWARD OPLER

There are six separate Apache tribes of the American Southwest: the Chiricahua, Jicarilla, Kiowa Apache, Lipan, Mescalero, and Western Apache. These tribes ranged over a substantial part of eastern Arizona, much of New Mexico, and sections of northern Mexico adjoining these states, as well as southeastern Colorado, western Oklahoma, and western, central, and southern Texas. The extent of Apache territory meant that some tribes were not in contact with others and that at the peripheries there might be frequent interaction with outside groups. Inevitably variation and differential borrowing occurred, which affected not only material culture but concepts as well. Thus only the Kiowa Apache participated in an annual Sun Dance, and only the Jicarilla perform an annual ceremonial relay race, probably inspired by eastern Pueblo examples. All except the Kiowa Apache mark a girl's pubescence by a complex ceremony; none but the Jicarilla has a boy associated with the girl in this event.

Nevertheless, a common core remains that identifies Apache religion. Prominent in this nucleus is the concept of supernatural power that pervades the universe and with which man can form a working relationship. This power manifests itself through divine beings of Apache legend, celestial bodies, living creatures, and familiar geographical features; there is little in man's world that is not potentially suffused with spiritual meaning. Sometime during his life a person is certain to require the protection that such power can give; power, too, is unfulfilled if it remains dormant. Consequently, although it is often man who seeks a power experience, frequently supernatural power sees man's need and proffers its services. In either case, the outcome is a vision experience in which a person is offered a ceremony, told of its uses, and given necessary directions.

Usually the power source first appears as an animal or heavenly body, changes to human guise, and leads the beholder to some sacred spot. There instruction proceeds if the individual man or woman is willing to accept the rite. The student learns the purposes of the ceremony and what ritual items to require initially from his clients. These gifts are actually offerings to power and may be turquoise, coral, small bags of pollen, or unblemished buckskin.

The recruit is taught the appropriate prayers and songs and what ceremonial articles to manipulate. He may learn that by means of this ceremony he will be able

65

to see an object that is sickening a patient and to "suck it out." He is given to understand that the ceremony exists mainly to ensure supernatural presence and help; without these, nothing can be accomplished. Power exerts itself when its earthly messenger is strong in belief and meticulous in carrying out directions. If his faith should waver, power will withdraw its support. Shamanism is the designation given to ceremonies that are individual in origin and dependent on constant interaction between the practitioner and the particular power. However, Apache religion also includes another kind of ritual, over which priests officiate.

Although obtaining a shamanic ceremony is a personal matter, and although power stems from many sources, this type of ritual is highly patterned. Four is the sacred number: songs and prayers usually occur in sets of four, and four ritual feints accompany the drinking of "medicine." The ceremonial circuit is clockwise, beginning with the east. There is a color-directional tie: ordinarily, black with east, blue with south, yellow with west, and white with north. The inventory of objects used for offerings to power is limited. Besides those already mentioned, they include eagle feathers, black flint blades, obsidian, specular iron ore, grama grass, red and yellow ocher, pieces of abalone shell, tobacco, and white clay. Rites normally begin at dark and continue until dawn for four successive nights. The procedures and symbols described thus far are present in priestly as well as shamanic ritual and unify Apache ceremonialism. In shamanism, however, the role of supernatural power is constantly remembered; for instance, the practitioner may introduce the rite by recounting the tale of its acquisition. Outsiders who witness an Apache shaman's legerdemain mistakenly cry fraud; the Apache understand that what they see is merely a dramatization of the interplay of invisible forces.

Some ceremonies may be held to find lost objects; others, to locate enemies or even to sway the affections of a member of the opposite sex. There are rituals, in which masked dancers play a prominent part, to ward off epidemics. More common are rites conducted over ailing people. The causes of illness are various: the supernaturals may be affronted; contact, often inadvertent, with an "unclean" animal or bird (particularly the bear, snake, owl, or coyote) may sicken a person; even to cross the tracks of such creatures may precipitate disaster; sickness can occur if one stands too near a place where lightning strikes.

Many of the maladies with which beneficent ceremonialists contend are not accidental. There is evil as well as good in the world. Some envious or vengeful people perform ceremonies to cause ailments. Power, too, has a dual nature. In fact, it may be evil power that suggests revenge. Sometimes, after aiding a ceremonialist to cure several patients, it tempts him to use the ritual for harmful ends. Some shamans interpret successive failures as proof that power has deceived them. The ritualist may suspect that what he thought was benign power is really capricious witchcraft, and he may refuse to conduct the ceremony thereafter. Fear of witchcraft is vivid and pervasive in Apache thought. Even the ghosts of those who in life were witches strive to stalk the earth doing mischief rather than going quietly to the underground land of the dead.

The knowledge gained by a shaman may be so personal that he may never pass it on. Others may agree to teach their ceremony to someone, but whether the student can practice successfully depends on the will of power. If the novice forgets details or fails to achieve results, it is assumed that power refuses to work through him. Even if an understudy finds favor with power, he is still to be considered a shaman rather than a priest, for what he accomplishes rests less on what he learned from another than on the rapport he maintains with the supernatural. As his intimacy with his power grows, a shaman may be taught additional uses for the ceremony. He may practice it only for his immediate family, or he may make more general use of it. Shamans may acquire several rites and employ each to combat a different malady.

The Apache also perform a series of life-cycle rites, over which, depending on the tribe or the occasion, either priests or shamans may preside. These occur when an infant is placed in the cradleboard, when a child takes his first steps, and when, during the following spring, his hair is shorn except for a few locks left to link him with the growing season and promote good health. A girl's puberty rite takes place soon after the first menses to ensure a long and happy life for her. The family must host a large number of friends for four days, procure special equipment, and obtain unblemished buckskins for her dress. Several ceremonialists have to be hired. One is a woman who will make the girl's costume, advise her, lead her to the ceremonial enclosure, and care for her during the four-day event. Another is the ritualist who prays for the girl and to whose songs she does stylized dances each night. To safeguard the well-being of those gathered for the occasion, a ceremonialist is employed to prepare a group of young men as masked dancers who impersonate mountain spirits, the protectors of Apache territories. Most tribes also engage in training practices that ritually prepare a boy for his first raid and warpath experience.

The shamanic principle is paralleled in all Apache tribes by the priestly model. In each tribe there is at least one rite that was painstakingly taught to the people by great supernaturals who were once among them. Early in mankind's existence, when monsters threatened man's survival, a divine maiden miraculously gave birth to a son who grew up to slay these threatening beings. The mother and her son taught the Apache the details of the female puberty rite and serve as exemplars of proper male and female behavior. The ceremonies they taught must be continued in the prescribed manner if all is to go well with the tribe. The practitioners of the rite do not claim divine inspiration but feel that they are performing a public service. When their ranks are thinned by death, an attempt is made to recruit young people as understudies. Such persons become true priests. They carry on traditional practices without the expectation that supernatural power will intervene. In priestly ceremonies there is none of the contest between good and evil so prominent in shamanism.

In every Apache tribe, religion is a combination of shamanic and priestly rites, but in differing proportions. Shamanism predominates among the Chiricahua and the Mescalero. The Jicarilla favor priestly ceremonies and tend to employ shamanism only in emergencies. Other tribes range somewhere in between. Yet, despite variations, common symbols and concepts knit all Apache ceremonialism into a recognizable and understandable whole.

BIBLIOGRAPHY

Basso, Keith H. *Western Apache Witchcraft*. Anthropological Papers of the University of Arizona, no. 15. Tucson, 1969. A very full account of Western Apache witchcraft by one of the foremost students of Western Apache culture.

Basso, Keith H. *The Cibecue Apache*. New York, 1970. A well-rounded account of the culture of one of the Western Apache subdivisions that devotes a good deal of space to a description of the religious system.

Goodwin, Grenville. "White Mountain Apache Religion." *American Anthropologist,* n.s. 40 (January–March 1938): 24–37. A succinct but informative overview of the belief system of the subdivisions of the Western Apache by an able scholar.

McAllister, J. Gilbert. *Dävéko, Kiowa-Apache Medicine Man.* With a summary of Kiowa Apache history and culture by W. W. Newcomb, Jr. Bulletin of the Texas Memorial Museum, no. 17. Austin, 1970. A valuable collection of stories concerning the shamanic achievements of a famous practitioner.

Opler, Morris Edward. *Myths and Legends of the Lipan Apache Indians.* Memoirs of the American Folk-Lore Society, vol. 36. New York, 1940. A volume of Lipan lore that contains much information about the religion of this tribe.

Opler, Morris Edward. *An Apache Life-Way: The Economic, Social, and Religious Institutions of the Chiricahua Indians.* Chicago, 1941. A basic study of all aspects of the culture in which the religion is fully described.

Opler, Morris Edward. "Adolescence Rite of the Jicarilla." *El Palacio* 49 (February 1942): 25–38. A compact description of the adolescence rite as it has developed among the Jicarilla.

Opler, Morris Edward. *The Character and Derivation of the Jicarilla Holiness Rite.* University of New Mexico Bulletin, whole no. 390; Anthropological Series, vol. 4, no. 3. Albuquerque, 1943. A detailed account of one of the major priestly ceremonies of the Jicarilla.

Opler, Morris Edward. "The Jicarilla Apache Ceremonial Relay Race." *American Anthropologist,* n.s. 46 (January–March 1944): 75–97. A study of another major Jicarilla ritual, showing the degree to which a borrowed ceremony has been shaped to conform to Jicarilla concepts.

Opler, Morris Edward. *Apache Odyssey: A Journey between Two Worlds.* New York, 1969. The heavily annotated autobiography of a Mescalero who describes many ceremonies that he witnessed or in which he participated.

7 NAVAJO

Louise Lamphere

The Navajo, whose population in the 1980s has been estimated at 170,000, now live primarily on the Navajo Nation (a reservation approximately the size of New England) in northern Arizona and New Mexico. Archaeological and linguistic evidence suggests that the Navajo were latecomers to the American Southwest, arriving between 1000 and 1525 CE. Through contact with the Spanish and Puebloan peoples they acquired horses, sheep, goats, and agriculture. Anthropologists believe that after the Pueblo Revolt of 1680, refugee Puebloan people living with the Navajo greatly influenced Navajo religion. Similarities in their origin legends, parallels between Pueblo and Navajo cosmologies, their use of masked figures in ritual, and their use of sand paintings probably date from this period.

COSMOGONY AND WORLDVIEW

The Navajo origin myth recounts their emergence from a series of underworlds onto the Earth Surface. Using a medicine bundle brought from the underworlds, in an all-night ceremony at the place of emergence, First Man, First Woman, and other Holy People set in place the "inner forms" of natural phenomena (earth, sky, the sacred mountains, plants, and animals), creating the present world. It was into this world that Changing Woman was born; she was impregnated by the sun and gave birth to twin sons, who killed various monsters that had been endangering the Holy People. Using the medicine bundle First Man had given her, Changing Woman created maize. She also created the Earth-Surface People, or the Navajo, from epidermal waste rubbed from her skin.

The Navajo creation myth indicates that there is no dichotomy between the natural and supernatural in Navajo religion. Further, the human (the Earth-Surface People) and the divine (the Holy People) are conceived of in terms of the same set of motivating forces: the notion of "wind" *(nilch'i)*; the concept of inner form *(bii'gistíín),* or "in-lying one" *(bii'siziinii);* and the opposing notions of "pleasant conditions," or harmony and balance *(hózhǫ́),* and "ugly conditions," or disharmony and disorder *(hóchǫ́').*

Wind is a unitary phenomenon that is the source of all life, movement, and behavior. However, wind has various aspects that have different functions and hence

69

different names. Before the Emergence, winds are said to have given the means of life (i.e., breath) to the inhabitants of the underworlds. After the Emergence, mists of light were placed along each of the cardinal directions and four sacred mountains were created in each direction. Each direction is said to have an "inner form" *(bii'gistíín)* as well as a closely associated wind. From the four directions these winds give the means of life, movement, thought, and communication to the natural phenomena, the Holy People, and the Navajo. Wind's Child is sent to guide and advise the Earth-Surface People. Finally, each Navajo also has a "wind within one" *(nílch'i bii'sizíínii)* that enters at birth and guides the individual.

Thus both natural phenomena and humans have inner forms or "in-lying ones" animated by wind. As Gary Witherspoon has written, "In most cases the Holy People of the fifth world are those who are the inner forms of various natural phenomena and forces, including animals. These in-lying ones are the controlling and animating powers of nature. Navajo ritual is designed to control the Holy People who are the inner forms and controlling agents of natural phenomena" (Witherspoon, 1983, p. 575).

The Holy People *(diyin dine'é)* are immune to danger, destruction, and death. They are not holy in the sense that they are virtuous but rather in the sense that they are powerful. It is a Navajo's responsibility to maintain harmonious relations between himself and the Holy People, though they may be persuaded to aid in the restoration of a person who has become ill through improper contact with them. In Navajo religion the term *hózhǫ́* refers to a positive or ideal environment. The phrase *sạ'áh naagháí, bik'eh hózhǫ́* ("long life, in accordance with happiness, harmony") occurs in most ritual songs and prayers and even more clearly exemplifies the Navajo ideal. As Witherspoon puts it, "The goal of Navajo life in this world is to live to maturity in the condition described as *hózhǫ́,* and to die of old age, the end result of which incorporates one into the universal beauty, harmony, and happiness described as *sạ'áh naagháí bik'eh hózhǫ́*" (ibid., p. 573).

Illness is thought to be a state of "ugly conditions" *(hóchǫ́')* that has resulted from the patient's contact with something "dangerous." Wyman and Kluckhohn (1938, pp. 13–14) list four groups of "etiological factors" that can produce sickness: (1) natural phenomena such as lightning, wind, and thunder; (2) some kinds of animals, including bears, deer, coyotes, porcupines, snakes, eagles, and fish; (3) coming into contact with ceremonial paraphernalia at inappropriate times; and (4) ghosts of Navajos, aliens, or witches, including werewolves. Illness may result from a direct attack, in which case the "weapon" *(deezláá')* or "arrow" *(bik'a')* of the animal or lightning is thought to lodge in the person's interior, or the "in-standing one" or wind *(nílch'i)* of a dangerous animal, a natural phenomenon, a witch, or a ghost may enter the body and become temporarily or permanently the "wind within one" of the person. The process of curing during a Navajo "sing" thus entails removing the "ugly things" (anger, weapons, or even the "in-standing one" that has entered the patient's body) if the person is to regain the state of *hózhǫ́.*

TYPES OF CHANTS

Anthropologists have identified twenty-four chant complexes; only about eight were well known and frequently performed in the 1970s; six were extinct and four were obsolescent. There has been little agreement among either Navajo consultants or anthropologists as to how these chants might be ordered into a system. (See Wyman and Kluckhohn, 1938; Haile, 1938; Reichard, 1950; Wyman, 1983; Witherspoon, 1983; and Werner et al., 1983, for various possibilities.)

The Navajo Blessingway is, however, one of the central ceremonies. Its myth (recounted in full in Wyman, 1970) recounts the events of the Navajo creation after the Emergence, and the activities of Changing Woman play a central role. The Blessingway ceremony, two nights in length, is used to prevent *hóchǫ'* and to preserve a state of *hózhǫ́,* or blessing. The Kinaalda, or girl's puberty rite, is another ceremonial that uses Blessingway songs and reenacts Changing Woman's first menstruation.

Enemyway *('anaa'jí),* in contrast, is designed to counteract contact with non-Navajos and to exorcise their ghosts. According to Wyman (1983, p. 541) it is one of a mostly obsolescent group of ancient war ceremonials and is now classed with other ceremonies labeled Evilway *(hóchǫ'ojí).* Enemyway lasts three nights, and much of its symbolism revolves around war and the exorcism of "ugly things"; the ceremony includes a mock battle and the shooting of a scalp.

Other chants (Shootingway, Beautyway, Mountainway, Nightway, and Navajo Windway, to name the most popular) are dominated by one of three ways of performing the chant: Lifeway, Evilway, and Holyway. Two chants can be conducted according to the Lifeway ritual, and there is a fundamental Lifeway chant called Flintway. Lifeway is used to treat injuries resulting from accidents; in it, the person who is undergoing treatment is painted red, the color of flesh and blood, which symbolizes a return to life and health. Evilway ritual is characterized by techniques for exorcising native ghosts and for chasing away "ugly things." Most chants are performed according to Holyway ritual, which is directed toward the Holy People and is concerned with the attraction of good and the restoration of the patient. I shall discuss the Holyway version of Navajo chants in more detail to illustrate the themes of Navajo ritual and the curing process itself.

Holyway Chants. Navajo Holyway chants are two, five, or nine nights in length (a "night" being counted from one sunset to the next). They consist of component ceremonies strung together in a specified order. Many chants include a bath, a sandpainting ritual, a sweat and emetic ceremony, and an all-night sing on the last night. Each component ceremony is composed of ritual acts that are directed against the etiological factor (for example, bears, snakes, or lightning) causing the illness that the ceremony is designed to cure.

The Navajo model of the cosmos as laid out in the creation myth is expressed in the setting of the ceremony itself. The chant takes place in a Navajo hogan, which is circular like the horizon. Movement during a ritual is always clockwise or "in the direction of the sun." Men sit on the south side of the hogan; women sit on the north side. The singer sits on the southwest side and the patient, when resting, sits on the northwest side. The east (where the door is located) is associated with *diyin;* prayer sticks and other offerings are deposited toward the east. The north is associated with *hóchǫ',* and objects that have been pressed against the patient in order to remove *hóchǫ'* are deposited toward the north. Each chant uses color and directional symbolism as a condensed code for ordering and interpreting the myriad of ritual actions that are performed during the chant.

During the sing, the singer uses a number of ritual objects including (1) the fetishes that are a permanent part of his pouch, (2) the objects constructed during the chant (e.g., prayer sticks and sand paintings) partly from the singer's supplies and partly from materials (such as ground stone, yucca root, and corn meal) obtained by the patient's relatives according to the singer's specifications, and (3) medicines prepared during the chant from the singer's supply of pollen and plant materials.

During the chant, ritual objects are combined with several kinds of ritual actions: prestations to the Holy People, actions that identify the patient with the supernatural, and actions of removal that rid the patient's body of "ugly conditions." Identification with the Holy People takes place through actions of "applying to" or "taking in"— for example, pressing articles from the singer's pouch against the patient's body to make him or her *diyin*. Other important ritual actions include feeding the patient "sacred food" or herbal medicine, pressing the sand from the supernaturals depicted in a sand painting on parts of the body, and inhaling the dawn's breath or *nilch'i* at the very end of the sing. There are also several actions that remove "ugly things": for example, the "unraveling ceremony" (where feathers or herbs are bound in bundles with strips of yucca, pressed against the patient, and then yanked off) and the forced vomiting during a sweat and emetic ceremony.

The three themes (prestation, removal, and identification) occur over and over again during the entire Holyway chant. They are repeated in each subceremony, in each prayer, and in each song set. However, one of these themes may be dominant or emphasized in a particular subceremony. During the prayer stick ceremony, in which a supernatural is compelled to aid a patient, prestations are important; during a sweat and emetic ceremony, the removal of *hóchǫ'* is crucial; and during a sandpainting ceremony the identification of the patient with the *diyin* is the focus of effort.

COMPARISONS

There are striking similarities between Navajo ceremonialism and that of the Apache, on the one hand, and the Pueblo, on the other. Both the Navajo and the Apache place emphasis on the central theme of long life, and both center their ceremonies on the individual, that is, on changing his or her state through prestation, the removal of evil objects, and identification with supernatural power. Like Pueblo religion, Navajo religion entails a view of the cosmos that is structured as a bounded universe where the present world is the top of several layered worlds through which the ancestors emerged. Navajo ritual replicates the cosmos more clearly than does Apache ritual; but, by using color, sex, and directional symbolism to do so, Navajo religion parallels Pueblo ritual and worldview (see Heib, 1979; Tedlock, 1979; and Ortiz, 1969).

The similarities between the ceremonies of the Navajo, the Apache, and the Pueblo suggest that there are unifying features to ceremonialism in native Southwest cultures. Southwest religion, like that of other Native American cultures, is closely tied to the natural environment. Native cosmologies are rooted in conceptions of time and space that lay out the local terrain in a particular way, imbuing it with supernatural meaning. Natural objects are made into ritual objects and are used to attract positive supernatural power, to remove dangerous power, and to represent sacred presence. Ceremonial specialists using these objects and ritual actions communicate with the supernatural in order to ensure that the natural and cultivated plant and animal life will continue to be abundant and that individual and communal health and prosperity are maintained.

BIBLIOGRAPHY

Aberle, David F. "The Navajo Singer's 'Fee': Payment or Prestation?" In *Studies in Southwestern Ethnolinguistics,* edited by Dell H. Hymes and William E. Bittle, pp. 15–32. The Hague, 1967.

Haile, Berard. "Navaho Chantways and Ceremonials." *American Anthropologist* 40 (January–March 1938): 639–652.

Heib, Louis. "Hopi World View." In *Handbook of North American Indians,* vol. 9, edited by Alfonso Ortiz, pp. 577–580. Washington, D.C., 1979.

Kaplan, Bert, and Dale Johnson. "The Social Meaning of Navajo Psychopathology and Psychotherapy." In *Magic, Faith, and Healing,* edited by Ari Kiev, pp. 203–229. New York, 1964.

Lamphere, Louise. "Symbolic Elements in Navajo Ritual." *Southwestern Journal of Anthropology* 25 (1969): 279–305.

Lamphere, Louise. "Southwestern Ceremonialism." In *Handbook of North American Indians,* vol. 10, edited by Alfonso Ortiz, pp. 743–763. Washington, D.C., 1983.

McNeley, James K. *Holy Wind in Navajo Philosophy.* Tucson, 1981.

Ortiz, Alfonso. *The Tewa World: Space, Time, Being and Becoming in a Pueblo Society.* Chicago, 1969.

Reichard, Gladys A. *Navajo Religion: A Study of Symbolism.* 2 vols. New York, 1950.

Tedlock, Dennis. "Zuni Religion and World View." In *Handbook of North American Indians,* vol. 9, edited by Alfonso Ortiz, pp. 499–508. Washington, D.C., 1979.

Werner, Oswald, Allen Manning, and Kenneth Y. Begishe. "A Taxonomic View of the Traditional Navajo Universe." In *Handbook of North American Indians,* vol. 10, edited by Alfonso Ortiz, pp. 579–591. Washington, D.C., 1983.

Witherspoon, Gary. *Navajo Kinship and Marriage.* Chicago, 1975.

Witherspoon, Gary. "Language and Reality in Navajo World View." In *Handbook of North American Indians,* vol. 10, edited by Alfonso Ortiz, pp. 570–578. Washington, D.C., 1983.

Wyman, Leland C. *Blessingway, with Three Versions of the Myth Recorded and Translated from the Navaho by Father Berard Haile.* Tucson, 1970.

Wyman, Leland C. "Navajo Ceremonial System." In *Handbook of North American Indians,* vol. 10, edited by Alfonso Ortiz, pp. 536–557. Washington, D.C., 1983.

Wyman, Leland C., and Flora Bailey. "Idea and Action Patterns in Navaho Flintway." *Southwestern Journal of Anthropology* 1 (1945): 356–377.

Wyman, Leland C., and Clyde Kluckhohn. *Navajo Classification of Their Song Ceremonials.* Memoirs of the American Anthropological Association, vol. 50. Menasha, Wis., 1938.

8

CALIFORNIA AND THE INTERMOUNTAIN REGION

Thomas Buckley

The Intermountain Region of North America is framed on the east by the Rocky Mountains of Canada and the United States and on the west by the Cascade and the Sierra Nevada ranges. Ethnographers customarily divide this region into two indigenous "culture areas," the Plateau and the Great Basin. The Plateau is bounded on the north by the boreal forests beyond the Fraser Plateau of British Columbia and on the south by the Bitterroot Mountains of Idaho and the arid highlands of southern Oregon and northwestern Montana. It includes the Columbia River's plateau and drainage in Washington, Oregon, and a small portion of northern California. The Great Basin is the area of steppe-desert lying primarily in Nevada and Utah but including parts of southern Idaho, western Wyoming, and western Colorado. It runs south from the Salmon and Snake rivers of Idaho to the Colorado Plateau, is bounded by the Colorado River on the south, and includes the interior deserts of southwestern California. "California," as an indigenous culture area, thus comprises the lands west of the Sierra Nevada crest to the Pacific Ocean, most of southern California and northern Baja California, and most lands north from there to the present Oregon border.

California and the Plateau have supported large and varied native populations. The Great Basin, with its exceedingly restrictive ecology, has always been less heavily populated and more culturally uniform than either California or the Plateau. Nonetheless, even in the Basin, sweeping areal generalizations can serve only as starting points in investigating both intra- and interareal diversity among native peoples, for the three areas are foci of cultural adaptation, expression, and influence, rather than impermeably bounded cultural or historical isolates.

Although the indigenous peoples of the Basin were all speakers of closely related Numic languages, the languages of the Plateau were more varied, and those of California had a truly extraordinary diversity. Broadly speaking, cultural and linguistic diversity were correlated in the three areas. In terms of religious practice, the greatest diversity was in California and the least in the Basin, with the Plateau falling somewhere between.

General Themes

The pervasiveness of religious concerns and behavior in the daily lives of all of these peoples is suggested by the range of religious themes that are common to the three areas, despite the diverse, area-specific expressions given them.

POWER

Significant contacts with European influences occurred in the three areas beginning in the eighteenth century and had achieved devastating impact by the mid-nineteenth century. As will be seen, European influence tended to elevate concepts of anthropomorphic creator figures to new eminence. Before contact, however, a widespread perception of a diffuse, generalized, and impersonal cosmic force, often referred to today as "power," was far more significant. This energic field of all potentials is a neutral, amoral, and generative presence that produces all things.

MYTHOLOGY

In some cases, power was first manifested by a world creator who, through it, brought the world into its present form. Such creators might be culture heroes and transformers, such as Komokums among the Modoc, a people interstitial between California and the Plateau. Komokums and many others like him acted in conjunction with earth divers to form the earth from a bit of soil raised from the depths of a primordial sea. In other cases, especially in north-central California, world creators are likely to be true creator gods, thinking the world into existence or bringing it forth with a word. In southern California we find creation myths of great metaphysical complexity and subtlety, such as those of the Luiseño, for whom creation arose by steps, out of an absolute void. Even here, however, we find a transformer, Wiyot, shaping the present world from an earth that preceded his existence, and this seems the more typical pattern. Such gods and heroes tend to become otiose after their work is accomplished, rather than lingering on as moral overseers.

Unlike the Californians, neither the peoples of the Basin nor those of the Plateau seem to have been much concerned with world origins. Yet they shared with Californians a profound concern for a variety of prehuman spirits—usually animals, but also celestial beings, monsters, and others—who aided in bringing the world to its present shape and in establishing culture. Thus, throughout the region one finds arrays of such prehuman beings, each exercising power for good or ill according to its innate proclivities. The actions of each are recounted in a broad spectrum of myths and stories. Commonly, one or more of these beings, most often Coyote but others as well, emerge as a trickster, undoing the good works of the heroes and creators through a peculiar blend of innocence, greed, and stupidity. Such tricksters may be creatively helpful as well as negatively influential, and sometimes creators and tricksters are one and the same, which accounts for the multivocality of existence. Often the trickster is the sibling of a culture hero, as Coyote ("little wolf") is of Wolf among the Shoshoni, Short-tailed Weasel is of Long-tailed Weasel among the Washo of the eastern Sierras, and Frog Woman is of Wiyot among the Luiseño.

SPIRITS AND PERSONAL POWER

Many animal spirits, including tricksters, remained in the world as sources of specialized powers for human beings. Other unique power potentials might reside in celestial and landscape features and in common, manufactured objects. People might encounter such spirits, usually in their anthropomorphic forms, in visions or in dreams. Through such encounters individuals gained spirit-helpers, enhancing the power innate in themselves and gaining particular powers that, through volitional control, brought success in specific endeavors. Vision quests in many different forms are found throughout the three areas.

Seeking increased, specialized power and protection through intentional encounters with spirit-beings was a primary concern of the religions of the Plateau. In the Basin, visions and personal powers tended to come to individuals spontaneously, at the spirits' will, and were not often sought through formal quests. In California, spirit encounters sometimes resulted from stringent austerities and Plateau-style questing, as among the Achomawi and Atsugewi in the northeast. Often they were sought through participation in initiatory "schools" of pubescent boys seeking power collectively under the tutelage of older initiates. Such schools were central to the visionary religions of the south and the elaborate dance and healing societies of northern California.

In many such California initiation schools, sodalities—secret, mythically chartered societies—were at the forefront. Membership in such sodalities was often restricted; males alone were accepted, and sometimes only those representative of elite kin groups. In parts of the Plateau, especially among the Nez Perce and the Tenino, specific guardian spirits might be transmitted through inheritance. In the notably egalitarian Plateau, however, this did not have the effect of centralizing both spiritual and social ascendency in elites, as did sodality membership in the more stratified of California groups.

More generally, both males and females had access to the spirits and, thus, to personal power. In the Plateau, young boys and girls alike often sought visions, although boys did so more frequently than girls. In the Basin, both males and females could receive spirit powers at any time during their lives, although it appears that men were more often so favored. The situation in California was more complex. In each of three major subareas, women were initiated into some groups but not into others and, among these groups, there were often varying, ranked degrees of male and female spirit acquisition and initiation.

Throughout the three culture areas, the specific spirits that one might encounter and the powers that they enabled were varied. Hunting or fishing skill, the ability to cure and to injure, success in courting and in fighting, finesse in crafts and in song making, gambling luck, wealth, wisdom, and many other potentials might be realized.

Although increased and specialized powers could be acquired and maximized through contacts with spirits, they could also be lost by offending those spirits through failure to adhere to taboos imposed in vision or dream; through misuse of songs, rituals, or power objects; through more general breach of custom, or simply through baffling happenstance. Every increase in an individual's power had its price.

SHAMANS

The shamans were the most powerful of people, the most respected for their spirit contacts, and the most feared. It was they who paid the highest price for their acumen. (*Shaman* here means a healer who obtains and exercises his powers through direct contact with spiritual beings.) In the Plateau, special effort was not usually exerted to obtain the guardian spirits that brought shamanic powers. Here, as in the Basin, both men and women could receive shamanic powers, although male shamans predominated. The same was largely true of Californians, although shamans among Shoshoni, Salinan, and some Yokuts groups were exclusively male, whereas in northwestern California female shamans vastly predominated, those who were the daughters and granddaughters of shamans having the greatest proclivity toward acquiring such powers.

Throughout the three areas, initial encounters with spirits capable of bestowing shamanic powers (sometimes volitionally sought in California and, to a lesser extent, in the Basin) were followed by intensive and often long-term training in the control of the spirit-power and an apprenticeship in its use under a recognized shaman. Such training might include initiation in the secrets of legerdemain, fire handling, and ventriloquism, on which shamanic performances often depended for their dramatic impact. Yet although shamans everywhere were expected to display their powers in such feats, and occasionally to best other shamans in public power contests, their primary function was as curative specialists, and the tricks of the trade were subordinate to success in this important function.

Theories of disease were fairly uniform. Illness came through magical objects projected into the sufferer's body by human sorcery or witchcraft. Again, ghosts or spirits whose rules for conduct had been ignored or whose special places had been defiled might make people ill. The spiritual essence of the patient could be called away by unseen beings or injured by a sorcerer or witch. Finally, one could be poisoned by a witch, either psychically or physically. In the Plateau all such power-related disease was distinguished from natural, physical illness; shamans treated only the former, whereas the latter were treated through exoteric remedies, often by lay specialists. Among the Washo of the Basin, however, all death was attributed to sorcerers.

As theories of spiritually induced disease were quite uniform, so were therapeutic measures. Shamans diagnosed the illness and then entered a trance through singing, dancing, and, occasionally, the ingestion of powerful substances. The shaman then sucked out the introjected objects and disposed of them or used his breath to blow off the "shadows" of offended spirits that had lodged in the patient's body. He might also heal through various forms of massage. Many shamans specialized in one or another approach to particular sorts of illnesses. Some, especially in the Plateau, traveled out of their bodies to find and retrieve the lost souls of patients or to regain these in other ways. Illnesses might be caused by the misdeeds of members of the community other than the patient himself, and both public confessions and the identification of sorcerers were common features of performances.

Shamans in most groups acquired other, noncurative powers and specialties as well. In the Great Basin, in southern California, and north through the central California subarea, rattlesnake handling was practiced by shamans specially related to this powerful creature and capable of curing its bites. Weather shamans who both caused and stopped rains were found in these areas as well. In the Basin, shamans served as hunt leaders, dreaming of quarry such as antelope, leading drives, and charming the game into enclosures. Other specialties abounded. Paiute shamans in the Basin and many in central and northern California became "bear doctors," imitating these animals and using their powers for both benign and malign ends. Others might gain the power to find lost objects, to predict the future, or to conjure, as among the Colville and the Kutenai of the Plateau, whose rites were similar to the shaking tent rites more common far to the east. Virtually everywhere, even among the Plateau and Basin groups whose shamans first obtained their powers without special questing, such practitioners often sought to augment their acumen through gaining additional spirit helpers, often seeking these in special places.

Power itself is neutral, its potential for good and ill being manifested at the discretion (or indiscretion) of those spirits, ghosts, or human beings who have more than usual control of it. Thus shamans were universally feared for their potential to use power in malign ways, as sorcerers. In the Basin and in much of California shamans were viewed with great suspicion; they were thought to induce or prolong illness in order to collect higher fees and to kill outright for a fee from an aggrieved party. Among the Mohave and other River Yuman groups in southeastern California, the killing of a shaman, on whatever grounds, was not considered reprehensible. Elsewhere shamans were killed only in the event of their patient's death. In northwestern California, shamans simply returned their fee should the patient die, greed being more commonly attributed to them than sorcery. The shaman's position was not always enviable, and, particularly in the Great Basin and Plateau, people tended to become shamans only at the behest of a spirit who could not be refused, or they refused to accept shamanic powers when opportunities to acquire them arose.

FIRST-FRUITS RITES

First-fruits rites, celebrated for a variety of resources throughout the region, were often conducted by shamans. This was true, for example, of the small, local first-salmon rites that were common along many of the rivers and streams of the Plateau, along the northern California coast south to San Francisco Bay, and among the Pyramid Lake Paviosto, the Lemhi Shoshoni, and some other groups in the northern Great Basin. In some cases, however, first-salmon and other first-fruits rites were incorporated into larger-scale renewal ceremonies, as in northwestern California, and were directed by specialized priests—intermediaries between the human and nonhuman worlds who, as holders of inherited and appointed offices, recited codified liturgies.

GIRLS' PUBERTY AND MENSTRUAL SECLUSION

The ritual initiation of females into adulthood at menarche and, often, the public celebration of this event constitute a second widespread ritual element in the religions of the three culture areas. In general, throughout the region women were isolated at menarche and placed under a variety of restrictions, their conduct during the time being thought to presage their future. Emphasis on girls' puberty tended to be greater among peoples more dependent on hunting than on gathering. Thus, periods of training might be as short as five days, as among the peoples of the western Basin, or extended as long as four years, as among the Carrier Indians of the northern Plateau. In coastal southern California, puberty was a community concern, and all young women reaching menarche during a given year were secluded and instructed together, sometimes being "cooked" in heated pits in a way reminiscent of the training of novice shamans to the north in California. Indeed, it can be argued that puberty rites in many groups represent a female equivalent of male spirit quests and sodality initiations. Such "cooking" of pubescent girls is found elsewhere, as among the Gosiute of the Basin. Communal rites are paralleled in the Plateau, where the Chilcotin, the Southern Okanogen, the Tenino, and the Nez Perce utilized communal seclusion huts for the initiation of young girls.

There were, however, no elaborate public female puberty celebrations in the southern Plateau, where girls' puberty was marked by simple elaborations of more general menstrual customs. Public ceremonies did occur, usually at the discretion of the girl's family, in the Great Basin—as among the Washo and others. Here, girls' puberty might be celebrated in conjunction with a Big Time, an intergroup gathering for shared subsistence enterprises, ritual, feasting, trading, dancing, gambling, and games. In California, girls' puberty dances were held by many northern groups as the year's ritual highlight—again, often in conjunction with Big Times. Occasionally, and especially among the Athapascan-speaking groups of the northwest, such dances were the prerogative of elite Californian families.

The prevalence of concern for female puberty in the three areas is clearly related to a concern for menstruation in general. Menstrual blood was viewed as among the most powerful of substances, highly dangerous if not properly controlled and, although often of positive virture to the woman herself, inimical to the welfare of others, especially males. The isolation and restriction of girls at menarche was thus widely repeated—although with far less elaboration—at each menses. Communal menstrual shelters were found in some Plateau communities and perhaps in parts of California. Elsewhere, a small hut for the individual menstruant was constructed, as in much of the Basin, or her movements were restricted to the family's dwelling, as among the River Yuman groups. Menstrual seclusion and dietary and other restrictions varied in duration from the time of the flow up to ten or twelve days, as in northwestern California.

SUDATORIES

Male concern for menstrual pollution and for other pollutants that might hinder the exercise or acquisition of power, or "luck," was certainly related to the prevalence of male sweating, carried out in a variety of sudatories in all three areas. Such sudatories might be small and temporary or large and permanent structures. In northwestern California, for example, "sweat houses" were sizeable, semisubterranean houses, men's clubs where all adult males slept, worked, and practiced rituals, as well as sweated. Among the Nomlaki substantial men's sweat houses were the domain of a male sodality, the *huta*. The religious nature of purification through regular sweating is evident in the veneration with which the sudatory was regarded. Among certain Plateau groups, such as the Sanpoil, the sweat house itself was the mundane manifestation of a powerful sweat-house god.

Major Religious Systems

In each area, and often in specifiable subareas, the general themes outlined above were manifested within the context of—and were given particular ideological inflections by—area-specific religious systems.

Among the peoples of the Great Basin, environmental conditions demanded small populations divided into highly mobile bands, reduced at times to the extended nuclear family, and expanding at more abundant times to small bands of such families. There was little need for social or political organization on a wider scale that would ensure the privileges of more complex kin groups or the territorial autonomy of a large political unit. By the same token, dispersed resources could not be collected in sufficient quantities to provide for the needs of frequent, large gatherings. Complex ritual systems depending on cyclic collective action did not develop in the Basin as they did in both California and the Plateau. By contrast, in these latter areas more sedentary peoples, enjoying richer resource bases and enacting more complex and farther-reaching kinship and political organizations, created religious systems through which large numbers of people were regularly assembled for collective ritual experience.

THE GREAT BASIN

Basin religion was largely an individual or small-band concern, and shamans provided spiritual leadership sufficient to the needs of most bands. Rituals, such as girls' puberty celebrations, that in other areas served as foci for large gatherings here tended to be small, family affairs. The healing performances of shamans might provide occasions for shared ritual participation, but such gatherings, too, were small, limited to band members, and not held according to a fixed schedule.

Large-scale Big Times did occur with some regularity among the Washo and Paiute of the western Great Basin, several bands gathering together for harvest of the more abundant wild crops (such as piñon nuts) for ritual, and for recreation. The Paiute reciprocated such Big Times with the Mono and Miwok of California. Interband antelope drives, sometimes in conjunction with Big Times, were ritually prepared and imbued with religious significance, as suggested by the many Basin rocks displaying petroglyphs and pictographs that date from the remote past through the nineteenth century.

The Big Times of the western Great Basin and California were supplanted in the eastern portion of the Basin area by other sorts of events. Ute and Shoshoni bands convened several times a year for "round dances." Among the Ute, a more ritually focused Bear Dance, marking the return of bears from hibernation and thus the renewal of the world in spring, was performed annually in late winter.

THE PLATEAU

In the Plateau the common western theme of personal spirit-power was honed to its greatest refinement and served as the basis for an areal religious system keynoted by collective "winter spirit-dances." Although there were a great many variations in the specifics of individual guardian-spirit quests and of winter dances among Plateau tribes, a generalized account may be offered as an introduction.

Among the Sanpoil-Nespelem and most other Salish groups, boys and many young girls began spirit questing at or before puberty, often when they were as young as six or eight. (Sahaptin groups placed less emphasis on spirit quests, and others, such as the Carrier, restricted them to certain males.) The child was sent out to fast, scour himself with rough foliage, bathe in cold pools, and keep vigils in isolated places. In dreams, as among the Carrier, or in visions, the supplicant was visited by an animal spirit or the spirit of an object or place. The spirit instructed the person in a song that often had an associated dance step, and sometimes revealed power objects.

In many groups, the supplicant, on returning from a successful quest, "forgot" both encounter and song. (The Kutenai, whose youths sought only a single, immediately effective spirit, present an exception.) Among the Salish, when the individual reached full adulthood, usually about age twenty-five for men, the spirit returned, often causing illness. With the aid of a shaman, the individual "remembered" the song and spirit. Once fully accepted, one's spirit became an intrinsic aspect of one's being, like a soul, a "partner" whose loss was life-threatening. Throughout their lives, people might seek different, additional spirits with associated powers and specialties.

During a two-month period in the winter, anyone who had a guardian spirit—a shaman or a layman—might sponsor a spirit dance. The dances, held in a winter lodge, lasted two or three nights and were scheduled so that people of a given locale might attend several in a winter. Under the supervision of shamans, dancers imitated their own guardian spirits, singing their songs and performing their dance steps. New initiates to whom spirits had recently returned used the occasion to legitimize their relationships with their spirits. Other components of the dances included feasting and the giving of gifts to visitors, the offering of gifts to spirits at a center pole, and shamans' displays and contests. The conduct of the audience was rigidly controlled during the dances, and in some groups their behavior was policed by officiants.

Among the Sanpoil, Colville, Kutenai, Kalispel, Spokan, Coeur d'Alene, and Flathead, a society of men possessing Bluejay as guardian spirit served this policing function. These "Bluejay shamans" identified entirely with Bluejay during the winter dance period, painting their faces black, keeping to themselves, and scavenging food. The Bluejay shamans perched in the rafters of dance houses during performances, swooping down on those who broke the rules of conduct. They also performed services as finders of lost objects and as curers, and were ritually returned to a normal state at the end of the dance period. Although the Bluejay shamans suggest an at least latent sodality structure in the southeastern Plateau, such sodalities were fully developed only in California.

CALIFORNIA

There were four major subareal ritual complexes in aboriginal California. Beyond serving as vehicles for religious expression, such complexes served important functions in social, economic, and ecological regulation, in ethnic maintenance, and, through creating unifying networks, in political organization.

Toloache. From the Yuman tribes of the south, north through the Yokuts and, in diminished forms, to the Miwok, the use of *Datura stramonium*—jimsonweed, or *toloache* (from the Nahuatl and Spanish)—was a common and central feature of religious practice. A psychotropic decoction was made from the root of this highly toxic plant and carefully administered to initiates by shamans or by specialized priests. After a period of unconsciousness the initiates awoke to a trancelike state of long duration during which, guided by adepts, they acquired animal or celestial spirit-helpers. Such collective, drug-induced vision questing was often undertaken by males at puberty and in the context of an extended "school," as among the Luiseño-Juaneño, the Cahuilla, the Ipai-Tipai, the Cupeño, and the Gabrielino. Schooling included severe physical ordeals, instruction in mythic cosmology carried out through dry painting, and in some cases the creation of rock art. In such groups as the Chumash and the Serrano, training was restricted to the sons of an elite. In all cases, the group of initiated men, and—among the Monache and the Yokuts—women, formed a sodality that bore defined religious, economic, and political responsibilities. Among the Chumash, such an organization provided the basis for a highly complex, elite socioreligious guild, *?antap,* led by priest-astronomers. Throughout the subarea, shamans made use of *toloache* in achieving curing trances.

In the extreme southeast, among the Mohave, the role of *toloache* was secondary to that of dreaming. Men learned clan myths through intentional dreaming and chanted these in long, collective "sings." Kin group solidarity was important to religious practice among other southern California groups as well, many keeping sib medicine bundles that were revealed only to *toloache* adepts.

Mourning Anniversaries. With their stress on ritual death and rebirth, the *toloache* religions of southern and central California reflected an overriding concern with personal and cosmic death and renewal. A second feature, the "mourning anniversary," accompanied the *toloache* complex. In broad outline, mourning anniversaries were large public gatherings in which effigies of the year's dead, together with large quantities of property, were burned on poles erected in circular brush shelters, the assembled audience mourning its collective losses. The occasion often served as a vehicle for girls' puberty celebrations, for the giving of new names, for honoring chiefs, and for expressing reciprocity between kin groups. Often an Eagle (or Condor) Dance, in which shamans displayed their power by slowly killing a sacrificial bird, formed an important part of the event.

The mourning anniversary, with many local variations, was practiced by the Basin peoples of the southern portion of contemporary California—the Chemehuevi, the Panamint, the Kawaiisu, and the Tubatulabal —as well as by virtually all groups in the southern California culture area. The practice extended northward through the *toloache*-using groups and beyond, being performed by the Maidu and Nisenan of northern California in conjunction with another religious complex, the Kuksu cult.

Kuksu. In northern California the *toloache* complex gave way to a second great ritual system, the Kuksu cult. The term *Kuksu* derives from the Pomo name for a creator-hero who is impersonated by masked dancers in the periodic performances that are the focus of the religious system. A parallel figure, Hesi, was prominent in the performances of groups in the Sacramento Valley and the Sierra Nevada foothills. The Hill Maidu expression of the complex featured a third such figure, Aki, who is found together with Hesi among the Northwestern Maidu. Kuksu and Hesi are sometimes found together among other groups.

Masked and costumed dancers impersonated these and other spirits and mythic figures in elaborate ceremonials performed in dance houses before large audiences during gatherings that lasted several days. Dances at various ceremonial centers were reciprocally supported. As with *toloache* religions, the various Kuksu religions provided collective "schools" for pubescent initiates who were, through cultic indoctrination and participation, conducted into secret, often ranked sodalities. Such sodalities could exercise great political and economic influence, as well as spiritual power. The Kuksu dances themselves returned the world to its pristine, mythic condition and often included first-fruits and curing elements in their scope. Intergroup trading, gambling, shamans' contests, and recreation were features of the Big Times that usually followed Kuksu performances.

Among groups that had both Kuksu and Hesi sodalities, as well as some others, participation was open to young men and also to some young women, as among the Cahto and the Yuki. More commonly, membership in such sodalities was restricted to males. In some groups, membership was further restricted to elite cadres who worked their way up through the sodality's ranked levels, as among the Pomo-speaking groups. In such groups a second sodality, the Ghost society, was open to all young men, as among the Patwin, and sometimes to women as well, as among the Eastern Pomo. These less prestigious sodalities presented masked dances that paralleled those of the Kuksu type and emphasized the honoring of the departed, the curing of ghost-disease, and the continuity of generations. Such themes were present in the mourning anniversaries prevalent to the south. Thus, the Ghost society was not found among groups in the Kuksu subarea (such as the Maidu and the Nisenan) that practiced mourning anniversaries.

World Renewal. Mythic reenactment, collective mourning, generational continuity, and world renewal are all motives present in the Kuksu religion that found other expressions in northwestern California, where a fourth areal ritual complex, the World Renewal cult, flourished. This complex featured cyclic ten-day ceremonials within more extended periods of ritual activity performed by specialized officiants. The various dances were given reciprocally at two- to three-year intervals at perhaps thirteen ceremonial centers in Yurok, Karok, and Hupa territories. Close equivalents of these World Renewal dances were held by Tolowa-Tututni, Wiyot, Chilula, and Shasta groups as well. The focal occasions were religious festivals, extended periods of public and private ritual, dancing, feasting, and communality that at times attracted several thousand participants. World Renewal festivals thus replaced both Big Times and mourning anniversaries in the northwestern subarea. However, the primary purpose of these large gatherings was the prevention of world disorder and the reaffirmation of interdependency. The world, potentially imbalanced by the weight of human misconduct, was "fixed" or "balanced" through the Jump Dance, the interdependence and abundance of all life reaffirmed and ensured through the Deerskin Dance. In both, teams of dancers displayed finery and power objects emblematic of the spiritual ascendency of their sponsors, and it was in this sense that such costumes and objects were considered "wealth."

The World Renewal religion was given different inflections by the different participating groups: the Yurok incorporated first-salmon rites and collective fishing as well as the rebuilding of a sacred structure; the Karok included "new fire" (new year) elements, as well as a first-salmon rite; and the Hupa celebrated a first-acorn rite, the rebuilding of a cosmographic structure, and so on. All stressed the reenactment, by priests, of the origins of the dances and their attendant rituals. The recitation of long, codified mythic scenarios was a central feature. School-like organizations of "helpers" were instructed by the priests. These organizations were similar to the initiatory sodalities of south and central California and included both men and women. Neither priests and their assistants nor dancers impersonated spirit beings, however, as was done in Kuksu performances or the spirit dances of the Plateau.

The sketches given here do not exhaust the aboriginal ritual inventories in any of the areas and subareas dealt with. There were many less prominent but no less meaningful ritual activities, both private and public. Throughout these areas religious knowledge and practice were fully integrated with social action. The European invasion of the American West, in disrupting ecological, social, and political systems, also disrupted religious systems.

Postcontact Religious Change

The religions of California, the Great Basin, and the Plateau have undergone thousands of years of slow change and development. They were probably changed most suddenly and drastically by the direct and indirect influences of Europeans and Euro-Americans that began in the eighteenth century.

The Roman Catholic missionization of California, beginning in 1769, had largely disastrous effects on the native populations of the area. Voluntary conversions took place, but forced baptism and forced residence in mission communities were more common. Ultimately, the successes of Catholic missionization north to San Francisco Bay were negated by the fearsome toll exacted by the diseases fostered by overcrowded missions and forced labor under the Spanish *encomienda* system. Success measured in lasting conversions was modest, and negative in terms of human welfare, but the missionaries contributed to native religious revitalization. For example, Catholicism seems to have provided the basis for a new high god, Chingichngish, in the *toloache* religions of the south. This moralistic, omniscient creator, which originated among the Gabrielino, also supplemented the mythic pantheons of the Luiseño-Juaneño, the Ipai-Tipai, the Chumash, and the Yokuts.

Other missionaries, primarily Protestant and Mormon, also made extended efforts in the nineteenth century in California, the Basin, and the Plateau. Yet the effects of later missionization were broadly similar: rather than supplanting native religions, Christianity provided symbolic means through which native religions found new forms to cope with the radically changing circumstances of life.

However, the effects of conquest were not limited to innovations informed by Christian ideology. The introduction of the horse onto the Plains and thence into the Plateau and the northwestern Basin in the early eighteenth century had an important impact on the peoples of these areas. Together with the horse came other Plains influences. Military sodalities were integrated into the religions of the Kutenai and the Flathead, as was the Sun Dance. The Sun Dance also spread to the Great Basin, where it was taken up by the Wind River Shoshoni and the Bannock and was introduced to the Utes by the Kiowa as late as 1890. [*See* Sun Dance.]

The preponderant contact phenomena evidenced in the religious life of all three areas, however, were the millenarian crisis cults inspired by a variety of "prophets" whose visions had been shaped by Christian influences. Typically, such visions occurred in deathlike states in which prophets met God or his emissary and received word of the coming millennium and the practices and moral codes that would ensure Indians' survival of it. Perhaps the best known of such crisis cults are the Paiute Ghost Dances of 1870 and 1890.

The first of these, initiated by the prophet Wodziwob in 1870, moved through the Basin and into central California. It was taken up by a number of California groups and moved north to the Shasta. The Ghost Dance doctrine stressed the destruction of the whites by the Creator, the return of the Indian dead, and the restoration of the earth to its pristine, precontact condition. It inspired a number of variants in the years following 1870. Most of these represented fusions of Kuksu-type and Ghost society dances with the new millenarianism. Such cults included the Earth Lodge religion practiced by many central and northern California peoples. Adherents awaited the millennium in large, semisubterranean dance houses. Other cults inspired by the 1870 Ghost Dance included the Big Head and Bole-Maru cults of the Hill Patwin, the Maidu, and the Pomo-speaking groups, and a succession of other local cults led by various "dreamers."

The 1890 Ghost Dance, initiated in 1889 by the Paiute prophet Wovoka, again spread through the Basin, this time moving east onto the Plains. It directly affected neither California nor the Plateau.

The two Ghost Dances are but the better known of a large number of similar efforts toward religious revitalization that flourished, particularly in the Plateau area, in the nineteenth century. In the 1830s, many prophets, not acting in concert, spread the Prophet Dance through the central and southern Plateau. This round dance, always performed on Sundays and reflecting belief in a high god, showed Christian influence, although some have argued that it had aboriginal precedents as well. The dance took many forms under the guidance of many prophets and dreamers, of whom the best known is perhaps Smohalla, a Sahaptin dreamer who revived the Prophet Dance in the 1870s in a form that spread widely.

In 1881 a Salish Indian from Puget Sound named John Slocum underwent what was by that time the established visionary experience of a prophet. Together with his wife Mary he inaugurated the Indian Shaker church, a Christian church in which the presence of God's power, signified by physical trembling ("the shake"), was used by congregants to cure the sick. This mixture of Christian and native shamanistic elements proved highly appealing, and the Indian Shaker church spread into the Plateau, where it was accepted by Yakima, Umatilla, Wasco-Tenino, Klamath, and, to a lesser extent, Nez Perce Indians. In northwestern California in 1926, churches were built by Yurok, Tolowa, and Hupa congregations. The Shakers' popularity in California began to wane in the 1950s, the result of internal schism, competition with evangelical Christian churches, and increasing stress on "Indianness" and the accompanying return to old ways.

These two apparently conflicting ideologies, based on the salvific powers of Jesus Christ, on the one hand, and on an Indian identity perceived as traditional, on the other, seem to have reached mutual accommodation in peyotism and its institutionalized expression, the Native American Church. The Peyote Way has been accepted by a large number of Basin Indians, spreading among the Ute, Paiute, Gosiute, and Shoshoni in the early twentieth century, its acceptance perhaps facilitated by the collapse of the 1890 Ghost Dance. The Washo received peyote from Ute believers in 1936.

Peyotism spread through the Basin despite the resistance of many traditionalists, becoming itself the basis for a new traditionalism. It was not, however, established in California, although Indians from such cities as San Francisco make frequent trips to take part in peyote meetings sponsored by the Washo and others in Nevada.

Many other postcontact religious systems, including the Sun Dance, continue to be enacted. Chingichngish remains central to religious life on the Rincon and Pauma reservations in southern California; Smohalla's Prophet Dance is still practiced as the basis of the Pom Pom religion of the Yakima and Warm Springs Indians; and Bole-Maru and other postcontact transformations of Kuksu religions are viable among Pomo and other central Californian groups. The Indian Shaker church survives in many communities.

Since the 1960s Indians of all three culture areas have made concerted efforts to reassert religious, as well as political, autonomy; indeed, the two realms continue to be closely intertwined. Traditional religious specialists and, in many cases, collective ritual activities have survived both conquest and christianization. Younger Indians are increasingly turning to elderly specialists and investing themselves in old ritual practices. Annual mourning ceremonies are still prominent in parts of southern California; northwestern Californians continue to dance in World Renewal rituals; and shamanism survives in the Basin, as does spirit questing on the Plateau. A myriad of other native ritual events and private practices continue throughout the region. Such state agencies as California's Native American Heritage Commission, as well as federal legislation such as the 1978 American Indian Religious Freedom Act, support these efforts to a degree. Withal, one can see the durability of the ancient ways, their persistence, and their ability to continue through modern transformations.

[*For further discussion of postcontact transformations of Native American religious systems, see* North American Religions, *article on* Modern Movements. *For more detailed information on particular movements, see* Ghost Dance; *sections on peyotism in* North American Indians, *article on* Indians of the Plains; *and* Psychedelic Drugs.]

BIBLIOGRAPHY

The most valuable sources in the beginning study of the religions of California, the Great Basin, and the Plateau are the pertinent volumes of the *Handbook of North American Indians,* 20 vols. (Washington, D.C., 1978–). Volume 8, *California,* edited by Robert F. Heizer, was issued in 1978, and volumes on the Great Basin and on the Plateau are forthcoming. Heizer's *California* volume to an extent supplants A. L. Kroeber's *Handbook of the Indians of California* (1925; reprint, New York, 1976), although this earlier work remains of interest.

Useful bibliographies can be found in the volumes of the new *Handbook* and in several other important sources: *Ethnographic Bibliography of North America,* 4th ed., 5 vols., edited by George Peter Murdock and Timothy J. O'Leary (New Haven, 1975); Robert F. Heizer, *The Indians of California: A Critical Bibliography* (Bloomington, Ind., 1976); Joseph P. Jorgensen, *Western Indians* (San Francisco, 1980); and Omer C. Stewart, *Indians of the Great Basin* (Bloomington, Ind., 1982).

Jorgensen's *Western Indians* is a computer-assisted distributional study with chapters on a number of pertinent topics, placing religious practices in ecological and political context. As such, it is a sophisticated continuation of earlier culture-element distribution surveys. One such study by Harold E. Driver, "Girls' Puberty Rites in Western North America," *University of California Publications in Anthropological Records* 6 (1941/42): 21–90, provides a comprehensive overview of its topic, an important one in all three culture areas under consideration here. Other such Western themes are explored in Willard Z. Park's *Shamanism in Western North America* (1938; reprint, New York, 1975) and in Erna Gunther's two analyses of first-salmon ceremonies in the *American Anthropologist* 28 (1926): 605–617 and in *Washington University Publications in Anthropology* 2 (1928): 129–173. Park's *Shamanism* contains a detailed account of Northern Paiute (Paviosto) shamanism and thus serves to introduce specific aspects of Great Basin religion, while Verne F. Ray's *Cultural Relations in the Plateau of North America* (Los Angeles, 1939) surveys the complexities of that area's religious life in a way that remains important.

There are various sources on the major religious systems of California. A. L. Kroeber and E. W. Gifford's "World Renewal: A Cult System of Native Northwestern California," *University of California Publications in Anthropological Records* 13 (1949): 1–56, gives good descriptive materials, although its interpretations are rather narrow. Edwin M. Loeb's "The Western Kuksu Cult" and "The Eastern Kuksu Cult, " *University of California Publications in American Archaeology and Ethnology* 33 (1932/33): 1–138, 139–232, are comparable, Kroeberian works. More recent studies include *?Antap: Californian Indian Political and Economic Organization,* edited by Lowell John Bean and Thomas F. King (Ramona, Calif., 1974), and Raymond C. White's "The Luiseño Theory of 'Knowledge,' " *American Anthropologist* 59 (1957): 1–19. The two, together, provide entrée into the study of southern Californian religions. White's essay is also included in a volume of largely theoretical papers, *Native Californians: A Theoretical Retrospective,* edited by Lowell John Bean and Thomas C. Blackburn (Socorro, N.Mex., 1976), which provides a number of stimulating interpretations of aboriginal California religious systems.

Finally, the *Journal of California and Great Basin Anthropology* (Banning, Calif., 1979–), succeeding the *Journal of California Anthropology* (1974–1979), publishes current explorations in the religions of California and the Great Basin fairly regularly.

9

THE NORTHWEST COAST

Stanley Walens

The peoples of the Pacific Northwest Coast of North America lived along a narrow strip of land that extends from the mouth of the Columbia River north to Yakutat Bay in Alaska. Cut off, for the most part, from the tribes around them by the rugged, impenetrably forested mountains that rise from the sea, and relatively isolated from one another by the scarcity of habitable beach sites, they developed a variety of distinct but intertwined local traditions.

For the sake of convenience, the Northwest Coast culture area has been divided into three subareas: the northern area was inhabited by the Tlingit, Haida, and Tsimshian peoples; the central by the Bella Coola, Nootka, and Kwakiutl groups; and the southern by the Coast Salish and Chinookan tribes of the Washington and Oregon coasts. While the cultures within each subarea shared some basic traits that distinguished them from one another, the bewildering variety of linguistic, social, political, and ideological variations within each area implied numerous migrations, acculturations, and cultural borrowings that make any retrospective synthesis of Northwest Coast culture a formidable task.

Adding complexity are the effects of contact with white culture, which did not begin until the late eighteenth century. The vast wealth introduced into the area by the sea-otter fur trade altered the balance of wealth and power that had existed in the aboriginal period. During the nineteenth century (usually referred to as the "historical" period, and the time frame for this essay) the peoples of the Northwest Coast underwent dramatic social change, including cultural efflorescence, drastic population decline, wholesale abandonment of ancestral villages, the formation of new composite villages, increased trade, and intermarriage between all of which contributed to the tribes, diffusion of religious traditions at a vastly accelerated rate. The indigenous peoples eventually, came under heavy governmental and missionary pressure to abandon all native customs.

MATERIAL CULTURE

The lives of the Northwest Coast Indians were entirely oriented toward the sea, on whose bounty they depended. The staple food of the area was salmon; varieties of salmon were smoked and stockpiled in immense quantities. However, many other types of fish, sea mammals, large land mammals, water birds, shellfish, and varieties of wild plants were also collected. Though food was plentiful, the rugged topography of the land limited access to food-collecting sites. Access to these sites was also controlled by an oligarchy of hereditary nobles (called "chiefs") who maintained their power primarily through ritual performances that legitimized their claims.

Northwest Coast technology was based on a complex of wood and animal products. Wood and tree bark, especially from cedars, were the fundamental materials and were used ubiquitously. Humans lived in houses, traveled in canoes, caught fish with hooks, trapped salmon in weirs, stored their belongings and were themselves interred in boxes, and wore clothing and ceremonial costumes all made from wood products. A system of symbolic correspondences between objects underlay the entire ceremonial system. Skins, flesh, and bones from animals were also used and played a critical symbolic role in religious activities.

SOCIAL ORGANIZATION

The basic principles of Northwest Coast social organization have been the object of much theoretical controversy. Traditional tribal appellations may lump together groups with similar languages but very different customs, and vice versa. Essentially the basic unit of social and political organization was the independent extended local family, defined by some degree of lineal descent and by coresidence in a single communal household in a single winter ceremonial village. (Winter was the season in which virtually all ceremonies were held.) Group membership was defined less by kinship than by concerted economic and ceremonial activity, though in the northern subarea suprafamilial kin groups played a role in setting the boundaries of a group. The head of each household was its political and spiritual leader, the inheritor and custodian of the house's aristocratic titles, and its ambassador to both human and supernatural worlds. All aristocratic titles in each area were ranked hierarchically for all ceremonial activities. Whether or not the hierarchical system created a class structure as well as a rank structure is a controversial theoretical question. While there was some social mobility, social position was primarily ascribed and inherited. However, all succession to rank had to be validated by the giving of a potlatch at which the heir recounted or reenacted in dance drama the family myths that proved the legitimacy of his claim; the potlatch also proved his personal power and spiritual worthiness by the heir's distribution of wealth to other chiefs. The potlatch was a major mechanism for promoting group solidarity, organizing labor, and maintaining the structure of the hierarchical system. [See Potlatch.] As one goes north within the area, hierarchical systems seem to increase in importance and are firmly embedded in a religious matrix. The peoples of the southern subarea seemed to put little emphasis on hierarchy and exhibited a social structure and religious ideology with more similarities to peoples of the Plateau and California areas than to the coastal peoples to their north.

BELIEF AND RITUAL

There was little synthesis of religious ideas and institutions on the Northwest Coast. Rituals and myths developed into a multiplicity of local traditions that directly integrated local history and geographical features with the more universal elements of creation. Different families and different individuals within families might have conflicting accounts of family history and its mythic events, giving the religion an atomistic quality that permitted a continual restructuring of ceremonies and renegotiating of meanings. However, much of the cognitive conflict that might arise from such discrepancies was mitigated by the fact that although there was an extraordinary amount of public ceremony most rituals were performed in secret and were known only to the rankholder and his heir.

Like the religions of other native North American peoples, the beliefs of the Northwest Coast Indians focused on the critical relationship of hunter to prey and on the set of moral principles that permitted that relationship to continue. Humans were thought to be essentially inferior to the rest of the world's inhabitants and were dependent on other creatures' good will for survival. Humans were important as mediators between different spirit realms because supernatural beings had granted them gifts of knowledge and insight about how the world operates and how they fit into the world. The features unique to Northwest Coast religion centered on the private possession and inherited control of the religious institutions by titled aristocrats. Access to the supernatural beings (called "spirits" by anthropologists because of their essential rather than corporeal nature) and their power was strictly under the control of chiefs, as was access to food.

Spirits. The origin of all power—both the power to control and, more importantly, the power to become aware—was in the spirit world, and the actions of spirit power, which gave form and purpose to everything, were visible everywhere. All objects, ideas, forces, and beings were believed to have inherent power that could be released and directed into human affairs, if correctly integrated into ritual action. The world was seen as filled with spirit power that could be reified in human rituals. Spirits, the personified categories of power, were less characters than ineffable forces. As a salmon could be brought into the human world when caught in a properly constructed net, so could spirit power be brought into the human world when caught in a net of properly constructed ritual action. Humans could never perceive the true nature of spirits, but they could see that the costumes—created as coverings for the spirits—became animated when the spirits covered themselves with them and danced.

An example may better explicate the idea of spirits as essences: the *sisiutl,* visible to humans in its manifestation as a huge double-headed serpent, was one of the most powerful spirits in Kwakiutl religion. It was the reification of all the inherent qualities and power of that which is wet and fluid—ocean, rain, blood, tears, and so on—and by extension all that is uncontainable and transitory and all that is insignificant in small quantities, life-sustaining in proper amounts, and dangerous in excess. The *sisiutl* thus provides a metaphor for a key ideological tenet of Kwakiutl thought: that the world is in motion and can be stopped (and thus perceived as a material entity) only temporarily; that human life, ritual, understanding, wealth, and power will come to pass but will flow away like water. The *sisiutl* was only one among hundreds of creatures depicted in Northwest Coast myth and ritual—each a vision, a realization, of the processual nature of the universe, and each a metaphorical statement of a fundamental philosophical idea.

The peoples of the Northwest Coast saw their world as one in which myriad personified forces were at work, competing for a limited supply of food and souls. Every human, every group, every species, and every spirit-being had its own needs, its own specialized niche in the food chain. All of their conflicting demands and needs had to be balanced against one another, and this could be achieved only through ritual, which was seen as a method of mediation between the various creatures of the universe. The world was filled with a seemingly endless variety of raptorial creatures who feed on human flesh and souls just as humans feed on salmon flesh. Man-eating birds and other animals, ogres, dwarves, giants, and monsters were believed to prey upon humans as raptorial birds prey upon mice (a frequent image in Northwest Coast myths).

Animals, which were seen as the material representations of spiritual beings, sacrificed themselves for the benefit of human survival because humans had agreed to sacrifice themselves for the benefit of the spirits. The metaphors of Northwest Coast ritual continually repeat the image of the responsibility of humans to support the spirit world. Humans and spirits, living off each other's dead, were intertwined in a reincarnational web. By eating the substance of each other's bodies, they freed the souls and permitted their reincarnation. If any link in the ritual chain was lost, the entire system of reincarnation broke down.

Food. Food was thus a sacramental substance, and meals were inherently ceremonial occasions. Northwest Coast religion placed a heavy emphasis on the control of food-related behavior, on the denial of hunger (which was thought to be a polluting desire), and on the ritual distribution of food and other material substances. The rules, taboos, and rituals associated with food are ubiquitous and enormous in number.

Of all the ceremonies directed toward the propitiation of the animals on which humans feed, those known collectively as the first-salmon ceremonies were the most widespread. These were sets of rituals performed every year in each area over the first part of the salmon catch of each species. Similar ceremonies existed for other species as well. The fish were addressed as if they were chiefs of high rank and were killed, prepared, and served in a ceremonious manner. Their released souls returned to the land of their compatriots to inform them of the proper treatment that they had been accorded. Like most other Northwest Coast rituals, these ceremonies were the property of individual chiefs, who performed them for the benefit of all of the people. All hunting was imbued with ceremony, since success in the hunt was strictly a matter of the proper ritual relationship to the hunted animal. The ceremonies associated with hunting were an important part of a family's inheritance.

Guardian Spirits. In theory, a person could obtain a guardian spirit by dedication to a regimen of self-mortification, abstinence, fasting, prayer, and ritual bathing. However, the most powerful contracts with the spirits were obtained in mythic times through the group's ancestors, and these contracts formed the basis of the rank system. Every ranked position was actually an embodiment of a spiritual contract—a covenant between the rankholder and the spirit world. The relationship between the ancestor and the spirit was the primary element of a family's patrimony and was constantly reaffirmed in ritual. As the living representative of the ancestor, the rankholder acted as an intermediary to the spirits on secular occasions and as an impersonator or embodiment of a spirit on sacred occasions.

The relationships between particular aristocrats and particular spirits were manifested in a system of "crests," which were images of spirits that have become allied with individual families. The right to depict the image of a spirit, or in some cases even to pronounce its name in public, was a fiercely guarded possession. All objects of spiritual importance were decorated with images of a person's guardian spirits. This gave the objects a name, an identity, and the ability to act as a conduit through which spirit power could be directed. While crest images acted on one level as emblems of a group's status, they were more than mere coats of arms—they were ritual objects of causal power. Most crest images presented representations of transformation, a key idea in Northwest Coast thought, which expressed the interlocked identities and destinies of humans and spirits. Through the crest, the identity of the aristocrat was connected to that of the spirit being, and through this connection the aristocrat's self expanded to a more cosmic identity. The widespread use of crest objects was graphic proof of the extent to which religious ideas permeated the entire fabric of Northwest Coast culture.

In addition to having shared destinies, humans and spirits were interrelated in that all creatures were considered to be human and to possess human souls. Each lived in its own place in one of the levels of the universe, where it inhabited a house, performed ceremonies, and otherwise acted like a human being. At the proper season, the spirits donned costumes and visited the world of humans, where they appeared in their transformed identity. Similarly, humans who appeared to themselves as humans put on costumes and appeared to the spirits as spirits.

With the exception of Frederica De Laguna's account of Tlingit culture (1972), Northwest Coast Indian ideas of the self, its components, and its relationship to the spirits are not well documented. It is clear that the soul was believed to have several material manifestations as well as several incorporeal components. A person was viewed as a combination of life forces and parts from different planes of existence, and therefore as having spiritual connections in many directions. Whatever their component parts, souls were thought to exist in only limited numbers, to undergo metempsychosis, to be transferred from one species to another, and to be reincarnated alternately in first a human and then either a spirit or animal being. A human death freed a soul for an animal or spirit, and vice versa, linking humans, animals, and spirits in a cycle of mutual dependency. Ideas about the soul and its nature seem to have been better codified among the Northern peoples, though this impression may be an artifact of the high quality of De Laguna's ethnography.

Shamanism. Connections to the spirit world could be made through inheritance or by acquiring, through a vision, the power to cure disease. All illnesses and death were considered a sickness of the spirit that was caused either by the magical intrusion of a foreign substance into the body or by the wandering or the loss of the soul. When methods for reestablishing one's spiritual purity failed to alleviate the symptoms, a curer (or "shaman") was called in. A shaman cured an illness by going into a trance during which his guardian spirits would fight with the soul of the disease or of the witch who had sent the disease. When the shaman came out of his trance, he was able to display a small object that symbolically represented the empty husk of the diseased spirit body. Shamanic paraphernalia, like other ritual objects, were formed and moved so as to direct the spirit power in the proper ways to effect a cure. Shamanic performances were dramatic events, with much stage illusion as well as singing, dancing, and praying.

Shamans acted as intermediaries between humans and the forces of nature and the supernatural, and were thought to be able to foretell the future, control the weather, bring success in war or in hunting, communicate with other shamans at a distance, and, most importantly, cure illnesses and restore souls stolen by witches or maleficent spirits. The shaman was believed both to control and to be inspired by the spirits with whom he was connected. Among the Tlingit, shamanic rituals were usually inherited, but among the central tribes they were obtained through visions. Shamans had to undergo strict regimens if they were to retain their powers; shamanism was a route to prestige but not to title, nor was it a lucrative profession. It was believed that the shaman received his calling involuntarily, but that, having been chosen, it was his responsibility to accept wholeheartedly the burdens of his profession.

Witches. Northwest Coast Indian beliefs about shamans were complemented by their beliefs about witchcraft. Witches were thought to be motivated by envy and jealousy, either conscious or unconscious, and there was no act, no matter how terrible, of which they were thought incapable. Patterns of witchcraft among the Northwest Coast Indians were parallel to those of other North American groups: it seems likely that few if any people practiced witchcraft, but accusations of witchcraft were an important means of articulating rivalry and competition. Among the central tribes, witches were generally thought to be shamans from enemy tribes; among the northern groups, where fear of witches was more prevalent, witches were thought to belong to the same kin group as their victims. Witches were thought to be under the compulsion of a possessive spirit, from whose influence the witch could be freed by torture. Occasionally witches died under torture or were executed despite their confession. The best protection against witches was to maintain spiritual purity through fasting and the correct performance of ceremonies. As long as the ceremonies were performed, the world existed in the proper balance, and witches could not do harm.

The causal principle underlying the ideas of the Northwest Coast Indians on the effectiveness of ritual lay in the idea that under the proper analogical conditions, the patterned motions or words of human beings have an inherent ability to coerce the spirits into parallel actions. Thus a human action could be magnified and intensified into a power that alters the state of the world. Human beings were conduits for supernatural power: although they possess no powers themselves, humans could become the vehicles of supernatural power if they observed the proper ritual actions. In creating analogies between themselves and the spirits, humans gained the ability to influence the actions of those more powerful than themselves.

Creation. Supporting the social and ritual systems was an extensive and varied body of myths and tales (which, except in the work of Claude Lévi-Strauss, have been little analyzed). There were few myths about the creation of the world as such, since the world was seen as a place of innumerable eternal forces and essences. Like other North American groups, the Indians of the Northwest Coast were less interested in how the world was created as material substance than in how it was made moral or how the inherent powers of the universe could be controlled for the benefit of its inhabitants. The creation of material phenomena—the sun and moon, human beings, animal species—is always secondary to the moral dilemmas presented in the myths and the resolution (or lack thereof) of those dilemmas. For example, though there are no myths about the sun being created out of nothing, there are many myths about the sun being placed in the sky, in order to fulfill its proper role by enabling people to see—reminding them of the continual motion and flux of the world and of the balance of light and darkness.

Transformers. Although there are few myths about a creator spirit (and those possibly developed after contact with whites), there are cycles of myths about a transformer or trickster figure who through his actions places the forces of the world in balance. The most detailed and integral of these is the Raven cycle found among the Tlingit (though each tribe had some form of trickster or transformer cycle, not always associated with Raven). Raven is a creature of uncontrollable desires and excesses, and in the act of trying to satisfy his desires, he inadvertently creates moral order and constraint. Incidental to each act of moral creation is the creation of some physical attribute of the world—a mountain or other geographical feature, or the color of a mallard's head or an ermine's tail—that serves to remind people of the myth and its moral import. Thus the world is made up of signs and images of mythic significance for those who know the stories behind them.

In general, the trickster cycles of the Northwest Coast parallel those of other areas in their nature and social function, although imagistically the Northwest Coast trickster stories more strongly emphasize the maintenance of the flow of wealth as representation of the correct motion of the universe. This image of flow—the release of wealth from its temporary container, whether it be the material wealth of a chief or the spiritual soul that is released from the body of a dead person when ravens begin to tear it apart—runs throughout the Northwest Coast mythology. However, not all Northwest Coast transformers are trickster figures: the Kwakiutl culture hero is one of a set of rather solemn mythic beings.

Myths of Origin. Every feature of the geographic, social, and ceremonial world had an origin myth that encapsulated it into the basic structure of power and ideology, and these myths formed the basic material for Northwest Coast religion and ceremony. No public ceremony occurred without the retelling—either in recital or a dance reenactment—of the origin myths of the people involved, which is to say that no ceremony took place without the reenergizing of the connection between humans and spirits. Clan and family myths were integrated individually into the larger corpus of hero mythology, so that every family and person of title was in some specific way linked to the events and forces of the universe. Myth is a depiction of the interaction of universal forces, and the retelling of the myth reactivates and redirects those forces.

Northwest Coast rituals, like myths, developed into a multiplicity of local traditions, resulting in the direct linking of local history to the more cosmic elements of creation. Ceremonies were always changing as new rituals were acquired through war, marriage, new visions, or the emigration of families. There was a constant renegotiation of the meanings and structure of all rituals and stories, as traditions coalesced, melded, or broke apart; conflicting versions of stories were constantly being reworked.

Winter Ceremonials. Spirit power was an essential part of the success of any task; thus there was ceremony in all human endeavor. Even so, there was a clear division of the year into secular (summer) and sacred (winter) seasons. Large-scale ceremonial performances were given in the winter. These were most important among the Kwakiutl and Nootka. Among the southern tribes there was a ceremony of spirit-possession and occasional rituals of world renewal similar to those of the peoples of northern California. Some scholars feel that the spirit-possession ceremony was more widespread until the beginning of the nineteenth century, when cultural change promoted the rapid efflorescence and diffusion of northern and central ceremonial forms, but the evidence for such a historical change is contradictory.

The narrative structure of the Kwakiutl winter ceremonials, like that of the family origin myths, was based on a simple set of images that were endlessly elaborated: a hero cuts himself off from the material world of humans, seeks or is kidnapped by spirits who take him to their home, learns the rituals of the spirits, obtains some of the spirits' power, and then brings the rituals back to the human world. He becomes frenzied as his frail human form attempts to contain the potency of the spirit power. During the ceremony the hero's fellow humans gradually came to control the power that threatened to destroy them, and it was they who "tamed" him. These rituals were performed in the most sensationalistic fashion, with elaborate stage effects and illusions, masked performances, complicated props, and stunning displays of strength and athletic agility.

The winter ceremonials were complex and changing ceremonies. All performances were carefully integrated into a larger dramatic structure with important ritual implications, depending on the number and type of dances being given, the guests' status, the time of the season, and a number of other factors. Each type of dance, of which there were hundreds, was a metaphorical connection to the spiritual universe. Just as the world is made up of people separate but interdependent, so were Northwest Coast rituals structured so as to place individuals in a web of mutual reinforcement. The agenda of dances was ordered so that each individual dance would contribute to their combined effect. One dance would act as contrast or catalyst for the next, giving added power to their combined performance. Feasts were carefully interspersed so as to distribute, in the form of food and wealth, the powers that had been brought into the human world through the preceding dances.

The rituals of the winter ceremonials were under the jurisdiction of groups called "dance societies" or "secret societies." Membership in these groups was inherited and strictly limited. A new member could be invested only upon the retirement of his predecessor, but there were many stages of initiation and many years of preparation before complete initiation. Most of the ceremonies of the dance societies were performed away from public scrutiny, to maintain private ownership of the rituals and to prevent the uninitiated from being harmed by the presence of immense spirit power. A small proportion of the ceremonies were performed only for members of the dance society or for a small group of aristocrats, and a very few were performed for the entire village. Yet even this small proportion of rituals went on for hours every day over a period of four or five months. In essence, then, the entire winter period was given over to ceremony—a fact that belies the usual claim by anthropologists that the peoples of the Northwest Coast were primarily interested in status.

Of all the winter-ceremonial performances, the most famous and widely discussed is the Hamatsa dance, which the Kwakiutl considered to be their most powerful ceremony. The Hamatsa dance seems to best encapsulate the ethos of Northwest Coast religious ideology. The *hamatsa* was a human who had been carried away by those supernatural creatures who preyed on the flesh and substance of human beings; while living with these supernatural creatures in their ceremonial house, the *hamatsa* took on their spiritual qualities (especially their affinity with death and killing); and when he returned to the land of human beings, he was possessed with the wild desire to eat human flesh. In a long series of rites, the members of the tribe gradually tamed his wildness through a series of pledges to sacrifice their wealth and (when they eventually died) their souls, to feed the spirits so that the world would remain in equilibrium. The violence and energy with which the *hamatsa* acted was a potent representation of the intensity of the struggle or task that humans had to accept if the world were to be kept moral. The burden of spiritual power demanded not a quiet acceptance but energetic activity, a ferocity for right action.

CONCLUSION

Although founded on the same basic philosophical principles as that of other native North American religions, Northwest Coast religion developed those ideas into a distinct set of social and religious institutions that were adaptable to the changing fortunes and histories of each village and its individual members. It was a system in which atomistic elements could be separated from their original relationships with each other and reformed in new combinations dealing in a powerful, cohesive, creative, and poetic way with the purposes and dilemmas of human existence.

Unfortunately, much of Northwest Coast culture was irrevocably altered or destroyed in the course of the nineteenth and early twentieth centuries. All Northwest Coast religion was illegal in Canada from 1876 to 1951, though enforcement of applicable laws was uneven, and some ceremonial life persisted. In the last several decades, there has been a new emphasis on the traditional rituals, but how much they retain of their original character and the place they hold in the lives of the people today are questions that remain to be answered. As North American Indians and scholars both reexamine the historical record to determine the significance of the Northwest Coast religion for the present, it can only be hoped that there will be new interpretations and understandings of what is unquestionably one of the most vibrant and fascinating of the world's tribal religions.

BIBLIOGRAPHY

Traditional trait-oriented surveys of Northwest Coast culture can be found in Philip Drucker's *Cultures of the North Pacific Coast* (New York, 1965) and in the excellently illustrated *People of the Totem* by Norman Bancroft-Hunt, with photographs by Werner Forman (New York, 1979). No synthesized scholarly accounts of Northwest Coast religion exist. The best ethnographic accounts of the beliefs of specific tribes are the many volumes by Franz Boas on the Kwakiutl, Philip Drucker's *The Northern and Central Nootkan Tribes* (Washington, D.C.,

1951), and Frederica De Laguna's *Under Mount Saint Elias* (Washington, D.C., 1972). Irving Goldman's *The Mouth of Heaven* (New York, 1975) and my *Feasting with Cannibals* (Princeton, 1981) both reanalyze Boas's materials and emphasize the critical role of religious thought in Kwakiutl life. Pamela Amoss's *Coast Salish Spirit Dancing* (Seattle, 1978) is the best account of contemporary Northwest Coast religious activity.

10 THE FAR NORTH

WERNER MÜLLER

Translated from German by Anne Heritage and Paul Kremmel

The North American sub-Arctic extends from Alaska to Labrador, a vast region comprising several vegetation zones. The tundra covers the area along the Arctic coast, a strip of treeless wilderness between one and four hundred miles wide, which protrudes deep into the interior in northern Alaska and in Canada west of Hudson Bay. The uniformity of this lichen-and-moss-covered plain is broken by the occasional shrubs of the bordering zone, which appear with increasing frequency farther south. The third zone, the "cold snow forest," begins, in western Canada, around the region of Great Slave Lake, Lake Athabasca, and Reindeer Lake. Countless fir trees interspersed with spruce, pine, birch, and poplar cover this region, which changes over into the prairie and the deciduous forests of the Atlantic East before reaching the border between Canada and the United States.

ADAPTATION TO CLIMATE

The inhospitable climate of the region, with its long, severe winters and short summers, shaped the culture of the native inhabitants. Since any form of cultivation was impossible, human existence was dependent on hunting and fishing. And here natural factors proved to be of some assistance. Large deer, such as caribou and moose, sought refuge in the forest zone in the autumn, then wandered back into the northern tundra in spring. This movement back and forth set huge herds of migrating caribou into motion, which facilitated big-game hunting and the accumulation of food reserves. In late winter, however, hunting was limited to stalking of small packs or isolated animals. Extensive river networks that abounded in fish, particularly salmon, provided food in the summer. Hunting and fishing, two seasonally varying activities—the one with lance and arrow, the other with hook and net—formed the basis of the sub-Arctic economy so long as the native population was isolated from outside influences. This alternation in economic life led to nomadism, which often involved a short-term relocation of housing. A round, dome-shaped house covered with bark or straw was erected in the winter; a rectangular, gabled lodge was preferred in the summer. Today these structures have given way to the conical tent, which in turn is beginning to be replaced by the log cabin.

The advancing Europeans encountered tribes belonging to three linguistic families: the Inuit (Eskimo) along the Arctic Ocean, the Athapascan in western Canada, and the Algonquian in eastern Canada. Among the Algonquian we also include the Abnaki of New Brunswick and Maine (Micmac, Malecite, Passamaquoddy, Penobscot, Abnaki), who have preserved vestiges of their sub-Arctic way of life up to the present. The non-Indian Inuit will not be treated here, as they are the subject of a separate article. [*See* Inuit Religion.]

The usual division leaves us twenty-four groups or tribes of Athapascan provenance and thirteen of Algonquian provenance. All are unmistakably shaped by the sub-Arctic way of life with its alternation between forest and water, its absence of any cultivation, and its biggame hunting in winter and fishing in summer.

Human existence in the sub-Arctic has always revolved around surviving the winters. January and February witness the worst side of the cold season: the temperature reaches its lowest point, the reserves are exhausted, the short days limit the hunter's range of movement, and the last caribou and moose in the vicinity of the winter camps have already been hunted down. This is a time of extreme hardship. The isolation of families—each has its own hunting grounds—is a hindrance to mutual help and support. The earliest reports tell of famine and starvation and of whole bands fatalistically facing their death.

The tool kit and hunting methods were not always adapted to environmental conditions. There were, for example, no procedures and devices for hunting the masses of waterfowl that appeared on the surfaces of the interior lakes in autumn, as Cornelius Osgood (1932, p. 42) observed. Likewise the Indians in the cordillera had little control over the important hare-hunting, which often failed owing to unexpected fluctuations in the hare population (*Handbook of North American Indians*, 1981, vol. 6, p. 376; hereafter referred to as *Handbook*).

By way of comparison, the Inuit cultures along the Arctic coast mastered every environmental difficulty: of their inventions one need only think of the igloo, fur clothing, seal hunting at the breathing holes on the ice, and oil lamps—a utilization of natural conditions not to be found among the Athapascan and the Algonquian. It is as though the interior sub-Arctic Indians had migrated from other regions and had somehow been stopped in the middle of the necessary relearning process.

MYTHOLOGY

The meagerness of the material culture stands in sharp contrast to the abundance of spiritual traditions. Even the common people, who are not counted among the elite shamans, have an immeasurably rich view of the world. The forests and waters teem with a host of beings of half-human, half-animal appearance, similar to the figures of early European popular superstition.

Thus the Athapascan-speakers fear the *nekani,* the "bad" Indians who wander about the wilderness and abduct children; the *nekani* do their mischief only in summer when there is no snow to reveal their tracks. The Algonquians tell of monsters like the cannibal Windigo, sometimes said to be as tall as a man, sometimes as tall as a tree; and of well-meaning dwarfs, water sprites, and shaggy creatures with razor-sharp faces that lead a shadowy existence in the thicket.

This multitude of frightening creatures has led to the erroneous impression that the spiritual world of the sub-Arctic Indians is a confusion of pure fantasy arising from fear and anxiety. In fact, virtually all Canadian mythologies display a careful chronological and figural order. Mythological tradition is structured by a series of epochs, beginning with the events of primordial time (such as the deluge). Likewise the mythical beings are subject to a hierarchical ordering, with great differences separating the important from the unimportant figures.

AGES OF THE WORLD

The mythical chronology falls into three stages (see Rand, 1894; Osgood, 1932; and Pliny Earle Goddard, "The Beaver Indians," *Anthropological Papers of the American Museum of Natural History* 10, 1916). In the earliest period there were no divisions between living creatures; each could assume any animal's form and discard it again at will. All moving creatures spoke a single language; no barriers stood in the way of understanding. The second period began with the birth of the culture hero, the great teacher and leader of mankind. Material and spiritual knowledge derived from him. The house, tent, snowshoe, sled, bark canoe, bow, arrow, lance, and knife—in short, all man's appurtenances—stem from him, as does knowledge of the land of the dead, the stars and constellations, the sun, the moon, and the calendar months. It was also he who had the muskrat dive into the waters after the Deluge and who then created a new world from the mud that was brought up, thus becoming a second creator (if there had been a first).

The activities of this hero are directed toward a single goal: providing mankind with a special position and, thus, severing man from the community of the world family. The constant struggle of the hero against malicious monsters also serves this purpose. Consequently, with the appearance of this archetype of the Herakles of antiquity the community of living creatures ceases: man remains man, and the animals remain animals. Man is no longer able to transform himself, nor can he understand the language of animals.

The present era is within the third epoch. Although the hero has disappeared, the special position of mankind remains and begins to expand. Only the shamans are able to cross the boundaries between the human and the extrahuman.

Individual tribes expand this universal chronology. The Koyukon, for example, the northwesternmost Athapascan tribe in Alaska, speak of no less than five world periods: (1) the hazy time before there was light on the earth; (2) the epoch when man could change into animals, and animals into men; (3) the time when the culture hero created the present state; (4) the past time of legends; and (5) the present as far back as memory reaches (*Handbook,* vol. 6, p. 595).

Unity of Life. The sequence of world epochs is more than a faded memory. It lives on today in traditional beliefs and customs that recall the events or conditions of those epochs—especially the earliest period, with its basic idea of the world family and the unity of all living creatures. Thus the Kutchin, a northern Athapascan tribe that inhabits the territory between the Mackenzie River delta and the upper Yukon, possess a special relationship with the caribou; every man, they believe, carries a small piece of caribou heart within himself, and every caribou a portion of human heart. Hence, each of these partners knows what the other feels and thinks (*Handbook,* vol. 6, p. 526). The Sekani of British Columbia believe that a mystical bond links man and animal (*Handbook,* vol. 6, p. 439); the Koyukon call the bear "Grandfather" and the wolf "Brother" (*Handbook,* vol. 6, p. 593); and the Chipewyan, who live west of Hudson Bay, identify with the wolf (*Handbook,* vol. 6, p. 279).

The names of certain Athapascan tribal groups—Beaver, Dogrib, Hare—point to familial ties with certain animals. In all of these examples we hear an echo of the earliest epoch, when a common language prevailed and all creatures had the ability to transform themselves and thus to overcome every barrier between them.

Also, the game that is killed is treated respectfully. The animal is addressed in familial terms; its death is mourned; its bones are protected from the dogs. Otherwise, the spirit "master" of the particular type of animal will withhold game from the hunter, subjecting him to hunger. The very concept of a master of the game teaches the Indians to show a religious reverence toward the nonhuman creatures of the world. They know that every animal form has a spirit protector and helper to whom the souls of the killed animals return and, if warranted, make complaints about ill treatment. They know that no game returns to earth without the consent of the master. Finally, they know that this consent is dependent on the keeping of certain religious prescriptions. Thus the activity of the hunter is a religious act: he is constantly aware of being watched by extrahuman beings.

The Culture Hero. The culture hero remains the most powerful figure within this hierarchy. Just as the different animals have their masters, mankind also has its overlord, who is at the same time the master of all masters. Thus we move from the series of mythical epochs to the mythical center of time. To the hunter, this heroic figure is an ideal that cannot be equaled. The Ojibwa on the northern side of Lake Superior liken this master to the captain of a steamboat or to the government in Ottawa; he directs all lesser masters (Diamond Jenness, *The Ojibwa Indians of Parry Island,* 1935, p. 30).

The culture hero is responsible, too, for the abundance and richness of sub-Arctic mythology. Around the camp fire or in the tent, the deeds of the hero, teacher, and friend of mankind provide the most important storytelling material. Other mythical figures are patterned after him, so there is a continuous expansion of the cycles of myths. The Koyukon are said to have "a highly developed and sophisticated repertory of myth and legend" (*Handbook,* vol. 6, p. 595); other groups are said to have a "deep respect for and attachment to their mythology" (*Handbook,* vol. 6, p. 195). The oral tradition is not understood merely as entertainment; the mythical stories confer a sacral dimension on it, which is still recognized by the Indians.

The figure of the hero is most clearly developed among the Algonquians of the Atlantic coast. The Micmac of Cape Breton Island, for example, call the teacher of mankind Kuloscap ("liar" or "deceiver") because he always does the opposite of what he says he will do. The stations of his life can still be read in the natural features of the landscape: Cape Breton Island abounds in references to the hero. Every large rock, every river, every waterfall, testifies to his deeds. All the sub-Arctic Indians have a similar mythical geography.

To the west of the Micmac other names for the culture hero appear. Among the Montagnais-Naskapi of Labrador he is called Little Man or Perfect Man; among the Cree on either side of James Bay, the One Set in Flames or the Burning One; among the Chipewyan, Raised by His Grandmother; among the Beaver Indians, He Goes along the Shore.

This last example brings us to the group of names found in northern Athapascan mythologies, which pay particular attention to the hero's unflagging wanderlust. In the regions around the large Canadian lakes, the Kutchin, Koyukon, and Kolchan speak of the Wanderer, Ferryman, Celestial Traveler, He Paddled the Wrong Way, He Who Went Off Visiting by Canoe, or One Who Is Paddling Around, designations that refer to a particular task of the hero. He is said to labor continuously to combat giants, cannibals, and monsters for the benefit of mankind. The mass of fantasy figures in whose deeds the mythologies abound—such minor heroes as Moon Boy, Moon Dweller, Shrew, Moss Child, Wonder Child, White Horizon, the Hero with the Magic Wand—follow the same path as the tireless figure of the Wanderer. The designation *First Brother* reveals that pairs of brothers also appear among these parallels to the great culture hero.

Robin Ridington's account of the religious culture of the Beaver Indians of Alberta is the most vivid report we have for an Athapascan people (*Swan People: A Study of the Dunne-za Prophet Dance,* 1978, pp. 13ff.). The emergence of a genuinely sub-Arctic world-genesis is remarkable in itself, but of equal importance is the picture of the culture hero Swan that Ridington brings to light. The Indians view this figure as a model, an example; they identify themselves with him almost completely. The young boy who through vision seeking acquires a helper and a "song," that is, his own personal "medicine power," not only follows this model; he is in reality Swan himself, a duplicate of the hero. The mature hunter who locates his game in dreams is an embodiment of an aspect of Swan, called Saya. In the myths, Saya eliminates the hostile monsters and teaches man how to hunt and how to avoid being hunted. Prepared and directed by dreams, daily activities become a repetition of primeval experiences.

The situation changes along the western rim of the Athapascan region in the cordillera and on the Alaskan plateau. Here the heroes appear in animal form. The story cycles are grouped around Raven or Crow, which suggests the probable influence of the Northwest Coast Indians, whose mythologies are dominated by the Raven, Yetl (*Handbook,* vol. 6, pp. 410, 502).

STORYTELLING AND RITUAL

The thriving, highly developed oral tradition that centers on the mythical leader of mankind is an original creation of the sub-Arctic. During the endless dark nights of the long winter, no one willingly leaves the camp. Outside, the man-eating giants roam about. The faintest sound is startling. All the inhabitants huddle around the hearth, listening to the storyteller whose tales contain the religious knowledge of generations. The loneliness of the taiga and tundra promoted the development of the art of storytelling. The practice of ritual requires the participation of large groups, as is immediately apparent in the cultic celebrations farther to the south (e.g., the Big House ceremony of the Delaware, or the Sun Dance celebrated by many Plains tribes). But in the sub-Arctic regions the harsh climate and difficult terrain made large groups immensely difficult to muster, especially in winter; this explains the predominance of the word in the religious life of the Indians of the Far North.

The tribes of the sub-Arctic perform only short, meager rituals such as the biannual Feeding the Fire, during which pieces of meat are thrown into the flames and the souls of the dead are asked to nourish the living just as the living themselves are feeding the fire. As Goddard pointed out in "The Beaver Indians," "this seems to have been the one important ceremony of the north" (p. 230). The New Year celebration of the Tanaina of Cook Inlet, British Columbia, begins as soon as the salmon start to swim upstream. The ritual signifies the renewal of nature with the coming of the warm period. Fresh grass is spread out before the house doors to serve as a bed for the first catch of fish, sweat baths are taken to refresh the body, the finest clothing is put on, and clouds of smoke from a lucky herb are made to swirl through the mild air (see Cornelius Osgood, *The Ethnography of the Tanaina,* p. 148).

The national holiday of the Micmac, Saint Anne's Day (26 July), is a blend of Christian and Indian traditions. Celebrated with canoe races, footraces, dancing, wedding ceremonies, baptisms, and feasting, it is certainly derived from an earlier tribal custom. Native rituals are also encountered in the sparse references to the calendar ceremonies, which were determined by the course of the sun. The Koyukon, for example, celebrate the winter solstice, a time at which they also honor their dead. It is, they say, the time "when the long and short days meet" (*Handbook,* vol. 6, p. 593.) Implicit in that phrase is a precise knowledge of the solstices, which were determined by observing when the sunrise positions on the horizon reached a standstill.

A sharper contrast between the dearth of ritual and the abundance and vividness of mythology is hardly imaginable. The distinctive one-sidedness of religions of the sub-Arctic is due to certain religious tendencies that emanate from the figure of a supreme being.

THE SUPREME BEING

In general, research on religions of sub-Arctic Indians tends to assume the absence of a belief in a supreme being. Lane's statement on the Chilcotin of British Columbia—"There was no belief in a supreme being" (*Handbook,* vol. 6, p. 408)—is supposed to be applicable to all Athapascan and Algonquian groups. Any hints of such a belief that do occur are assumed to be due to Christian influence.

This simplistic assumption might never have arisen had its supporters referred to the dictionary compiled by the French priest Émile Petitot (1876). Under the entry "Dieu" Petitot distinguishes between native terms for the deity and those that came into circulation as a result of missionary activity, some time after 1850. Among the first category are found the following: *The One by Whom One Swears, Vault of the Sky, The One through Whom Earth Exists, Eagle, Sitting in the Zenith, The One Who Sees Forward and Backward, Having Made the Earth, The One through Whom We Become Human.* Alongside these early native names appear the Christian terms *Creator, Father of Mankind, The One Who Dwells in Heaven,* but the first two Christian terms are also found among the early native designations, and Petitot includes them in both categories. He evidently wanted to indicate that the designations *Creator* and *Father of Mankind* existed before the missionaries arrived.

The missionary Silas Tertius Rand, who worked among the Micmac along the Atlantic coast of New Brunswick in mid-nineteenth century, also noted word formations that referred to the supreme being as creator—for example, *He Creates Us* and *Our Forebear.* Frank Gouldsmith Speck's work among the Algonquian tribes to the south confirms this interpretation: they, too, speak of *Our Creator* and *Our Owner*. Osgood is correct in assuming that the conception of a supreme divine being is genuine (1932, p. 132). Here the work of missionaries activated and strengthened an archaic belief but by no means created it.

Ridington's research on the Beaver Indians provides conclusive evidence of the correctness of Osgood's assumption. In the beginning, Ridington reports, the tribe resisted christianization. Around 1900 the Beaver finally accepted Roman Catholic baptism, but their conversion remained nominal. "They had," Ridington observes, "assimilated Catholic ideas in enrichment of their own traditions rather than giving them up in favor of the religion of the missionaries" (*Handbook,* vol. 6, p. 358).

This resistance probably explains the Beaver's preservation of their own account of the creation of the world. In the beginning, it is related, Heaven Sitter drew a cross on the surface of the primeval sea. He then commanded Muskrat to bring up a clump of mud from the bottom of the water. Heaven Sitter then placed this piece of earth at the center of the cross and ordered it to grow. The earth was created as a disk divided into four parts, since four paths lead from the center to the edge of the sky, at the cardinal points. The connection from east to west marks the path of the sun. Up and down, that is, heaven and earth, meet at the intersection in the middle, so that six directions come together in the middle point of the world: four vertical lines and two horizontal lines. This bundle of directions continues to order daily life. The Beaver sleep with their heads pointing toward the sunrise; they see in the path of the sun a reenactment of creation, for that body renews itself every day (*Handbook,* vol. 6, p. 354).

No parallels of this cosmic myth have ever been discovered among other Athapascans, so here it is important to consider the entire continent, especially since the diving of animals is a prominent motif of creation myths found elsewhere in North America.

The motif appears in two versions. In one version the diver descends into the primeval sea of the beginnings; in the other, which refers to a much later occurrence, the diver descends into the waters of the deluge. The cause in each case is clearly differentiated: the creator is the prime mover over the primeval waters; the culture hero, over the waters of the deluge. It is the culture hero who drifts on his raft across the watery waste and who, in instigating his animal passengers to dive, functions as a second creator.

The frequent occurrences of this myth reveal a surprising geographical distribution. The deluge variant is predominant in the middle of the continent and deep into the Canadian North; the primeval sea variant is found in areas bordering on this region: on the western Prairies, in California, along the lower Mississippi, in the Southeast, and on the Alaskan plateau. It looks as if the deluge myth displaced the primeval sea myth, pushing it into the coastal regions. Both versions are mutually exclusive; where the deluge appears, there is no primeval sea.

The geography of the creation myth lends itself to the following interpretation: deluge and animal diver represent a more recent variant of the ancient myth of creator and water genesis. Its dispersal corresponds exactly to the borders of the Athapascan and Algonquian linguistic families; no other group could have invented and preserved this new version. They are the ones who attributed to the culture hero what once belonged to the sphere of the creator.

A shifting of religious emphasis becomes evident here. The creator withdraws, and the hero moves into theforeground. This explains the faint contours of the supreme being and the intensive development of the heroic cycles. The appearance of the Athapascans and the Algonquians sets in motion a tendency that leads to a dethronement of the supreme god. He loses his most important task, the creation of the world. This explains why the sub-Arctic mythologies almost never speak of a creation; rather, they tell only of a second genesis from the watery wastes of the deluge. The Beaver tradition is the unique example of the retention of both versions by a single group: here we find the primeval sea *and* the deluge, the creator *and* the hero (Ridington, *Swan People,* p. 13; Pliny Earle Goddard, "Beaver Texts," *Anthropological Papers of the American Museum of Natural History* 10, 1917, p. 344).

This shifting of basic values, that is, the eradication of the supreme being and the ascendancy of the hero, must have begun long before the first contact with Europeans, for the attempt to degrade the creator can be seen even in the names for the deity. Names that recall Janus figures, like *The One Who Looks Forward and Backward,* are totally unsuitable for a supreme being who has relinquished the function of world-orderer to the culture hero. Likewise, the name *Boatsman* is linked to the wandering hero but not to the regent of the universe.

The contrariness of these two key religious figures is quite evident. The hero is closely identified with man and with man's goals and purposes. The supreme god, however, encompasses the world in its entirety; he is the cosmos itself. "He is in the sun, moon, stars, clouds of heaven, mountains, and even the trees of the earth," according to the Penobscot (Speck, "Penobscot Tales," p.4). The Naskapi likewise declare, "He is a spirit like the sun, moon, and stars, who created everything including them" (Speck, 1935, p. 29).

The reason that ritual in the sub-Arctic never progressed beyond the meager initial phases thus becomes clear. Cultic celebrations for a cosmic, universal god require a cosmic foundation, and to be effective they require the presence of all inhabitants of the "world house"—human beings, animals, and plants—as only the prayers, songs, and drumming of the whole world community reach the ear of the universal god. But this basic idea is contrary to the sub-Arctic way of life. The harsh, hostile environment tends to isolate people; it prevents any kind of community and thus hinders communal celebrations. As soon as the northern wasteland gives way to the southern deciduous forests, there suddenly appears the unique religious poetry of the Big House, Midewiwin, and Sun Dance. With these rituals, which encompass the world in its entirety, the supreme god begins to live as the creator at the crown of the universe. [*See* North American Indians, *article on* Indians of the Northeast Woodlands, *and* Sun Dance.]

The sub-Arctic and its culture hero are left behind. The myth clearly prophesies the direction the hero is moving toward. One day the timeless Wanderer will return, and it is then that the earth will go up in flames (Speck, "Penobscot Tales," pp. 5f.).

SHAMANISM

The all-encompassing rituals mentioned above form the bulwark of human life in more southerly latitudes. They incorporate everyone into the cosmic unity of life. These universal celebrations provide an indestructible shelter within the world house and prevent isolation of the individual. In the taiga and tundra, however, the individual is dependent on himself. When he needs help, the sub-Arctic Indian turns to the shaman. It is he who provides the only help when bad weather spoils the hunt, when the game withdraws into inaccessible places, when fewer fish swim upstream, when disease announces the loss of the soul, and when continued misfortune bespeaks the attack of a hostile shaman.

Dreams, Songs, and Journeys. The shaman has reliable dreams; he foresees future events; he disperses evil spirits; he sings effective songs or incantations. The word *shaman* derives from Tunguz and is thus a foreign term in Indian languages. Indigenous names, equivalents of "clairvoyant," "dream doctor," "singer," and "dreamer" (*Handbook*, vol. 6, pp. 660f.), or "shadow man," "arrogant one," and "head full of songs" (Petitot, 1876, p. 224) are far more descriptive than such nebulous European designations as *medicine man, sorcerer,* and *magician.*

The shaman's important and essential characteristics are attained through dreams. The visions befall selected candidates. The chosen must have a "peculiar aptitude" (*Handbook*, vol. 6, p. 607), but family inheritance can also play a role. The strength of a shaman depends on spirit helpers that are either acquired through dreams or inherited from his father or his maternal uncle. Every hunter has one such helper, acquired in the years of childhood through dream-fasting, but the shaman has at least half a dozen. The spirits manifest themselves in the form of animals, in natural phenomena such as the sun and the moon, or in the souls of deceased shamans (*Handbook*, vol. 6, p. 409).

Every spirit helper has its own song, and when a shaman incants a spirit's song, the spirit addressed hurries to help his master. The activity of the shaman alleviates much more than everyday cares. It is believed that his spirit leaves his body every night, travels on lengthy visits to the sky, and learns there everything he desires to know. When his spirit returns from its flight accompanied by the shaman's helpers, the drum on the wall begins to sound without being touched. His song is heard far and wide, and his body dances six inches above the ground (John Alden Mason, *Notes on the Indians of the Great Slave Lake Area,* 1946, p. 40).

These "journeys" establish the reputation of a shaman. While his body lies rigid and motionless on the floor, his soul hastens through far-off spaces and unknown lands, encounters mythical figures, and receives their instruction. The few reports we have indicate that the images in these dream experiences are the same as those found in the tribal mythologies. The visionary sees in his trance only what he knows. His dream journeys revitalize religious knowledge; without the continual confirmation through dreams, the mythical images would be forgotten. The shaman is thus the most important preserver of tribal traditions.

There once lived among the Hare Indians a powerful sorcerer who was called Nayeweri ("he who was created by thought"). One autumn as he saw the birds flying toward the warm lands, he followed them and soon came to the foot of the sky. There a huge cave opened up, and out of it a river flowed. The cave was the winter abode of the souls of the dead. In the summer they roam the earth, but with the approach of the cold, they fly with the migratory birds southward to this cave.

Nayeweri looked around but could see the souls only up to their knees. Some were casting nets, others paddled around in their canoes, while others were danc-

ing. In front of the cave stood a tall tree; with the help of that tree Nayeweri climbed up to the sky. For two days his body lay lifeless on the earth, but on the third day Nayeweri returned from his journey and rose to his feet.

(adapted from Petitot, 1876, p. xxxi)

What the visionary saw here is based on an idea common to all Canadian Indians: the southwest is the home of the dead. This is a familiar image in the conceptual world of the hunter. The Micmac place their ancestral home in the southwest, and even the Narraganset, an Algonquian people who inhabited a maize-growing region on the coast of Rhode Island, locate their land of the dead in the southwest, which is also said to be the source of their maize and beans (Rand, 1894, p. 110 and n. 2; and Roger Williams, *A Key into the Language of America,* 1643, pp. 7, 70).

The world cross of the Beaver Indians, which the creator drew on the surface of the primeval sea and which formed the basis of the earth disk, also belongs to these dream images. When preserved as a graphical representation on a drumhead, the image is without doubt based on a dream experience. We do not know a great deal about these experiences, but the few pieces of evidence available to us display a fundamental characteristic of shamanistic epiphanies: their pictorial nature. They are painted on bark or leather with sticks and colors and are also sewn as patterns on articles of clothing. They are thus never meant to express abstractions, as the indiscriminate use of the word *medicine* would suggest.

The Shaman's Drum. Pictorial representations are mostly to be found on the drum, the most important accessory of the shaman. Physically the drum consists of a skin-covered wooden hoop. The upper side is painted with numerous figures, all illustrations of dream experiences. Animal tendon into which pieces of bone have been twisted is stretched across the drumhead. When the drum is beaten with a wooden stick, the bone fragments begin to vibrate; they "sing."

Speck (1935) reports that the Labrador shamans believe that their drums are living beings capable of speaking and understanding human language (p. 175). The close association of drum and drummer is also indicated by the Penobscot word for "shaman": he is the "drum-sound man."

The drum is used to induce a trance in the drummer; the vibrating and buzzing sound dulls the consciousness and opens the way for the "journey." At the same time the drum beckons the helping spirits, as can be seen in the following drumming song from the Passamaquoddy:

I sit down and beat the drum, and by the sound of the drum I call the animals from the mountains. Even the great storms hearken to the sound of my drum.
I sit down and beat the drum, and the storm and thunder answer the sound of my drum. The great whirlwind ceases its raging to listen to the sound of my drum.
I sit down and beat the drum, and the spirit-of-the-night-air comes and listens to the sound of my drum. Even the great storm-bird will cease moving his wings to hearken to the sound of my drum.
I sit down and beat the drum, and the spirit-under-the-water comes to the surface and listens to the sound of my drum, and the wood-spirit will cease chopping and hearken to the sound of my drum.

I sit down and beat my drum, and the great man with long red hair will come out of the deep and hearken to the sound of my drum.
The lightning, thunder, storms, gales, forest-spirit, whirlwind, water-spirit and spirit-of-the-night-air are gathered together and are listening to the sound of my drum.

(John D. Prince, "Notes on Passamaquoddy Literature,"
Annals of the New York Academy of Sciences 13, pp. 385f.)

This song, with its pictorial richness, also testifies to the worldliness of the shaman-istic conceptions. The shaman lives with the realities of the world, not in the un-reachable hereafter. Even the spirits are a part of this world; they sit and listen, and participate in the life of the cosmic house.

The Shaking Tent. In addition to the drum, the eastern Canadian Algonquians use another device to communicate with the spirits: the shaking tent, which is a specially built cylindrical structure with a framework of thick poles. The top of the tent re-mains open so that the spirits can enter. As soon as the shaman crawls into the tent and begins to sing, the posts, which are dug in deeply, start to shake. The beckoned spirits can be heard rushing by; animal cries arise; the shaman asks questions; and the spirits respond. The whole tent sways as if battered by a storm. Those assembled outside are also allowed to pose questions about lost articles, cures for illnesses, and the threatening designs of hostile persons. The séance ends when all the partic-ipants are satisfied (*Handbook,* vol. 6, p. 251).

A certain bewilderment is noticeable in the reports of Europeans who have wit-nessed the ceremony, all of them sensible and discerning men. They have affirmed again and again that the shaman crawls into the tent alone and, further, that a single person could not have the strength to move the deeply sunken posts as much as a finger's breadth. They assert, too, that the shaman could not possibly produce the confusion of different sounds simultaneously. To them, the whole phenomenon re-mains incomprehensible and inexplicable. The usual talk of deception and charla-tanry misses the point. The search for purely rational or empirical explanations can-not come to grips with the kind of spiritual powers to which sub-Arctic peoples have access.

BIBLIOGRAPHY

Our earliest sources on sub-Arctic Indian religions are two myth anthologies compiled by missionaries. *Legends of the Micmacs* (New York, 1894) is the work of Silas Tertius Rand. Around the middle of the nineteenth century Rand wrote down what the Indians at his mission in New Brunswick related to him. The publication followed several decades later.

Around the same time the monk Émile Petitot was working among the northern Athapas-cans. His *Traditions Indiennes du Canada Nord-Ouest* (Paris, 1886) is to this day the most comprehensive collection of texts from the region between the upper Yukon and Mackenzie rivers. Equally indispensable is his comprehensive *Dictionnaire de la langue Dènè-Dindjié* (Paris, 1876). The author lists the vocabulary in four parallel columns: French, Montagnais, Hare, Loucheux (Kutchin). Individual entries offer deep insight into the religion of the Indians of the time.

The transcribing of the oral tradition was continued in numerous collections. Volume 10 of the *Anthropological Papers of the American Museum of Natural History* (1917) contains the

"Chipewyan Texts" by Pliny Earle Goddard (pp. 1–66) and "Chipewyan Tales" by Robert H. Lowie (pp. 171–200). The *Journal of American Folk-Lore* 30 (1917) published the "Kaska Tales" by James Teit (pp. 427–473). The "Passamaquoddy Texts" by J. Dyneley Prince appeared in the *Publications of the American Ethnological Society* 10 (1921): 1–85.

With the rise of modern anthropology a special problem emerged: the widespread inability of the younger generation of researchers to understand and grasp the meaning of the religious heritage of the Indians. A mechanistic worldview reduced religious values to sociological catch-words; fashionable sociological theories blocked the understanding of alien ways of thinking. Frank Gouldsmith Speck's *Naskapi: The Savage Hunters of the Labrador Peninsula* (1935; re-print, Norman, Okla., 1977) is one exception. Speck was one of the few researchers who recognized that the so-called primitive cultures are steeped in religion and are guided by the spiritual side of life, not by the material.

In comparison to this superb work Cornelius Osgood's otherwise laudable study on the Athapascans appears somewhat pedantic. The author fails to grasp that religion is more than knowledge. He nevertheless takes a positive step by treating religious elements not as material for sociology but as values *sui generis*. Among his numerous publications are: "The Ethnography of the Great Bear Lake Indians," *Bulletin of the National Museum of Canada* 70 (1932): 31–97; *Contributions to the Ethnography of the Kutchin* (New Haven, 1936); and *Ingalik Mental Culture* (New Haven, 1959).

The same shortcomings mark the *Handbook of North American Indians,* vol. 6, *Subarctic,* edited by June Helm (Washington, D.C., 1981). The impression often arises that this collection of short studies is dealing with "religionless" peoples. One exception here is Robin Ridington's article on the Beaver (pp. 350–360).

11 INUIT

Inge Kleivan

The Inuit (Eskimo) live in the vast Arctic and sub-Arctic area that stretches from the eastern point of Siberia to eastern Greenland. Of the approximately 105,000 Inuit, 43,000 live in Greenland, 25,000 in Arctic Canada, 35,000 (plus 2,000 Aleut) in Alaska, and 1,500 (plus a small number of Aleut) in the Soviet Union. Language has been used as the basic criterion for defining the Inuit as an ethnic group. The "Eskimo languages" (as they are invariably referred to) are divided into two main branches, Inuit and Yupik. Inuit is spoken from northern Alaska to eastern Greenland, forming a continuum of dialects with mutual comprehension between adjacent dialects. Varieties of Yupik are spoken in Siberia and in southern Alaska as far north as Norton Sound.

The word *Eskimo* seems to be of Montagnais origin and has been erroneously believed to mean "eater of raw meat." The word *Inuit* means "people." *Inuit* as a self-designation is used primarily in Canada and, to some extent, in Greenland (where the more common self-designation is *Kalaallit*). *Yupik* means "a real person," just as *Inupiat,* which is the self-designation in northern Alaska, means "real people." *Inuit,* however, is the common term used to designate themselves collectively by the members of the Inuit Circumpolar Conference, an organization established in 1977 by representatives from Greenland, Canada, and Alaska.

Traditionally the Inuit are divided into many geographic groups. The members of each group, or band, were connected through kinship ties, but the band was without formal leadership. The nuclear family was the most important social unit, but the extended family often cohabited and worked cooperatively. Dyadic relationships, such as wife-exchange partners and joking partners, were also common.

Today, most Inuit live in the so-called Arctic area, north of the treeline and the 10°C July isotherm. The Inuit were hunters who adapted to the seasonal availability of various mammals, birds, and fish. Hunting sea mammals with harpoons was characteristic, but hunting inland during the summer was also part of the subsistence pattern of many Inuit. A few groups in northern Alaska and in Canada have spent the entire year inland, hunting caribou and fishing for arctic char. In southern Alaska, the wooded valleys along the long rivers were inhabited by Inuit who relied upon the great run of the fish as well as the migrations of sea mammals and birds.

Most Inuit in Canada lived in snow houses during the winter; others settled in winter houses built of stone and sod or wood. Stone lamps that burned blubber were used for heating, lighting, and cooking. Skin boats and, except in southern Greenland and Alaska, dog sledges were used for transportation; kayaks were used for seal hunting and large, open umiaks for whale hunting. Although some Inuit are still hunters and fishermen, today's Inuit societies are modernized. Money economy has replaced subsistence economy; modern technology and education have been introduced; television plays an important role; and so on. Except for the small population in Siberia, the Inuit have become Christians, and even the Inuit in Siberia no longer observe their religious traditions.

Historically, the Inuit held many observances to insure good hunting, and in the small and scattered hunting and fishing communities many local religious practices were observed. Generally, ritual life was more elaborate in Alaska than in Canada and Greenland. In Alaskan settlements there were usually one or more big men's houses, called *qarigi* among the Point Barrow Inuit and *qasiq* among those of the Bering Sea, where people gathered for social and religious feasts. In Canada, the Inuit built temporary festival snow houses, but no eyewitness accounts exist of festival houses in Greenland.

RELATIONS BETWEEN MEN AND ANIMALS

According to eastern Inuit religious tradition, each animal had its own *inua* (its "man," "owner," or "spirit") and also its own "soul." Within the western Inuit religious tradition, the *inua* seems to have been identical to the soul. The idea of *inua* was applied to animals and implements as well as to concepts and conditions (such as sleep). Lakes, currents, mountains, and stars all had their own *inua,* but only the *inua* of the moon, air, and sea were integral to the religious life of the Inuit.

Since the Inuit believed that the animals they hunted possessed souls, they treated their game with respect. Seals and whales were commonly offered a drink of fresh water after they had been dragged ashore. Having received such a pleasant welcome as guests in the human world, their souls, according to Inuit belief, would return to the sea and soon become ready to be caught again, and they would also let their fellow animals know that they should not object to being caught. When the season's first kill of an important species of seal was made, the meat was distributed to all of the inhabitants of a settlement. This practice divided the responsibility for the kill among the entire community and increased the possibility of good hunting.

Inuit rituals in connection with the polar bear are part of an ancient bear ceremonialism of the circumpolar regions of Eurasia and North America. In southern Greenland, for example, the head of a slain polar bear was placed in a house facing the direction from which the bears usually came so that the bear's soul could easily find its way home. During the five days that the soul was believed to require to reach its destination the bear was honored: its eyes and nostrils were closed so that it would not be disturbed by the sight and smell of human beings; its mouth was smeared with blubber; and it was given presents. [*See also* Bears.]

Whaling was of great social, economic, and ritual importance, especially among the North Alaska Inuit. In the spring, all hunting gear was carefully cleaned, and the women made new clothes for the men. The whales would not be approached until everything was cleaned. During the days before the whaling party set out, the men slept in the festival house and observed sexual and food taboos. The whaling season terminated with a great feast to entertain the whales.

TABOOS, AMULETS, AND SONGS

Unlike cultic practices in connection with the deities, which had relatively minor significance, taboos, amulets, and songs were fundamentally important to the Inuit. Most taboos were imposed to separate the game from a person who was tabooed because of birth, menstruation, or death. A separation between land and sea animals was also important in many localities, reflecting the seasonal changes in hunting adaptation. An infringement of a taboo might result in individual hardship (for example, the loss of good fortune in hunting, sickness, or even death), but often, it was feared, the whole community would suffer. Usually a public confession under the guidance of the shaman was believed sufficient to reduce the effect of the transgression of a taboo.

Amulets, which dispensed their powers only to the first owner, were used primarily to secure success in hunting and good health and, to a lesser degree, to ward off negative influences. Parents and grandparents would usually buy amulets for children from a shaman. Amulets were usually made up of parts of animals and birds, but a wide variety of objects could be used. They were sewn on clothing or placed in boats and houses.

One way to increase the effect of the amulets was through the use of food totems and secret songs. Used primarily to increase success in hunting, secret songs and formulas were also used to control other activities and were often associated with food taboos. Songs were either inherited or bought. If a song was passed on from one generation to the next, all members of the family were free to use it, but once it was sold it became useless to its former owners.

RITES OF PASSAGE

In many localities in Canada and Alaska, women had to give birth alone, isolated in a small hut or tent. For a specified period after the birth, the woman was subjected to food and work taboos. Children were usually named after a person who had recently died. The name was regarded as a vital part of the individual, and, in a way, the deceased lived on in the child. The relationship resulted in a close social bond between the relatives of the deceased and the child.

The family celebrated particular stages in a child's development, especially in connection with subsistence activities. For example, when a boy killed his first seal, the meat was distributed to all the inhabitants of the settlement, and for each new important species a hunter killed, there was a celebration and ritual distribution.

Death was considered to be a passage to a new existence. There were two lands of the dead: one in the sky and one in the sea (or underground). The Inuit in Greenland considered the land in the sea more attractive because people living there enjoyed perpetual success in whale hunting; those in the sky, on the other hand, led dull existences. It was not the moral behavior of the deceased that determined the location of his afterlife, but rather the way in which he died. For example, men who died while whaling or women who died in childbirth were assured of an afterlife in the sea. Conceptions of the afterlife, however, differed among the Inuit. The Canadian and Alaskan Inuit believed the most attractive afterlife was found in the sky. Some Inuit had either poorly conceptualized beliefs in an afterlife or no beliefs at all.

While death rituals usually included only the nearest family members and neighbors, the Great Feast of the Dead, celebrated in the Alaskan mainland from the Kuskokwim River to the Kotzebue Sound, attracted participants even from neighboring villages. The feast was given jointly, and the hosts' social status was demonstrated by the quantity of food, furs, clothing, and implements that were given away.

The Bladder Feast, an important calendar feast celebrated in Alaska from Kodiak Island to Point Hope, was held in midwinter. At this feast, the bladders of all the seals that had been caught during the previous year were returned to the sea in order that their souls might come back in new bodies and let themselves be caught again. The skins of all the small birds and animals that the boys had caught were displayed in the festival house, and gifts were given to human souls, to the souls of the seals, and to those who were present.

SHAMANS

In Greenland and Canada, the shaman (*angakkoq*) played a central role in religion. In Alaska, however, where it was common for an individual to become a shaman as the result of a calling, many rites did not demand the expertise of the shaman. Prospective shamans often learned from skilled shamans how to acquire spirits and to use techniques such as ecstatic trances. In Greenland and Labrador, the apprentice was initiated by being "devoured" by a polar bear or a big dog while being in trance alone in the wilderness. After having revived, he was ready to become master of various spirits.

Shamans in Greenland always used a drum to enter a trance. Masks were also instrumental, especially in Alaska, both in secular and religious connections. The shaman might summon his familiar spirits to the house where a séance was taking place, or he might go on a spiritual flight himself. The Canadian shaman might, for example, go down to the *inua* of the sea, that is, the Sea Woman, to get seals. In Alaska, a shaman on Nunivak Island would go to the villages of the various species of animals in the sea. In the Norton Sound area he would go to the moon to obtain animals for the settlement.

Although shamans were the principal revealers of unknown things, some other people could also acquire information from the spirits by using a simple technique called *qilaneq*. It required that an individual lift an object and then pose questions, which were answered affirmatively or negatively according to whether the object felt heavy or not.

Shamans also functioned as doctors. For example, they would suck the sick spot where a foreign object had been introduced or try to retrieve a stolen soul. Sorcerers—often believed to be old, revengeful women—were also common, and shamans were sometimes called to reveal them. There were instances, however, in which the shaman himself was accused of having used his power to harm someone; in such cases the shaman could be killed.

THE DEITIES

The Inuit of Canada and Greenland believed that the *inua* of the sea, the Sea Woman, controlled the sea animals and would withhold them to punish people when they had broken a taboo. Franz Boas (1888) transcribed the name given to her by the Inuit on Baffin Island as *Sedna,* which probably means "the one down there." [*See* Sedna.]

The Inuit of eastern Baffin Island ritually killed Sedna during a feast that was held when the autumn storms came and whose purpose was to make sealing possible again. The Sedna ceremony included, *inter alia,* a ritual spouse exchange and a tug-of-war, the result of which predicted the weather for the coming winter.

While Sedna represented the female principle of the world, the *inua* of the moon, Aningaaq, represented the male principle. An origin myth tells how he was once a man who committed incest with his sister. She became the sun, he the moon. Otherwise the sun played no part in the religion of the Inuit, but the moon was associated with the fertility of women. He was recognized as a great hunter, and some Alaskan Inuit believed that the moon controlled the game. [*See* Aningaaq.]

The air was called Sila, which also means "universe" and "intellect." The *inua* of the air was a rather abstract but feared figure; if it was offended when taboos were broken, it would take revenge by bringing storms and blizzards.

The Raven appeared, primarily in Alaska, as a creator, culture hero, and trickster in a cycle of myths that included those of the earth diver and the origin of the light. The Raven, however, played a negligible role in religious practices. [*See* Tricksters, *article on* North American Tricksters.]

The differences between and sometimes vagueness in Inuit religious ideas may be related not only to their wide and scattered distribution but also to the fact that their societies had a loose social organization and were without a written language before contact with the Europeans. For all Inuit, however, a close and good relationship with the animals on which they depended for their survival was believed to be of vital importance.

BIBLIOGRAPHY

An excellent survey of Inuit culture from prehistoric to modern times is given in the *Handbook of North American Indians,* vol. 5, edited by David Damas (Washington, D.C., 1984). The best survey of Inuit religion is Margaret Lantis's article "The Religion of the Eskimos," in *Forgotten Religions,* edited by Vergilius Ferm (New York, 1950), pp. 311–339. Lantis is also the author of *Alaskan Eskimo Ceremonialism* (New York, 1947). This well-documented book is based primarily on literary sources, but it also contains Lantis's field notes from Nunivak. A review of the religion of the Inuit in Canada and Greenland has been written by Birgitte Sonne and myself as an introduction to a collection of plates that illustrate the religious life of these people in *Eskimos: Greenland and Canada* (Leiden, 1985), vol. 8, pt. 2, of the series "Iconography of Religions." A strong visual impression of the Bering Sea Inuit culture in the nineteenth century is found in William W. Fitzhugh and Susan A. Kaplan's *Inua: Spirit World of the Bering Sea Eskimo* (Washington, D.C., 1982). This is a fascinating book that examines how the spirit world manifests itself in all areas of the life of these Inuit. A study of the religion of two Inuit groups in Canada is given in J. G. Oosten's *The Theoretical Structure of the Religion of the Netsilik and Iglulik* (Mappel, Netherlands, 1976). Information that has been gathered on rituals in connection with animals is presented in Regitze Søby's article "The Eskimo Animal Cult," *Folk* (Copenhagen) 11/12 (1969–1970): 43–78. The position of the Inuit shaman has been analyzed by Birgitte Sonne in "The Professional Ecstatic in His Social and Ritual Position," in *Religious Ecstasy,* edited by Nils G. Holm (Stockholm, 1982), pp. 128–150, and by Daniel Merkur in his *Becoming Half Hidden: Shamanism and Initiation among the Inuit* (Stockholm, 1985).

Among the many valuable and often quoted books by Knud Rasmussen is *The Netsilik Eskimos: Social Life and Spiritual Culture* (Copenhagen, 1931). This book presents material that Rasmussen collected from various groups of Inuit who had had limited contact with the Euro-American world. Among the many valuable studies on the Alaskan Inuit, two should be mentioned: Robert F. Spencer's *The North Alaskan Eskimo: A Study in Ecology and Society* (Washington, D.C., 1959) and Ann Fienup-Riordan's *The Nelson Island Eskimo: Social Structure and Ritual Distribution* (Anchorage, Alaska, 1983).

An extensive bibliography for Inuit religion is given by John Fisher in his article "Bibliography for the Study of Eskimo Religion," *Anthropologica,* n.s. 15 (1973): 231–271.

12 THE NORTHEAST WOODLANDS

John A. Grim and Donald P. St. John

Northeast Woodlands peoples occupy an area within 90° to 70° west longitude and 35° to 47° north latitude. The region can be divided into three smaller geographical areas: (1) the upper Great Lakes and Ohio River Valley region, (2) the lower Great Lakes, and (3) the coastal region. Their settlement patterns varied from the northern nomadic hunting groups of extended families through combined bands in semisedentary villages to relatively permanent agricultural settlements. The organization of lineage descent was matrilineal among the Iroquoian-speaking peoples, matrilineal or bilateral among the coastal Algonquian-speaking peoples, patrilineal or bilateral among the upper Great Lakes and Ohio River Algonquian- and Siouan-speaking peoples. Population density in the Northeast varied. At the time of first contact with Europeans the number of persons per hundred square kilometers was ten to twenty-five in the upper Great Lakes and Ohio River areas; twenty-five to sixty in the lower Great Lakes region; and among the coastal Algonquian from three hundred in the Virginia–North Carolina area and decreasing northerly to fewer than twenty-five in the more northern regions of New England (Driver, 1969).

The most prominent tribes, divided according to language group, are (1) Algonquian-speaking (Southern Ojibwa, Ottawa, Potawatomi, Menomini, Sauk, Fox, Kickapoo, Miami, Illinois, Shawnee, Narraganset, Mohican, Delaware, Nanticoke, and Powhatan), (2) Iroquoian-speaking (Huron, Erie, Neutral, Petun, Seneca, Oneida, Onondaga, Cayuga, Mohawk, and Tuscarora), and (3) Siouan-speaking (Winnebago, Tutelo).

The oldest ethnographic material that scholars now rely on deals with these people as they were originally situated. However, significant materials have been gathered subsequently as different tribes either migrated or reorganized on reservations.

These Indian peoples began a period of intense movement in the seventeenth century or earlier, which has continued for many tribes into the present century. Although discussion of these movements will not be undertaken here, no treatment of the religious life of these people can be attempted without acknowledging the intensely disruptive experiences of the past four centuries. The severing of cultural and religious ties to specific geographical locations has been seen by some Native American religious leaders not simply as a loss of natural resources but as a sacrificial event with profound consequences for the survival of individual tribes and their religious practices. In particular, the loss of ancient ancestral sites has disrupted the linkage between the North American Indian peoples and the land through which the power and meaning of their religious culture manifested itself.

COSMOLOGICAL BELIEFS

The cosmological beliefs of the Northeast Woodlands peoples involve the concept of power as manifested in the land, in the dialectic of the sacred and the profane, and in patterns of space and time. According to the mythic thought of these peoples, power is that transformative presence most clearly seen in the cycles of the day and the seasons, in the fecund earth, and in the visions and deeds of spirits, ancestors, and living people. This numinous power is so manifestly present that no verbal explanation of it is adequate; rather it is itself the explanation of all transformations in life. While generally regarded as neutral, power may be used for good or ill by individuals.

Power. This all-pervasive power is expressed among Algonquian-speaking tribes by the word *manitou* or one of its linguistic variants. *Manitou* is a personal revelatory experience usually manifested in dreams or in visions of a spirit who is capable of transformation into a specific human or animal form. The efficacy of power is symbolized as "medicine," either as a tangible object reverently kept in a bundle or as an intangible "charm" possessed internally. The term *manitou* is used here to indicate both the singular form of power as the binding concept throughout the highly individual Algonquian belief systems and as the plural form of tutelary spirits who embody such binding force. *Manitou,* in its various contexts, has both noun forms that indicate entities that empower and verb forms that indicate a moral responsibility to cultivate power.

The belief in *manitou* can be found among the coastal Algonquians from New England to North Carolina. Similarities may be seen in the name for the Great Manitou: for the Narraganset he was Kautantowwit and for the Penobscot, Ktahandowit. The Delaware worshiped as Great Manitou a spirit called Keetan'towit, who had eleven assistants (*manitowuks*), each having control over one of eleven hierarchically organized "heavens." The most ancient of the *manitou* was Our Grandfather, the great tortoise, who carries the earth on his back. The Virginia Algonquians called those *manitou* who were benevolent *quiyoughcosuck;* this was also the name given to their priests. The evil *manitou* were called *tagkanysough.* Southeast Woodlands influences led to the depiction of *manitou* in carvings and statues, usually found in the sacred architecture of the North Carolina and Virginia Algonquians.

The Huron concept of *oki* referred both to a superabundance of power or ability and to spirit-forces of the cosmos, or guardian spirits. An *oki* could be either benevolent or malevolent. The supreme *oki,* Iouskeha, dwelt in the sky, watched over the seasons and the affairs of humans, witnessed to vows, made crops grow, and owned the animals. He had an evil brother, Tawiskaron.

The Iroquois *orenda,* a magico-religious force, was exercised by spirit-forces called Otkon and Oyaron; it was present in humans, animals, or objects that displayed excessive power, great ability, or large size. The Iroquois had a dualistic system whereby all of the spirit-forces deemed good were associated with the Good Twin and all of those deemed evil with his brother the Evil Twin.

The Land. In many of the mythologies of the peoples of the Northeast Woodlands this cosmic power was intimately connected with the land. In their origin myth, the Menomini relate that they came into existence near the mouth of the Menominee River in Wisconsin; here two bears emerged from the earth and became the first man and woman. Near Fond du Lac, where a prominent rock ledge projects into Lake Winnebago, three thunderbirds descended and also became humans. Thus the Menomini use sacred stories associated with the local landscape to mark their origin as well as to relate the division of the tribe into earth and sky clans. The interweaving of tribal myth and sacred geography serves to integrate the community into both personal and cosmic levels of meaning. The intimate relationship of these Algonquian speakers with the land was reflected in their image of the land as Nokomis ("grandmother earth"), who nurtured her grandchildren. This intimacy of kinship with the earth was also part of an elaborate hierarchical perspective that located the earth within a vast schema of layers of power in the cosmos. Both the Algonquian speakers and the Siouan-speaking Winnebago developed cosmologies in which the heavens above and the earth regions below were seen as layered in hierarchies of beneficial and harmful spirits. The highest power was the supreme being called Great Spirit by the Potawatomi, Ottawa, Miami, and Ojibwa; Master of Life by the Menomini, Sauk, and Fox; Finisher by the Shawnee and Kickapoo; and Earthmaker by the Winnebago. This "great mysterious" presence maintained a unique relationship with the last and weakest members of creation, namely, human beings.

Spirit-forces. Power and guidance entered human existence from the cosmic spirit-forces, from the guardian spirits of individuals and medicine societies, and from spirits of charms, bundles, and masks. Dreams, in particular, were a vehicle for contacting power and thus gaining guidance for political and military decisions. New songs, dances, and customs were often received by the dreamer and were used to energize and reorder cultural life; dreams channeled power as consolation and hope during times of crisis, and often initiated contact between visionary power and the shamans. One means of describing the human experience of this cosmic power is through the dialectic of the sacred and the profane.

This dialectic is useful even though the Northeast Woodlands peoples did not draw a sharp distinction between the sacred and profane. The dialectic refers to the inner logic of the manifestation of numinous power through certain symbols. Profane objects, events, or persons might become embodiments of the sacred in moments of hierophany. This manifestation of the sacred in and through the profane frequently became the inspiration for sacred stories and mythologies that narrated the tribal lore. Among the Winnebago and other Northeast Woodlands peoples, narrative stories were distinguished as *worak* ("what is recounted") and *waika* ("what is sacred"). Telling the *worak* stories of heroes, human tragedy, and memorable events was a profane event, whereas narrating the *waika* stories evoked the spirits and was therefore a sacred ritual. Thus the ordinary act of speaking could become the hierophany that manifests power. Not only narrative but also the interweaving of sacred space and time gave real dimensions to cosmic power.

Sacred Space. A place of orientation that provides individuals or groups with a sense of both an integrating center and a cosmic boundary is called "sacred space." This concept is exemplified by the Medicine society's rite, which originated among the Ojibwa and was transmitted throughout the eighteenth century to the other tribes of the upper Great Lakes. For this Medicine rite a special lodge was constructed of arched trees, covering an earthen floor with a rock and an elaborate pole in the center. These items varied slightly throughout the area of the ritual's diffusion, but in every instance they were used to delineate sacred space and to symbolize the cosmos. For the Winnebago, the arched trees of the lodge symbolized the water spirits (snakes who occupied the four cardinal directions). For the Potawatomi the earthen floor was Nokomis ("grandmother earth"). Among the Sauk the central stone in the lodge indicated the abiding presence of power. For the Ojibwa, originators of this ceremony, which they called Midewiwin ("mystic doings"), the pole symbolized the cosmic tree that penetrated the multilayered universe and united all the assembled *manitou.*

Iroquoian and coastal Algonquian peoples lived in rectangular "longhouses" or "big houses," in groups comprised of several matrilineally connected families. That the longhouses and big houses were seen as microcosms is most clearly reflected in the symbolism of the Delaware big house. The floor and ceiling represented the earth and sky, respectively. There was a door where the sun rose and a door where the sun set, and these doors were connected by the ceremonial Good White Path, symbolizing the journey human beings make from birth toward death. The fact that there was a door, an opening toward the west, and the fact that the dances eventually circled back, point to the Delaware hope in an afterlife and, for some, a rebirth. In the center of the big house stood a post with a carved face that was made from a tree and that symbolized the *axis mundi;* from its base the post was believed to run upward through the twelve cosmic levels, the last being the place of the Great Manitou. This post was the staff of the Great Manitou, whose power filled all creation. Power manifested in the spirits was symbolized by the faces carved into low posts situated around the inside of the big house.

Sacred Time. The period of contact with sustaining power is "sacred time." Such contact was believed to occur in the movement of the seasons, the fecundity of nature, and the personal life cycle. Among the native peoples of the upper Great Lakes, time was also sacralized in the narratives and rituals that reconstituted the mythic time of *manitou* revelation. During the Menomini Mitawin, or Medicine rite, while the origin myth of the ceremony itself was narrated, the society members imagistically participated in the original assembly of the *manitou* who began the ceremony in mythic time. Such an evocation of relationship with cosmic powers and identification with them in the oral narratives structured an experience of sacred time.

The Delaware Big House ceremony evoked powers that made possible the transition from the old year of chaos to the new year of cosmos. The origin myth narrated during that ceremony set the context for a renewal of the earth and of the tribe's binding relationships with the spirit-forces. The myth related that long ago the very foundation of life itself, the earth, was split open by a devastating quake. The forces of evil and chaos erupted from the underworld in the form of dust, smoke, and a black liquid: all creatures were struck with fear at these events. The humans then met in council and concluded that the disruptions had occurred because they had neglected their proper relationship with the Great Manitou. They prayed for power and guidance. The *manitou* spoke to them in dreams, telling them how to build a house that would re-create the cosmos and how to conduct a ceremony that would evoke the power to sustain it. This ceremony would establish their moral relationship with the *manitou,* and by the carvings of their *mesingw* ("faces") on the posts an identification with each of these cosmic forces would occur as one moved ritually along the Good White Path. Furthermore, the recitation of puberty dream-visions would renew and revivify the individual's relationship with his or her personal *manitou.* The old time was one of impurity, symbolized by dirt and smoke. To make the transition into sacred time everyone and everything had to be purified, including attendants, reciters of dreams, and the big house itself. Purifying fires burned on either side of the center post. Persons or objects in a state of impurity, such as menstruating women, were always excluded from the big house.

CEREMONIAL PRACTICES

Some understanding of the rich and complex ritual life of the Northeast Woodlands peoples can be obtained by considering selected ceremonies concerned with subsistence, life cycles, and personal, clan, and society visions.

Subsistence. Through subsistence rituals, tribes contacted power to ensure the success of hunting, fishing, or trapping; gathering of herbs, fruits, or root crops; and agricultural endeavors. Among the Sauk and Menomini there were both private and public ceremonials for hunting that focused on sacred objects generically labeled "medicine." The large public medicine-bundlesof three types were believed to have been obtained by the trickster–culture hero Manabus from the Grandfathers, or *manitou* spirits. The first hunting bundle, called Misasakiwis, helped to defeat the malicious medicine people who tried to foil the hunter's success. Both the second bundle, Kitagasa Muskiki (made of a fawn's skin), and the third (a bundle with deer, wolf, and owl skins), fostered hunting success. Each bundle might contain a variety of power objects such as animal skins, miniature hunting implements, wooden figures, herbal preparations, and often an actual scent to lure animals. The bundle's owner obtained the right to assemble or purchase such a bundle from a personal vision. Songs, especially, evoked the powers of the bundle; these songs often recalled the agreement between the visionary and the *manitou* as well as the prohibitions and obligations that impinged upon the owner of a bundle. In this way the bundle owner, and the hunters he aided, thwarted the evil ones and contacted the *manitou* masters of the hunted animals. Thus power objects from the environment, the empowered hunters, and the ritually imaged *manitou*-spirits, functioned together to bring sustenance to the people.

Although the growing season varied within the Northeast, most of these peoples practiced some form of agriculture. With the introduction of agriculture new symbol complexes developed, giving meaning and power to this new subsistence activity and integrating it into the larger cosmic order. The northern Iroquois, for example, linked together woman, earth, moon, and the cycles of birth and death.

According to northern Iroquois mythology, agricultural products first emerged from the dead body of the Creator's mother. Out of her breasts grew two corn stalks, and from her arms and body came beans and squash. Her death had been caused by the Creator's evil minded brother, who was frequently associated with winter and ice. In giving birth to winter the Earth Mother "dies," but she brings forth life in the spring. The gathering of plants and the planting of crops were also the practical

tasks of Iroquois women. Consequently, these women played a key role in sched-
uling and celebrating the ceremonies marking the yearly cycle of life: the Our-Life-
Supporters Dances, the Bush Dance, and the Maple, Seed Planting, Strawberry, Raspberry, Green Bean, Little Corn, Green Corn, and Harvest rituals.

The spirit of the Earth Mother was also made into the Moon by her son, the
Creator (or Master) of Life. Grandmother Moon was connected with life, as it was
her duty to watch over all living things during the night. The monthly cycle of the
moon and the yearly cycle of vegetation were associated with the mystery of life,
death, and rebirth; women and the earth were seen as connected because they both
have the power to bring forth and nourish life.

The domestic ceremony of apology for taking life is also found among all these
Northeast Woodlands people. This simple ceremony illustrates the moral character
of the force that was believed to bind the cosmos together. The ceremony consisted
of a spoken apology and a gift of sacred tobacco for the disturbance caused to the
web of life by cutting trees, gathering plants, or taking minerals. For example, William Jones, in his *Ethnography of the Fox Indians* (1939), quotes a Fox tribesman as
saying: "We do not like to harm trees. Whenever we can, we always make an offering
of tobacco to the trees before we cut them down. If we did not think of their feelings
. . . before cutting them down, all the other trees in the forest would weep, and
that would make our hearts sad, too" (p. 21). This ceremony is both a thanksgiving
for the blessing of a material boon and an acknowledgment of the environmental
morality that binds the human and natural worlds.

Life Cycles. Life-cycle rites of passage are illuminating examples of these peoples'
recognition that the passage through life's stages required a structured encounter
with power. These ceremonies included private actions that invoked power at lim-
inal moments such as menstruation, marriage, and birth. For example, menstruating
women withdrew to specially constructed lodges, and the marriage ceremony was
generally validated by an extensive exchange of gifts between families. Similarly,
conception was ensured by protective fetal spirits, and new birth required a period
of seclusion for purification of the mother and cradle-amulets for the child. Although
there were taboos surrounding pregnancy and delivery, there were no elaborate
birth rituals among the northern Iroquois or coastal Algonquians. Other life-cycle
ceremonials, however, were marked by elaborate ritual activities, such as naming,
puberty, and death ceremonies.

Birth and Early Childhood. Naming ceremonies arise both from the belief that
humans are born weak and require power for growth and survival as well as a belief
that new life should be introduced into the cosmos. Generally, two types of naming
ceremonies have been found. Among the Southeast Woodlands tribes a child was
given an ancestral clan name. This situated that child in the clan lineage and empowered the child by directly connecting him or her to the ancestral vision embodied
in the clan medicine bundles. Another ceremony associated with the Menomini,
Potawatomi, Ojibwa, and Ottawa, but occasionally practiced by the other groups,
involved naming by virtue of a dream vision. In this ritual a person was chosen by
the parents to undergo a fast or a sweat lodge purification so that they might receive
a name for the child from the *manitou.*

Among the Iroquois and Delaware the naming ceremony, which was conducted in the longhouse, was the most significant ritual of early childhood. Delaware parents were attentive to their dreams for a revelation of the name. They would give their child to an elder in the big house who would announce the child's name and offer prayers of blessing for it. A similar ceremony would be conducted for an adult who decided to change his or her name due to a significant deed or because the first name no longer seemed appropriate. The Huron pierced the ears of the child and named it shortly after birth; the child's name then belonged to the clan and could not be used by another member of the tribe. The Iroquois named their children either at the Green Corn ceremony in the summer or before the Midwinter ceremonies. A child who resembled a dead ancestor might be given his or her name since it was believed that the name might have some of the ancestor's personality. The name remained the child's exclusive privilege and the focus of his or her early spiritual formation until the puberty ceremonials.

Puberty. It is uncertain whether the puberty rites of the Algonquians of Virginia and North Carolina involved a vision quest. However, the vision quest was part of the puberty rites of all of the upper Great Lakes peoples with variations according to the tribe. Some southern Ohio River groups such as the Shawnee emphasized less ecstatic experiences such as a boy's first kill. Among the Potawatomi, however, on specially designated mornings the parents or grandparents would offer a youth in his or her early teens a choice of food or charcoal. Encouraged to choose the charcoal and to blacken their faces, the youngsters were taken to an isolated place, often to perch in the limbs of a tree. There, alone, they fasted for dream visions. Although boys and girls might undertake vision quests, many tribes in this area had special ceremonies for girls.

The northern Iroquois, the Delaware, and the coastal Algonquians secluded girls in huts during their first menstruation. Among the Delaware the girls observed strict rules regarding food, drink, and bodily care; while in seclusion they wore blankets over their heads, and they were not permitted to leave the huts until their second menstrual period. This rite signified a girl's eligibility for marriage. There is evidence that some northern Iroquoians did not seclude their women during menstruation, although certain taboos had to be observed.

Among the Kickapoo a young girl was isolated from the village in a small hut during her first menses. Tended by her female kin, the girl followed strict prohibitions. Her dreams, like those of the isolated youth in the forest, were of special importance. Accounts of these momentous visions and dreams speak of encounters with tutelary *manitou* who bestowed blessings. Visions of such entities as wind, trees, fire, or birds, were all considered symbolic indications of the young person's future life. A successful dreamer might narrate part or all of his or her dream to an elderly family member or a shaman empowered to interpret dreams. This dream-vision was a means of acquiring psychic integration and spiritual strength so as to meet the challenges of life and death.

One of the most striking puberty rites was the Huskanawe of the Algonquians of Virginia. This rite was undergone by boys selected to be future chiefs and priests, positions of great importance in a highly stratified society. The ceremony began with the ritual tearing away of the children from their mothers and fathers, who had to accept them thenceforth as "dead." The boys were taken into the forest and were sequestered together in a small hut. For months they were given little to eat and were made to drink intoxicating potions and take emetics. At the end of this period of mental and emotional disorientation, they completely forgot who they were, and they were unable to understand or speak the language they had known. When the initiators were sure that the boys had been deconditioned, they took them back to the village. Under close supervision from their guides, the boys formed a new identity; they relearned how to speak and were taught what to wear and the intricacies of the new roles now assigned to them. As rulers or priests they had to be free from all attachments to family and friends. Their minds had been cleansed and reshaped so that they might see clearly and act wisely. Their claim to authority and their power to lead others rested on their successful ritual transition to a sacred condition.

Death. The form of death rites varied widely among the Northeast Woodlands peoples. In the tribes of the upper Great Lakes area, bodies were usually disposed of according to the individual's wishes or clan prerogatives for scaffold exposure, ground burial, or cremation. Among the Fox, death was a highly ritualized event announced to the village by a crier. The members of the deceased's clan gathered for a night of mourning. The clan leader addressed the corpse, advising it not to look back with envy on those still alive but to persevere in its journey to the ancestors in the west. After burial there were the rituals of building a grave shed and installing a clan post as a marker. A six-month period of mourning then followed, during which time a tribesperson was ceremoniously adopted to substitute for the deceased person, especially at memorial feasts.

Burial practices differed among the peoples of the lower Great Lakes and coastal region. The Algonquians of Carolina buried common people individually in shallow graves. The Algonquians of Virginia wrapped the bodies of common people in skins and placed them on scaffolds; after the decay of the flesh was complete, the bones were buried. The rulers of both peoples, however, were treated differently. After death their bodies were disemboweled and the flesh was removed, but the sinews were left attached to the bones. The skin was then sewn back on to the skeleton, after being packed with white sand or occasionally ornaments. Oil kept the body's oils from drying. The corpses were placed on a platform at the western end of the temple and attended by priests.

The Nanticoke and other tribes of the southern Maryland and Delaware peninsula area practiced a second ossuary interment, in some cases preceded by an inhumation and in others by scaffold burials. The rulers of most of these tribes were treated like those of the Algonquians of Virginia and North Carolina. Some of the southern Delaware also had a second ossuary burial, but the main tribal group had one inhumation only; no special treatment for chiefs was noted.

The Huron and some Algonquian groups had two inhumations, the second one in an ossuary. Their Feast of the Dead was conducted at periodic intervals of ten to twelve years. At that time all of the bodies buried during the preceding decade were disinterred, their remaining flesh was removed, and after a ten-day ceremony the skeletons were reburied. Village bands solidified alliances in these ceremonies in which the bones were deliberately mixed. This was a symbol of the unity that should exist among the living. The Petun followed the Huron, while the Neutral and Wenro had a scaffold burial followed later by burial in an ossuary. The Wyandot and Iroquois had only one inhumation but had an annual or semiannual feast for the dead. Eastern New York State, including Long Island, may mark the northern coastal border of secondary burials.

These life-cycle ceremonials were an integral part of every tribesperson's passage through life. Indeed, in the Winnebago Medicine rite the image of human aging in four steps is presented as a paradigm of all life. However, such ceremonial rites of passage can be distinguished from certain personal, clan, and group rituals.

Individual, Clan, and Group. Power objects given by the *manitou,* such as medicine bundles, charms, and face-paintings, became the focus of personal rituals, songs, and dances. An individual evoked his or her spirit and identified with it by means of rhythmic singing, drumming, rattling, or chanting; one would then channel the power brought by the spirit to a specific need such as hunting, the healing of sick people, or, in some cases, toward more selfish ends.

The Huron owned power charms *(aaskouandy).* Many of these were found in the entrails of game animals, especially those who were difficult to kill. Charms could be small stones, tufts of hair, and so on. One of the abilities of a power charm was to change its own shape, so that a stone, for example, might become a bean or a bird's beak. *Aaskouandy* were of two types: (1) those that brought general good luck and (2) those that were good for one particular task. The particular use of a charm would be revealed to its owner in a dream.

An individual or family might collect a number of charms and keep them in a bundle consisting of, for example, tufts of hair, bones or claws of animals, stones, and miniature masks. The owner was periodically obliged to offer a feast to his charms, during which he and his friends would sing to the charms and show them honor. The owner usually established a relationship to the charm spirit, similar to that between an individual and a guardian spirit, although charm spirits were known to be more unpredictable and dangerous than guardian spirits. An individual or family who wished to get rid of a charm had to conduct a ritual and bury it; even then uneasiness surrounded the event.

Among the Huron and Iroquois, there were masks that had to be cared for in addition to a charm or bundle. A person acquired a mask through dreaming of it or having it prescribed by a shaman. A carver would go into the forest and search for a living tree; basswood, cucumber, and willow were the preferred woods. While burning tobacco, he recited prayers to the tree spirit and the False Face spirits. The mask was carved into the tree and then removed in one piece. The finishing touches, including the eye-holes (which were surrounded with metal) and the mouth hole, were added later. If the tree had been found in the morning, the mask would be painted red; if in the afternoon, black. The hair attached to the mask was horsetail.

Because the mask was considered sacred and full of power the owner had to treat it correctly. He would keep it in a cloth carrier with a turtle rattle placed in the hollow side. If a mask was hung on a wall, it had to face the wall, lest some unsuspecting person be possessed by it. Periodically the mask would be fed mush and anointed with sunflower oil. If a mask fell or if a person dreamed of his mask, he would burn tobacco to it. One or two small bundles of tobacco were also hung inside the mask. The owner of a mask belonged to the False Face society and engaged in its curing rituals. The mask not only brought the owner power and protection but also the ability to heal the sick.

Personal power could overwhelm individuals, causing them to seek only self-aggrandizement. The Shawnee have myths that relate the origin of witchcraft to that mythic time when a crocodile's heart, which was the embodiment of evil, was cut out and carried home to the village by unwitting tribespeople. While the tribes of the Northeast fostered belief in contact with power, they also condemned the misuse of such power in sorcery. They tried to control their exceptional personalities by threatening the return of all evil machinations to the perpetrator. Nonetheless, witch societies have been prominent in Menomini history. Even though these destructive medicine practices were at times pervasive among the Northeast Woodlands tribes, their many religious societies never completely abandoned the constructive use of power.

These religious societies could be either temporary or permanent. Participants were usually selected according to criteria based on clan membership, on blessing from the same tutelary spirit, or on personal conduct and achievement. Their ceremonial activities, including narrative rituals, feasts, dances, and games, all had sacred meaning because they were performed to honor clan ancestors, guardian spirits, or departed society members. The Miami and Winnebago each had religious societies formed around clan war-bundles. The Kickapoo still have clan societies that hold spring renewals centered on their ancestral bundles. Vision societies also developed among individual Winnebago, Sauk, Fox, Kickapoo, Illinois, Miami, and Shawnee people who had received vision revelations from the same *manitou* spirit. Throughout this region societies also formed around those warriors or braves whose heroic acts in battle were seen as special signs of personal power. So also the Potawatomi Southern Dance temporarily brought together tribespeople who still grieved for deceased relatives. The medicine societies and other groups, such as the Dream Dance (or Drum Dance) and the Native American Church, admitted tribespeople who felt called to these societies and were willing to submit to the societies' ethics.

At present the primary medicine society among the Iroquois is the Society of Medicine Men (also known as Shake the Pumpkin) to which most members of other societies belong. This society is dedicated to the medicine animals who long ago promised to heal humans in exchange for ceremonies and feasts.

The Society of Mystic Animals includes the Bear, Buffalo, Otter, and Eagle societies; members of each group take its tutelary spirit as their own when they are healed by it. The Little Water Medicine society guards and cures with the most potent of Iroquois medicines, which come from parts of animals, birds, and plants. Rituals to renew the power of this medicine are held several times a year. The Little People society (also known as Dark Dance) receives power from its relationship with the "little people" who live in stream banks, forests, and underground.

The False Face society is one of the most popular Iroquois societies. As described above, the wooden faces represent spirits of the forest who appear to people in dreams. The society has its own curing ceremonies, but it also participates in the Midwinter ceremony. The Husk Faces are agricultural correlates of the False Faces; they are dedicated to the spirits of maize, beans, and squash. Besides having private curing ceremonies, members of the Husk Face society are doorkeepers at the longhouse when the False Faces perform and also function as police during Longhouse ceremonies.

RELIGIOUS PERSONALITIES

The shaman is the most important religious figure among the upper Great Lakes and Ohio River native peoples. Primarily a healer and diviner, the shaman contacts power by means of a trance and channels that power to specific needs. Shamans are known by a variety of names derived from the calls to their vocation they have received by way of visions, as well as from their particular healing functions. Generally, four shamanic vocations are found among the northeastern Algonquian peoples. There are also a number of shamanic techniques. Both the shamanic vocations and techniques are documented from the seventeenth century.

The most celebrated shamanic figure among the Algonquian peoples is the shaking-tent diviner and healer, whom the Ojibwa call *tcisaki*, the Menomini *tcisakos* and the Potawatomi *tcisakked*. Among the Ojibwa, this shamanic figure received the vocation after a dream "call" from the *manitou* called Mistabeo had occurred four times. The *tcisaki*'s technique was to enter a special lodge that swayed when the *manitou* arrived. The *tcisaki* then mediated between the spirits and the audience during a question-and-answer session in which the location of a lost object or the cause of an illness was sought. In the case of illness, the diviner might determine the cause of the sickness while inside the shaking tent and then come out to perform a sucking cure.

Another ancient shamanic profession is that of the tube-sucking curer whom the Ojibwa called *nanandawi*. Several *manitou* could give this healing vocation, but the Thunderer was especially favored. The sucking curer often used the bones of raptorial birds to suck the affected area and to remove objects believed to have been shot into a person by malicious witches. The curer would partially swallow as many as seven bones down his esophagus; he would apply the bones, which projected out of his mouth, to the area of the patient's body that was being treated.

The manipulation of fire for healing purposes is also an ancient shamanic vocation; the Ojibwa call this healer *wabeno,* the Menomini called him *wapanows,* and the Potawatomi, *wapno*. The traditional call to this vocation came from Morning Star, who was imaged as a *manitou* with horns. The *wabeno,* working individually or in a group, healed by using the heat of burning embers to massage and fascinate his patients.

The final shamanic personality I shall consider here is the member of one of the medicine societies. For example, the Ojibwa Mide, or Medicine society, is composed of the tribe's recognized shamans and candidates initiated into the society as well as healed patients. Thus the healing shamans and ritually initiated members perform together with the healed patients during the ritual. There is a basic difference in technique between the members of these shamanic societies and the individual shamanic healers previously discussed. Among individual healers, healing through spontaneous trance is central, whereas within shamanic societies, transmission of sacred knowledge is primary and trance states are more formally structured and are of secondary importance. Thus the role of the religious leader in the medicine societies can be more accurately described as that of a shaman-priest.

Shamanism among the Huron and the Iroquois of the seventeenth century was primarily an individual enterprise, although a few societies did exist. In subsequent centuries the Iroquois channeled shamanistic powers and skills into the growing number of medicine societies, as described above. The central concern of the Huron shamans was the curing of illness. Illness was caused by either (1) natural events, (2) witchcraft, or (3) desires of the soul. The first could be handled by an herbalist or other practitioner. The second and third required the diagnostic and healing abilities of a shaman *(arendiwane),* including divining, interpreting dreams, sucking, blowing ashes, and juggling hot coals.

The *ocata* was a shaman skilled in diagnosis. In the case of a hidden desire of the soul whose frustration was causing illness he would seek to have a vision of what was desired. To do this he might gaze into a basin of water until the object appeared or enter into a trancelike state to see the object or lie down in a small dark tent to contact his spiritual allies to assist him.

The spirit-ally *(oki)* was won after a long fast and isolation in the forest; it could take the form of a human, an animal, or a bird such as a raven or eagle. Sometimes the power and skill needed to cure would come through a dream. There were shamanic specialists who handled hot coals or plunged their arms into boiling water without injury; frequently a power song, which allowed the person to accomplish this, was sung. Other shamans cured by blowing hot ashes over a person or by rubbing the person's skin with ashes.

Witchcraft was combatted by the *aretsan;* usually the *aretsan* would suck out the evil spell that the witch had magically injected into his victim. Still other shamans could see things at a distance, cause rain, persuade animal guardian spirits to release game, or give advice on military or political matters.

Outside of these established vocations, certain shamanic techniques were available to all lay people among the tribes of the Northeast. These included tattooing, naming, divining, bloodletting, induced vomiting as a cure, weather control, and herbal healing. However, at times individual shamans or shamanic societies were so strong that they absorbed these and other curing practices as their exclusive prerogative.

Other outstanding religious personalities included the war chiefs, who led war bundle ceremonies and war parties, and the peace chiefs, who did not go to fight but who acted as mediators, working for peace within the tribe as well as between separate tribes. The Menomini chose hereditary war chiefs from the Bear clan and peace chiefs from the Thunderer clan. All Northeast Woodlands tribes used a war and peace chief system, but the clan totems from which these leaders were selected often differed from band to band.

Occasionally singular religious figures appear in the ethnohistory of the Northeast Woodlands peoples. The Winnebago have had sacred clowns and "contraries" who performed ritual actions backward or in a humorous manner to accentuate the ambiguity of life. Transvestite men such as the Miami "whitefaces" wore women's clothes and did women's work; occasionally they gained reputations as healers or diviners because of their unusual call and personal abilities. Among other exceptional personalities were the ecstatic visionaries often called "prophets." The Delaware prophet Neolin called for a rejection of white influences and a return to the old ways and inspired many to join Pontiac's uprising in the 1760s. The famous Shawnee prophets Tecumseh and Tenkswatawa initiated a nativistic movement uniting many woodland peoples against American expansion in the late eighteenth and early nineteenth centuries. Handsome Lake, of the Seneca, inspired a reformed way of life for the Iroquois in the early nineteenth century. During the same period the Kickapoo prophet Kenekuk led a religious movement that fostered his people's accomodation to some American cultural influences. The Winnebago prophet Wabokieshiek began a short-lived revitalization of traditional values during Black Hawk's War in the 1830s. These and other minor prophets received revelations concerning the need to transform specific historical situations. They represented a shift in religious thought among these native peoples from the predominantly individual concern and responsibility for harmony with cosmic powers in nature to a more structured ethics based on an interior religious imperative.

Northeast Woodlands peoples have struggled to maintain their traditions into the present period. Not only have they endured the cultural inroads of a variety of Christian missionaries, but these native traditions have also persisted in the face of tribal fragmentation and degradation. This struggle was reflected in the life of the Seneca leader Handsome Lake; he was able to give focus to his people's plight by drawing on the spiritual power of dreams that came to him during an illness brought on by drunkenness and despair. The traditional sanction of dreams and visions in native Northeast Woodlands religions continues into the present revitalization of the sweat lodge, the vision quest, and medicine-wheel gatherings. The relevance of these traditional ceremonies to contemporary needs is highlighted by the growing participation of non-Indians in these meditative rituals.

[*For detailed treatment of one Northeast Woodlands tradition, see* Iroquois Religion. *See also* Shamanism, *article on* North American Shamanism, *and the biographies of Handsome Lake, Neolin, and Tecumseh.*]

BIBLIOGRAPHY

Anthropological Papers. New York, 1907–. These volumes, published by the American Museum of Natural History, contain extensive materials on the religious beliefs and practices of Northeast Woodlands peoples as, for example, in Alanson Skinner's *Social Life and Ceremonial Bundles of the Menomini Indians* and *Folklore of the Menomini Indians,* in volume 13, parts 1 and 3 (New York, 1915).

Beverley, Robert. *The History and Present State of Virginia* (1705). Edited by Louis B. Wright. Chapel Hill, N.C., 1947. A primary document on the Virginia Algonquians drawing on the author's own observations and those of earlier sources, written and verbal. More sensitive than most works of the period regarding both the native peoples and the natural environment.

Blair, Emma, ed. and trans. *The Indian Tribes of the Upper Mississippi Valley and the Region of the Great Lakes* (1911). 2 vols. New York, 1969. A fine collection of primary documents describing the upper Great Lakes and Ohio River native peoples during the seventeenth and eighteenth centuries.

Bureau of American Ethnology. *Annual Reports* and "Bulletins." Washington, D.C., 1888–. These reports and bulletins present materials on native peoples' beliefs and religious practices which, however, often need further interpretation. Special mention can be made here of the following monographs published as "Bulletins of the Bureau of American Ethnology": *The Midewiwin or 'Grand Medicine Society' of the Ojibwa,* no. 7 (1885–1886), and *The Menomini Indians* no. 14, (1892–1893), both by Walter J. Hoffman; *Ethnography of the Fox Indians,* no. 125 (1939), by William Jones; *Contributions to Fox Ethnology,* 2 vols., nos. 85

(1927) and 95 (1930), and *The Owl Sacred Pack of the Fox Indians,* no. 72 (1921), by Trumen Michelson; and *The Winnebago Tribe,* no. 37 (1915–1916), by Paul Radin.

Driver, Harold E. *Indians of North America.* 2d ed., rev. Chicago, 1969. Somewhat dated in parts but overall good statistical information on all Native American tribes, including those of the Northeast.

Flannery, Regina. "An Analysis of Coastal Algonquian Culture." Ph.D. diss., Catholic University, 1939. A detailed classification of cultural topics and documentation for all areas of coastal Algonquian life, drawn mostly from sixteenth- and seventeenth-century documents.

Greeman, Emerson F. *The Wolf and Furton Sites.* Occasional Contributions, Museum of Anthropology, University of Michigan, no. 8. Ann Arbor, 1939. Study of a woodland archaeological site of proto-historical period.

Grim, John A. *The Shaman: Patterns of Siberian and Ojibway Healing.* Norman, Okla., 1983. A study of the Ojibwa shaman that, in addition, traces broad patterns of shamanic expression. Includes an extensive bibliography on the religious figure of the shaman.

Hallowell, A. Irving. "Ojibwa Ontology, Behavior, and World View." In *Culture in History: Essays in Honor of Paul Radin,* edited by Stanley Diamond, pp. 19–52. New York, 1960. An important analysis of the categories and orientations of Ojibwa ethnometaphysics that is helpful in interpreting the religious practices of these woodland peoples.

Harrington, Mark R. *Religion and Ceremonies of the Lenape.* New York, 1921. The first and still the best work on the religion of the Delaware in the late nineteenth and early twentieth centuries.

Hewitt, J. N. B., ed. "Iroquois Cosmology," part 1. In *Bureau of American Ethnology Twenty-first Annual Report,* pp. 127–339. Washington, D.C., 1899–1900.

Hewitt, J. N. B., ed. "Iroquoian Cosmology," part 2. In *Bureau of American Ethnology Forty-third Annual Report,* pp. 449–819. Washington, D.C., 1925–1926. The best collection of Iroquois cosmogonic myths available.

Hultkrantz, Åke. *The Religions of the American Indians.* Berkeley, 1979. An overview of phenomenological patterns of religious expression among tribal peoples of North America that is helpful in interpreting the various ethnographies.

Kinietz, W. Vernon. *The Indians of the Western Great Lakes,* 1615–1760. Occasional Contributions, Museum of Anthropology, University of Michigan, no. 10. Ann Arbor, 1940.

Landes, Ruth. *Ojibwa Religion and the Midewiwin.* Madison, 1968.

Landes, Ruth. *The Prairie Potawatomi.* Madison, 1970. Both of Landes's works explore, from an anthropological perspective, selected myths and rituals associated with the presence of religious power.

Radin, Paul, ed. *The Road of Life and Death.* New York, 1945. Contains the text of the Winnebago Medicine rite with some commentary by Radin on the circumstances that prompted Crashing Thunder (Jasper Blowsnake) to narrate this esoteric lore. This book also includes Big Winnebago's autobiography, as edited by Paul Radin.

Speck, Frank G. *A Study of the Delaware Indian Big House Ceremony.* Harrisburg, Pa., 1931. The foremost study of the Big House ceremony among the Delaware of Oklahoma.

Sturtevant, William C., and Bruce Trigger, eds. *Handbook of North American Indians.* Rev. ed. Washington, D.C., 1981. An excellent overview of the specific tribal groups in this area with a brief treatment of religious beliefs and practices.

Thwaites, Reuben Gold, ed. *The Jesuit Relations and Allied Documents . . . , 1610–1791* (1896–1901). 73 vols. in 39. Reprint, New York, 1959. An indispensable work especially on the tribes of "Huronia" and "Iroquoia" as related by Jesuit missionaries.

Tooker, Elisabeth. *Native North American Spirituality of the Eastern Woodlands.* New York, 1979. Ethnographic selections from the religious rituals of various Northeast Woodlands peoples with some general interpretative sections.

Trigger, Bruce G. *The Children of Aataentsic: A History of the Huron People to 1660.* 2 vols. Montreal, 1976. Excellent reconstruction of the history, culture, and religion of the Hurons, relying on the earliest documents available.

Trowbridge, C. C. *Meearmar Traditions.* Occasional Contributions, Museum of Anthropology, University of Michigan, no. 7. Ann Arbor, 1938. A study of the Miami people.

Trowbridge, C. C., *Shawnese Traditions.* Edited by W. Vernon Kinietz. Occasional Contributions, Museum of Anthropology, University of Michigan, no. 9. Ann Arbor, 1939.

Williams, Roger. *The Complete Writings of Roger Williams* (1643). 7 vols. Edited by Reuben A. Guild et al. New York, 1963. Especially valuable for information on the Narraganset is "The Key into the Language of America" found in volume 1.

13 IROQUOIS

Donald P. St. John

The League of the Iroquois consisted, at the time of contact with Europeans, of five "nations" (the Mohawk, Oneida, Onondaga, Cayuga, and Seneca). In 1724, these groups were joined by the Tuscarora to form the Six Nations of the Iroquois. These tribes form part of a larger complex of Iroquoian-speaking peoples. The northern language group of which the members of the league are a part also includes the Saint Lawrence Iroquois, Huron, Wyandot, Susquehanna, Nottoway, Erie, Wenro, and Neutrals. The Cherokee form the southern language group. The separation between the northern and southern groups probably occurred between three and four thousand years ago, with further dialects developing over time.

Geographically, the early-seventeenth-century Iroquois inhabited the area from 42° to 44° north latitude and from 74° to 78° west longitude. In the late seventeenth century, the League of the Iroquois controlled territory from the Mohawk Valley in the east to Lake Erie in the west, and from Lake Ontario in the north to the mountains of western and south-central New York State and northwestern Pennsylvania in the south.

At contact the Iroquois were a matrilineal and matrilocal people living in clusters of longhouses situated on hilltops. The villages were usually palisaded and semipermanent. The men involved themselves in hunting, fishing, and making war; the women took care of the fields and gathered berries, nuts, and roots. The clan mothers elected the fifty sachems, or chiefs, who guided the external policies of the league from Onondaga.

COSMOLOGY

The cosmological structuring of space into three tiers provides the Iroquois with the basic categories with which to interpret human experience. The sky world and the underworld represent extremes of both a spatial and an existential nature. The sky world is order, goodness, warmth, light, and life. The underworld is chaos, evil, coldness, darkness, and death. In the in-between world—the world of ordinary human experience—the qualities of both worlds are intertwined in a myriad of ways. One of the ways is cyclical, as when night follows day; another is antagonistic, as when good struggles with evil.

Mythically, this world was the creation of two twins, one good and the other evil. The former, the Master of Life, was the creator of flora and fauna. He held the sky world in mind at all times while creating living things, and he gave customs to humans modeled after those of the sky world. His brother tried to imitate his creative acts, but what issued instead were all of the nasty, noxious, and monstrous forms of life. The evil twin is described as cold and hard, like ice and flint, and his influence is believed to infect all areas of existence. Each of the twins left behind spirit-forces and other manifestations of his orientation and power. The general thrust of Iroquois religion is toward increasing and renewing the power of those forces that sustain life and reducing or eliminating those forces that diminish life, such as disease and pain.

COMMUNITY RITUALS

To live in harmony with the spirit-forces is the essential requirement of Iroquois religion. These fundamental relationships that sustain community life are renewed, intensified, and celebrated in the calendrical cycles of the Longhouse religion. This final form of the Iroquois ceremonial cycle crystallized in the nineteenth century under the influence of the Seneca prophet Handsome Lake (1735–1815). [*See the biography of Handsome Lake.*] The Longhouse religion, as it is practiced today, is a synthesis of elements from the hunter-gatherer traditions of the Middle Woodland and early Late Woodland periods (300–1000 CE) and the agricultural complex that gradually took hold during the Late Woodland period (1000–1500 CE).

The fundamental attitude of the Iroquois community toward the benevolent spirit-forces of the universe is thanksgiving. Thus all Iroquois ceremonies begin and end with a thanksgiving address, a paean to all the forces of earth, sky, and the sky world that create, support, and renew life. The address is divided into three main parts. The first part includes prayers of thanksgiving for the earth, waters, plants and trees, animals, birds, and the "three sisters" (the staple Iroquois foodstuffs—maize, beans, and squash). The second section gives thanks to those spirit forces that have greater power: wind, thunder, sun, moon, and stars. The final section gives thanks to the spiritual guides of the Iroquois: Handsome Lake, the creator, and the Four Beings (protectors of humans and messengers from the creator to Handsome Lake).

The epitome of the synthesis represented by the Longhouse religion is the Midwinter festival. Concentrated into its eight days are all of the major themes and components of Iroquois ceremonialism. The first half of the Midwinter rite is the older and contains many elements from the hunting-forest complex that centered on shamanic practices. It is given over to the symbolic expulsion of the old year through rites of confession, ashes-stirring, and dream fulfillment, as well as medicine-society curing ceremonies, False Face society rituals, and the White Dog sacrifice (no longer practiced). These expiatory and cathartic rituals clear the path for the new year and for the second half of the festival, whose structure largely reflects the farming-village complex. The "four sacred rituals"—a feather dance, a skin (or drum) dance, a personal chant, and a bowl game—are considered the gifts of the creator, modeled after ceremonies in the sky world. A tobacco invocation, a kind of thanksgiving address, beseeches all of the spirit-forces to bless the people during the coming year. Both the Our Sustenance Dances and the performance by the Husk

Faces anticipate a fruitful agricultural season. The yearly ceremonial cycle unfolds from the Midwinter festival and returns to it.

While the ceremonial cycle may vary slightly from longhouse to longhouse, a representative list would include the Midwinter festival, the Bush Dance, and the Thanks-to-the-Maple, Seed Planting, Strawberry, Raspberry, Green Bean, Thunder, Little Corn, Green Corn, and Harvest ceremonies.

MEDICINE SOCIETIES

Not only has Iroquois religion been concerned with affirming and intensifying life, it has also been concerned with countering those things that diminish life. The spirit-forces that assist humans in this battle revealed themselves long ago and entered into covenants with individuals, families, and societies. Through fasting, dream-visions, and ecstatic states, the ancient shamans sought to divine the causes of illness, pain, famine, and sudden or widespread death. Other shamanic specialists had their own ceremonies and skills that brought healing power. At times groups of shamans who possessed similar secrets joined together into sodalities. With the demise of individual shamanism, these "medicine societies" grew in importance in Iroquois life and became the preserver of the ancient shamanic traditions.

The significance of medicine society rituals in Iroquois life differs from that of the communal ceremonies. The latter are thanksgiving-celebrative, follow the agricultural cycle, are directed toward the major spirit-forces, and are held in the longhouse. The former are power-evocative and occasional, invoke the tutelary spirit of the particular medicine society, and are usually conducted in private homes. Membership in a society is generally limited to those who have been cured by one of that society's rituals. The medicine societies have their own myths, songs, dances, prayers, costumes, and ritual paraphernalia. A listing of Iroquois medicine societies and their major characteristics follows.

1. *The Society of Medicine Men* (also known as Shake the Pumpkin) is the largest medicine society. Most members of the other societies also belong to it. The society began with a covenant relationship between the medicine animals and its founders. In return for feasts offered in their honor, the animals promised to cure diseases, ease pain, and get rid of bad luck. Practices of this society, such as juggling red-hot coals and wearing masks without eye holes, are quite ancient.
2. *The Company of Mystic Animals* includes the Buffalo, Otter, Bear, and Eagle societies. In varying degrees the members imitate their tutelary animals in their dances, songs, and practices. They continue the shamanic tradition in which humans and animals communicate with, and can be transformed into, one another.
3. *The Little Water Medicine society*, like its ally in the Eagle society, was originally associated with war and the healing of wounds received in war. The Iroquois say that its medicine, concocted from parts of animals, birds, and plants, is the most potent made by any society. Ceremonies are held at night, several times a year, to renew the medicine.
4. *The Little People society* (also known as Dark Dance) also holds its ceremonies at night. This society fosters a good rapport with the *jo-ga-oh* ("little people"), elf-like spirits who help humans in a variety of ways and who adopt many different forms for mischievous purposes.

5. *The False Face society* is the favorite of the Iroquois. The wooden masks worn by its members are filled with power. Reverence and ritual surround both their carving and their care. The most common practices of the Faces today were noted among the Huron by seventeenth-century observers: blowing ashes, handling hot coals, imitating hunchbacks, and carrying sticks. It is quite possible that the Faces came to the Iroquois from the Huron. The False Face society holds rites for cleansing the community of disease in the spring and fall. It sponsers rites at Midwinter both for its own members and for the broader community in the longhouse and performs individual curing rites when needed.

6. *The Husk Faces* are dedicated to the agricultural spirits. They also cure by blowing ashes and handling hot coals. During Midwinter they burst into the longhouse and announce that they are going to the other side of the world to till the crops.

7. *The Towii'sas society* is a woman's society honoring corn, beans, and squash. It participates in the Green Corn ceremony and also has its own curing ceremonies.

8. *The Ohgiwe society* conducts ceremonies for people who have been dreaming of ghosts. A feast is held to feed the ghost and to dissuade it from bothering the living. Just as the sharing of food brings harmony into human relationships, so does it harmonize relations between living and dead. The Iroquois both respect and fear the dead and therefore conduct a number of feasts for them. In addition to the feasts conducted by the Ohgiwe society, there is a community Feast of the Dead (also called Ohgiwe) that is held annually or semiannually. All souls, but especially those of the recently deceased, are invited. Songs and dances are performed, and a post-midnight feast is held. There are also frequent family feasts for the dead during the winter months. These celebrations both fulfill the family's obligations to the dead and serve as a means of bringing together relatives of the deceased.

THE INDIVIDUAL

In traditional (i.e., pre-nineteenth-century) Iroquois lore, access to the power and guidance of the spirit-forces was not limited to the community (through its collective ceremonial life) nor to the curing societies. The individual Iroquois had an array of spiritually vital allies, including charms, medicine bundles, guardian spirits, and his or her own soul.

The most common medium for communication with these forces was the dream-vision. During puberty rites or shamanic training a guardian spirit would reveal itself to the individual through the dream-vision. The spirit could take the form of a human being, or animal, or a bird such as a raven or crow. An intimate and powerful relationship was established between the person and the guardian spirit. A person who had such a friendship had greater inner power and confidence than one who did not. The guardian spirit revealed its desires in dreams. To ignore this ally or to fail to understand its desires could result in illness. Such an illness signified a dangerous disruption of the relationship between spirit-forces and humans. Should someone become ill, his dreams would be consulted to ascertain what the guardian spirit desired. Sometimes the efforts of everyone in the community would be needed to fulfill the dream. They willingly undertook this.

Similarly, an alienation could occur between a person's ego and soul. The Iroquois believed that the soul was the source of biological as well as mental well-being. Dreams were its language. To lose touch with or deny the desires of the soul could cause it to revolt against the body. Dreams were carefully investigated in order to avoid such a possibility or to remedy it when illness occurred. The dream-guessing rite that even today forms a part of the Onondaga Midwinter festival was performed quite frequently by the seventeenthcentury Huron. The ill person's soul's desire would be given in riddle form; whoever guessed it correctly had to fulfill the desire. This might involve an object, a feast, the performance of a particular ritual, or any of a number of other actions.

Dreams were also thought to contain warnings about future events—events whose actual occurrence might be prevented by acting out the dream and thereby fulfilling it. Thus, a warrior who dreamed that he had been captured, bound, and tortured by an enemy might, upon waking, ask his fellow tribesmen to tie him up and make cuts or burns in his flesh in order that the greater pain and shame predicted by the dream might be avoided. Dreams also affected hunting, fishing, military, and political plans.

There was no aspect of life among the ancient Iroquois and Huron that was not touched by the dream. Religiously it played both a conservative and an innovative role. That is, it confirmed within an individual's experience the culturally transmitted religious system while also initiating changes in the beliefs and rituals that constituted this system. It would not be going too far to say that most of Iroquois religion was constructed of dream material. Through this building process, the individual hierophany became symbolized and available to all. The last series of significant changes introduced into Iroquois life by the dream resulted from the revelations given to Handsome Lake, which were eventually institutionalized into the present-day Longhouse religion.

Today the majority of Iroquois live on reservations in Canada and New York State. Perhaps one-fourth of the approximately twenty thousand Iroquois adhere to the traditionalist Longhouse religion. In addition to the ceremonies described above, they perform partial recitations of the *Gaiwiio* ("good word") of Handsome Lake on the first mornings of both the Midwinter festival and the Green Corn ceremony. This formalization of the dream-vision revelations received by the prophet from 1799 until his death in 1815 provides the moral, ceremonial, social, and theological context in which followers of the Longhouse religion live. A complete recitation by an authorized preacher may occur every other fall at a meeting of the Six Nations, depending upon which longhouse is sponsoring the meeting.

BIBLIOGRAPHY

The main source for information on seventeenth-century Huron religion, which also provides some insight into Iroquois life, is *The Jesuit Relations and Allied Documents,* 39 vols. (1896–1901), edited by Reuben Gold Thwaites (New York, 1959). The nineteenth century marked the beginning of modern studies on Iroquois religion. Midcentury produced Lewis H. Morgan's classic *The League of the Ho-de-no-sau-nee, or Iroquois* (1851; reprint, New York, 1966). The most complete collection of Iroquois cosmological stories is found in J. N. B. Hewitt's "Iroquois Cosmology," which was published in two parts in the *Annual Report of the Bureau of American Ethnology* 21 (1899–1900) and 43 (1925–1926). An excellent, thorough study of the Midwinter festival is found in Elisabeth Tooker's *The Iroquois Ceremonial of Midwinter* (Syracuse, 1970). For an introduction to and translation of a thanksgiving address, see Wallace L. Chafe's "Seneca Thanksgiving Rituals," *Bureau of American Ethnology Bulletin*

183 (1961). A much more thorough, if complex, comparison of several thanksgiving addresses along with a study of other events in the ritual cycle is M. K. Foster's *From the Earth to Beyond the Sky: An Ethnographic Approach to Four Longhouse Speech Events* (Ottawa, 1974). Valuable information on the medicine societies, along with the only full translation at present of "The Code of Handsome Lake" (i.e., the *Gaiwiio*), is found in a collection of Arthur C. Parker's writings, entitled *Parker on the Iroquois,* edited by William N. Fenton (Syracuse, 1968). Fenton has done this century's most important work among the Iroquois. Among his numerous articles, special mention should be made of "An Outline of Seneca Ceremonies at Coldspring Longhouse," *Yale University Publications in Anthropology* 9 (1936): 3–22; and "Masked Medicine Societies of the Iroquois," in the *Annual Report of the Smithsonian Institution* (Washington, D.C., 1940), pp. 397–430. An indispensable collection of articles on the Iroquois and their neighbors can be found in the *Handbook of North American Indians,* vol. 15, *Northeast* (Washington, D.C., 1978).

14 THE SOUTHEAST WOODLANDS

Charles Hudson

The Indians who were the aboriginal inhabitants of the southeastern United States lived in a region whose boundaries were approximately the same as those of the contemporary South, that is, extending from about 95° west longitude eastward to the Atlantic coast and from about 37° north latitude southward to the Gulf of Mexico. The Indians of the Southeast Woodlands were linguistically diverse. Muskogean was the most important language family, but four additional language families were present: Iroquoian, Siouan, Algonquian, and Caddoan. Both prehistoric and historical forces shaped the cultural and social characteristics of the Southeast Indians.

In the late prehistoric, or Mississippian, period (800 to 1540 CE) the Indians of the Southeast developed a form of social organization and a belief system that appear to have been generally uniform throughout the region. The Southeast Indians farmed the rich, easily tilled alluvial soils on the margins of the larger rivers, and their villages and towns lay along these same rivers. They were organized into chiefdoms, societies ruled by chiefly lineages whose members possessed higher status than commoners, although the social distance between chiefs and commoners varied from society to society and from time to time. These chiefdoms were highly militaristic, and their young men vied with each other in winning war honors.

The Southeast Indians shared a common history in the eighteenth and nineteenth centuries because the region of the United States that was best for their hoe agriculture was also ideally suited for plantation agriculture. Hence, they became enmeshed in the wars that Britain, France, and Spain waged for supremacy in the South, and in the early nineteenth century they held title to vast tracts of land that southern planters wished to cultivate, using the labor of black slaves. At that time most of the Southeast Indians were "removed" from their land and forced to migrate to the present state of Oklahoma. Only a few Cherokees, Choctaws, Catawbas, and Seminoles evaded removal. Their descendants still live in the South.

Various estimates of the Indian population of the Southeast Woodlands have been proposed for the period just prior to European exploration in the sixteenth century. They range from a low of 170,000 to a high of perhaps 1.7 million. But whatever the Indians' aboriginal population, beginning in the sixteenth century they began to suffer from a series of European epidemic diseases that caused very heavy loss of life. By 1755, they may have numbered only about 50,000 to 70,000. It is clear that this demographic collapse caused extensive social and cultural change. The Indians' social structure became less stratified, and their religious and ritual life was simplified. The most detailed information on Southeast Indian religious beliefs and practices was collected in the late nineteenth and early twentieth centuries, although some good information was collected by eighteenth-century observers, and this is complemented by scattered information from the sixteenth and seventeenth centuries. Some threads of continuity can be discerned among beliefs and practices throughout this four-hundred-year period.

THE BELIEF SYSTEM

The Southeast Indian conception of the cosmos resembled, in its broad outlines, the cosmologies of many other New World peoples. The Southeast Indians believed, for example, that this world—the earth on which they lived—was a circular island that rested upon the waters. The sky above was thought to be a vault of stone, in the form of an inverted bowl. At dawn and at dusk, the bowl rose so that the sun and the moon, two principal deities, could pass beneath it at the beginning and end of their transit through the heavens.

In addition to the earth on which they stood and the world in which they lived, the Indians believed that an upperworld existed above the sky vault and that an underworld existed beneath the earth and the waters. The upperworld was peopled by the sun and the moon, and by large, perfect archetypes of all the creatures that lived on the earth. The underworld was peopled by spirits and monsters living in a chaotic world full of novelty and invention.

For the Southeast Indians, the upperworld was a place of structure, regularity, and perfect order. Its opposite was the underworld, a place of chaos and disorder, as well as fecundity. The Indians appear to have attempted to steer a middle course between the compulsive order of the upperworld and the mad chaos of the underworld. They believed, for example, that in the beginning there were only two worlds, the upperworld and the underworld, and that this world had been created when soft mud was brought up from beneath thewaters to form the island earth. Moreover, they believed that the island was suspended rather precariously from the sky vault by four cords, one in each of the four cardinal directions. They appear to have believed that man's inability to behave strictly in accordance with moral and religious precepts weakened the cords, and thus they feared that the earth would one day sink beneath the waters.

The Southeast Indians believed that certain kinds of beings were more pure, more sacred, than others. Sacred beings were those that seemed able to resist or to stand above natural, mundane constraints. Sacred plants included cedar, pine, spruce, holly, and laurel, because they remained green in winter while other trees shed their leaves. Sacred animals included the owl and the cougar, because both were able to go about in darkness, and they therefore possessed a terrible advantage over animals that could not see in darkness. Sacred people included priests and medicine men, who lived more completely in accordance with sacred precepts than did ordinary people. Hence, the Indians' priests and medicine men were believed to possess powers that ordinary people did not possess.

The sun, the chief upperworld deity, was represented on earth by sacred fire. The smoke that rose from sacred fire connected this earthly world with the upperworld. The Southeast Indians believed that when they behaved badly in the presence of sacred fire, their behavior was immediately known to the sun. The medium that connected people in this world with the underworld was the water in creeks and rivers, which were thought to be avenues or roads to the underworld. The Cherokee personified rivers and streams, calling them "the long person." Fire and water were considered opposites. As such, fire and water were one of an extensive series of opposed forces and beings in the Southeast Indian belief system.

The Cherokee, and probably other Southeast Indians, classified living beings into large categories, and the relationships among these categories were important structural features of their belief system. The three categories of living beings were people, animals, and plants. People, as hunters, preyed upon animals, and because they sometimes killed animals thoughtlessly or carelessly, the animal world became angry and resentful. As a way of getting revenge upon people, the spirits of the animals sent them diseases. The deer, for example, afflicted careless or thoughtless hunters with crippling rheumatism or arthritis. Plants, the third category of beings, were believed to be friends of people and, as such, were the sources of most medicines. These three categories and the interrelationships among them shaped the Southeast Indians' conception of illness as well as their theory of medicine.

Each of these three categories was further subdivided into smaller categories. People were divided into matrilineal clans. Plants were classified in terms of an elaborate taxonomy. Animals were divided into birds, four-footed animals, and vermin, the latter category including fish, snakes, and other creatures inhabiting the watery realm. Many of these animals were invested with symbolic value. In Southeast Indian thought, each of these three animal categories was epitomized by a particular species. The rattlesnake, the most feared venomous snake in the Southeast, was the epitome of the vermin category, and the Virginia deer, the region's most important game animal, was the epitome of the four-footed animals. Birds may have been epitomized by two creatures—the bald eagle, the supreme bird of peace, and the peregrine falcon, the supreme bird of war. If frequency of occurrence in late prehistoric art is a reliable measure of symbolic importance, then the peregrine falcon was clearly the more important of the two birds.

In addition to the animals that epitomized the normal categories, the Southeast Indian belief system recognized an extensive series of anomalous beings that did not fit neatly into a single category. In each case, these anomalies were given special symbolic value. For example, the Venus's-flytrap *(Dionaea muscipula)* and the pitcher plant *(Sarracenia purpurea),* because they "catch" and "digest" insects, were considered to be plants that behave like animals. The Cherokee believed that the roots of both plants possessed extraordinary magical powers.

The bear was considered anomalous because it is a four-footed animal that possesses certain characteristics reminiscent of people: it is capable of bipedal locomotion; the skeletal structure of its foot closely resembles the human foot; it is as omnivorous in its diet as people are; and its feces resemble human feces. In Cherokee mythology the bear is depicted as a buffoon who attempts to act as humans act, but who fails because of his clumsiness and because he is, after all, an animal.

The most anomalous being in the Southeast Indian belief system was a monster formed of the parts of many creatures. There is evidence that the Indians considered this monster to be an actual being, not a creature whose existence was exclusively spiritual. The Cherokee called this monster the *uktena*. Its body was like that of a rattlesnake, only much larger, the size of a tree trunk. It was believed to live on the margins of the known world, in deep pools of water and near high mountain passes. If a person merely saw an *uktena,* it could cause misfortune, and to smell the breath of an *uktena* brought death.

In the art of the late prehistoric Southeast Indians, images of creatures similar to the *uktena* are incised on shell and pottery. They are serpentine in shape, but they also have wings, deer horns, the teeth of herbivores or carnivores, and other non-snakelike features. Moreover, according to Cherokee mythology the first *uktena* was created when a man was transformed.

The *uktena* was not, however, merely an evil creature from which no good could come. The Cherokee believed that the *uktena* had a blazing crest on its forehead, which, if it could be obtained, was the most powerful means of divination. This crest was in the form of a crystal, and one could gaze into it and see the future reflected, just as a tree is reflected in a quiet pool of water.

Both in their form and in the role they played in the larger belief system, the *uktena* and other serpentine monsters resemble both the feathered serpent of the Aztec and the dragon of Eurasia. Why these imaginary monsters should have been structurally similar remains to be explained.

WITCHCRAFT

The Southeast Indians explained many of the events in their lives as reward and punishment meted out by spiritual beings who acted according to known standards of behavior. For example, young men who were too careless or headstrong to observe certain taboos and rules of behavior could endanger their own safety and the safety of their comrades in warfare. And women were required to segregate themselves during their menses; if they failed to do so, their mere presence was thought to be polluting and could spoil any serious enterprise. Thus the Southeast Indians explained some of the misfortunes in their lives as having emanated from a just principle—bad things happened when people behaved badly.

But this principle could not explain why morally virtuous people suffered misfortune, nor why morally corrupt people experienced remarkable success. The Southeast Indians believed that occurrences of this kind were caused by the mysterious agency of witchcraft. That is, they believed that witches were real people living in their communities who were irredeemably evil and who caused certain misfortunes to befall virtuous people.

The witchcraft beliefs of the Southeast Indians are largely known through historical sources. Hence they cannot be known in the same detail as similar beliefs documented in societies that have been studied more recently through firsthand observation. But enough is known to make it clear that in the Southeast, as elsewhere, witchcraft beliefs grew out of the powerful tensions and ambivalences that exist in small-scale societies. In such societies, people do powerfully affect the lives of one another, and because of this they are forever examining one another's behavior with the most exacting scrutiny, searching for motives and intentions. Witchcraft beliefs thrive in such a social climate.

In Cherokee myths witches are depicted as irredeemably evil people who can take on the appearance of any person, four-footed animal, or bird. Witches are thought particularly likely to assume the appearance of a horned owl or a raven. The Cherokee took pains to stay up all night at the bedside of anyone who was seriously ill because they believed that witches were especially likely to attack such weak and defenseless people. They believed that witches stole the remaining days, months, or years of life of the ill person, extending their own lives by adding this time to their own. For this reason, the Cherokee believed that witches were often old people.

The Cherokee believed that witches' activities could sometimes be discovered through divination. This was especially necessary in the case of people who were ill. The medicine man who was taking care of the afflicted person would rake up a cone-shaped mound of coals in the fireplace and then sprinkle some pulverized tobacco *(Nicotiana rustica)* on the cone. Using the mound of coals as a kind of compass, the medicine man would recognize the direction of a witch's presence by the place on the cone where the sparks flared. If the particles clung together and flared with a loud burst, the witch was just outside the house. The Cherokee believed that a witch could be killed merely by learning his or her identity. Deceit and deception were at the core of witchcraft, and without these a witch could not exist.

RITUALS

The Southeast Indians acted out their beliefs about the world in rituals at both small and large junctures in their lives. In their everyday lives they observed taboos and avoidances that devolved from their fundamental categories of thought. Fire and water, for example, symbolized the opposition of the upper world and the underworld; accordingly, the Southeast Indians had a taboo against extinguishing fire with water, except on the occasion of someone's death, when this act perhaps symbolized the dissolution of a human life. Many additional taboos and avoidances were predicated on other categorical oppositions and anomalies. For example, males and females were strictly separated on certain occasions; some Southeast Indians prohibited cooking birds and four-footed animals in the same pot; and children were forbidden to touch moles because of their anomalous life beneath the ground. The Southeast Indians bore their prohibitions and taboos constantly in mind.

Immersion in water was a ritual that all Southeast Indians were supposed to perform each day, although some practiced it more faithfully than others. One was supposed to go to a moving stream at dawn and immerse oneself in the life-renewing water, even if ice was on the water. This ritual appears to have been kept most strictly by males, and particularly by younger males, upon whose vigor the defense of the society depended.

All important transitions of life were underscored by rites of passage. Mothers generally gave birth in the small houses where women sequestered themselves during menstruation. Before the newborn baby was allowed to suckle, it was taken to a creek or a spring and dipped into the water. Then bear oil was rubbed all over the baby's body. The father of a newborn baby was required to fast for four days.

Marriages were sealed by a series of exchanges. The kinsmen of the groom first collected gifts that were then presented to the kinsmen of the bride. In the marriage ceremony itself, the most essential acts were the killing of a deer or a bear by the groom, symbolizing his role as meat producer, and the cooking of a corn dish by the bride to symbolize her role as corn producer.

The principal concern of young men in the aboriginal Southeast was acquiring war honors, which they earned by meritorious deeds of valor. At each juncture in their military careers, a new name was bestowed upon them at a ceremony in their honor. The young men to be honored rubbed bear oil over their bodies and wore special clothing. The beloved old men delivered orations on the valor of the young men, and they admonished others to observe sacred precepts.

In curing illness, Southeast Indian priests and medicine men relied upon rituals as much as upon herbal medicines. As has been seen, they believed that many diseases were caused by vengeful spirits of the animals they had slain. If, for example, a medicine man concluded that his patient's disease had been caused by a vengeful fish spirit, he might invoke a kingfisher spirit or heron spirit to fly down and snatch away the offending fish spirit. Or if the illness happened to be rheumatism caused by an angry deer spirit, the medicine man might require the patient to drink a medicine made of several different ferns, and he would then invoke a terrapin spirit to come and loosen the rheumatism from the patient's bones. Moreover, the medicine man might give his patient a number of taboos and avoidances to observe, such as eating no salt, wood ash lye (a food seasoning), or hot food and avoiding squirrels, cats, bison, or any other animal that humps its back like a person with rheumatoid arthritis.

Funerals were the rites of passage around which the Southeast Indians organized their most elaborate rituals. In the late prehistoric era, and in some places even in the early historical era, the death of an important person could cause several other people to submit to voluntary death so that they could accompany the dead person to the otherworld. The interment of an important person's body was the occasion of a solemn ceremonial with much mourning. Months later the body was dug up and the bones cleaned and placed in a basket or box that was kept in the temple. Less important people received less elaborate treatment, but even they might be buried with some of their possessions, as well as with containers of food for their journey to the otherworld. In some cases, favorite pets were killed and interred with their masters.

In addition to a multitude of everyday taboos and avoidances, life-crisis rituals, and rites of passage, the Southeast Indians organized periodic ceremonials that were performed on behalf of the entire society. There is evidence that the Southeast Indians in the late prehistoric period performed a series of such rituals throughout the year. But by the eighteenth century only one of these was widely performed—the Green Corn ceremony. This ceremony was performed when the kernels of the late corn crop filled out and could be roasted and eaten as green corn. Hence, the precise time when the ceremony was performed varied from late July to early September, and in the extreme south it could even come in June.

The Green Corn ceremony was a first-fruits ceremony and a rite of thanksgiving, but it was also an important vehicle in the Southeast Indians' never-ending quest for purity. In fact, the Green Corn ceremony was a ritual means of purifying an entire society.

When the principal men of a society decided on the date on which the ceremony was to begin, they announced it to all the towns. On the appointed day the people assembled and began by eating a feast of the old year's food, for the eating of the new corn was forbidden until near the end of the ceremony. Next, the men cleaned and refurbished all the public structures, and the women did the same for their households, throwing away old pottery and artifacts and replacing them with new. A strict avoidance was imposed between the sexes, so that a man could not touch even a female infant for the duration of the ceremony.

In the next episode of the ceremony, the men fasted for a day and two nights while repeatedly drinking emetics and vomiting up the last vestiges of the old year's food. During this period of fasting the men discussed all the social conflicts and crimes of the previous year. Many of these were resolved at this time, and all was forgiven except murder. People who for various crimes, such as adultery, had fled from the town or had been expelled could now return to society with their crimes forgiven.

Next came the crucial rite of renewal. All fires were extinguished, and all the people fell into absolute silence, as if time had stopped. Then one of the priests, using a fire drill, kindled a new, pure fire, and from this fire all fires in the households were made anew. This marked the beginning of a new year. Afterward all appeared in their finest clothes, and the Green Corn ceremony ended with feasting and dancing. Then it was as if the entire social order had been cleansed and purified.

CHRISTIAN MISSIONS AND MODERN RELIGIOUS MOVEMENTS

The christianization of the Southeast Indians began in the late sixteenth century, when the Spanish built a mission system along the Georgia coast and in northern Florida. An early missionizing attempt by the Jesuits failed, but beginning in 1583 the Franciscans laid the groundwork for a mission system that endured until the late seventeenth and early eighteenth centuries. The Spanish friars taught the mission Indians Roman Catholic dogma, and they taught some of them to speak Spanish; a few Indians even became literate in the language. The missionaries also introduced European grains, vegetables, and fruits. The friars were able to maintain their missions only in the coastal regions; they were never able to missionize effectively in the interior, although a few attempts were made.

The Spanish mission system was rapidly destroyed after the British founded the colony of South Carolina in 1670. In their new colony the British quickly set about building plantations to be worked with slave labor. They armed Indian mercenaries to aid in their attacks on the Spanish missions. They enslaved many of the Indians and put them to work alongside the African slaves. By 1705, the Spanish mission system among the Southeast Indians had been completely destroyed.

Throughout the eighteenth century the Southeast Indians were caught up in the competition among the British, French, and Spanish for supremacy in the Southeast. The French sent a few missionaries to the Indians, but they were relatively ineffective. In the British colonies the Anglican Society for the Propagation of the Gospel did some mission work, although never with great enthusiasm. John and Charles Wesley also attempted for a time to missionize the Indians of the Georgia colony, but without success.

The first serious attempt after the Spanish to missionize the Southeast Indians came in the late eighteenth and early nineteenth centuries, when several Protestant groups began working among the Indians. It was also at this time that a nativistic movement swept through one group of Southeast Indians, the Upper Creek, with disastrous results. Partly stimulated by a visit from the Shawnee leader Tecumseh, who attempted to unite the Indians against the Americans, a number of prophets arose among the Upper Creek who believed that they could expel the Americans through combining religious and military action. This led to the Creek War of 1813–1814, which ended in a decisive defeat of the Indians. [*See the biography of Tecumseh.*]

At the very time when nineteenth-century Protestant missionaries were trying to "civilize" the Southeast Indians by teaching them not only Christianity but also modern agricultural and mechanical arts, pressure was building among southern planters to "remove" the Indians from their land. Ultimately the planters had their way, and beginning in the 1830s almost all the Indians of the Southeast Woodlands were forced to migrate to the Indian Territory, now Oklahoma.

Although fragments of the old Southeast Indian belief system have lingered on, often in an underground way, such beliefs have become curiosities in the twentieth century. In some places descendants of the Southeast Indians attend "stomp dances," but similar dances are performed by many modern American Indians. In a few places the Green Corn ceremony continues to be performed, although it lacks the powerful and pervasive meaning it once had.

BIBLIOGRAPHY

A definitive book on Southeast Indian religion remains to be written. Introductions to the subject can be found in my books *The Southeastern Indians* (Knoxville, 1976), in which see especially chapters 3 and 6, and *Elements of Southeastern Indian Religion* (Leiden, 1984), which is mainly concerned with iconography. A useful introduction to late prehistoric and early historical iconography and religion is James H. Howard's *The Southeastern Ceremonial Complex and Its Interpretation* (Columbia, Mo., 1968). The best specialized work on late prehistoric iconography is *Pre-Columbian Shell Engravings from the Craig Mound at Spiro, Oklahoma*, vol. 1 (Cambridge, Mass., 1978), by Philip Phillips and others. A useful survey of the Green Corn ceremony is John Witthoft's *Green Corn Ceremonialism in the Eastern Woodlands* (Ann Arbor, 1949), and the Black Drink ceremony is surveyed in a series of papers in *Black Drink* (Athens, Ga., 1979), edited by me.

Information on the religious beliefs and practices of the Cherokee is richer than for any other Southeast Indian group. See especially James Mooney's "Myths of the Cherokee," in the *Nineteenth Annual Report of the Bureau of American Ethnology* (Washington, D.C., 1900), and James Mooney and Frans M. Olbrechts's *The Swimmer Manuscript: Cherokee Sacred Formulas and Medicinal Prescriptions* (Washington, D.C., 1932). See also Raymond D. Fogelson's "An Analysis of Cherokee Sorcery and Witchcraft," in *Four Centuries of Southern Indians* (Athens, Ga., 1975), edited by me; James Mooney's "The Cherokee River Cult," *The Journal of American Folklore* 13 (1900): 1–10; and Frans M. Olbrechts's "Some Cherokee Methods of Divination," in *Proceedings of the Twenty-third International Congress of Americanists* (New York, 1930). Most of the available information on Creek religion is surveyed in John R. Swanton's "Religious Beliefs and Medical Practices of the Creek Indians," in the *Forty-second Annual Report of the Bureau of American Ethnology* (Washington, D.C., 1982). The Spanish mission period is surveyed in John Tate Lanning's *The Spanish Missions of Georgia* (Chapel Hill, N.C., 1935) and in Mark F. Boyd, Hale G. Smith, and John W. Griffin's *Here They Once Stood: The Tragic End of the Apalachee Missions* (Gainesville, Fla., 1951).

15 HISTORY OF THE STUDY OF NATIVE NORTH AMERICANS

RAYMOND D. FOGELSON

The religions of North American Indians manifest considerable complexity and diversity. In 1492 several hundred cultural groups practiced distinctive forms of religion. While we customarily begin the documentary record at the time of initial European contact, discoveries in archaeology have extended religious perspectives far back into prehistory. Burial mounds in the Midwest, Southeastern ceremonial sites, abandoned *kiva*s in the Southwest, stone medicine wheels on the Plains, California petroglyphs, and other remains all evoke the antiquity of North American religions.

Despite its intrinsic value for comparative religion, the field of indigenous North American religions has been undercultivated by religious scholars. Too often dismissed as "primitive," these religions have been generally relegated to an undifferentiated residual category shared with other religions of primal peoples around the world. Interest in these religions has been limited to their supposed evolutionary position as stages logically antecedent to what are commonly called the "great religions," which command the allegiance of the majority of the world's population. Rarely, until recently, have North American Indian religions been studied as valid subjects in their own right. Nevertheless, research has revealed intricately structured rituals and ceremonies, myths densely packed with symbolic meanings, cosmologies that embrace subtle relations with nature, and highly elaborated varieties of individual religious experience.

One difficulty in studying native North American religions is that their institutions tend to be much less obviously compartmentalized than those of the so-called great religions. Their religious beliefs and practices pervade many spheres of practical activity; for example, among the Nootka constructing a canoe is considered a religious act, as is Hopi horticulture, the rabbit drive of the Rappahanock, the Paiute piñon gathering, and so on.

A second problem confronting students of North American Indian religions is the absence of literacy in traditional native societies. Lacking bodies of orthodox written doctrine, they have depended on oral and visual transmission of religious tradition. Such modes place a premium on mnemonic devices, rhetorical skills, and tacit understandings gained through participation. The absence of written texts has in the past allowed considerable flexibility in adapting to change and permitted considerable latitude for idiosyncratic interpretation.

147

A third difficulty is that the religions of North American Indians are typically dynamic. Efforts to depict or reconstruct these religions as timeless, fully integrated systems of belief and action are usually doomed to failure. Religious movements are recurrent features in North American history and prehistory. These movements, usually inspired by prophecy, originated within particular tribes but often spread beyond tribal boundaries. Deeply embedded in many of these religions are many reintegrated traits that ultimately derive from early contacts with Christianity.

EARLY OBSERVERS

The study of North American religions begins with the early European explorers. Many explorers carried with them strong Christian theocentric biases that denied the existence of religion in aboriginal societies. People who went naked and lived communally, who practiced polygamy, anthropophagy, and human sacrifice were sometimes judged as less than human. What served as religion to the Indian was disdainfully dismissed by the European newcomer as devil worship, idolatry, or irrational superstition. However, since part of the European mission to explore and settle the New World was religiously motivated, earnest efforts were made to convert the heathens to the "true faith" through both coercion and persuasion.

Later explorers of the interior regions were scarcely more perspicacious than their predecessors concerning native religions. Older stereotypes persisted: Indians were said to be haunted by demons, their religious practitioners were derided as conjurors, jugglers, and imposters, and their rites were regarded as ridiculous and absurd. On matters of religion, the accounts of the explorers replay their presuppositions with monotonous regularity.

Nevertheless, in the performance of their evangelical tasks, missionaries sometimes mastered native languages and were able to penetrate the belief structures of their potential converts. The Recollet and Jesuit fathers bequeathed an unprecedented record of seventeenth- and eighteenth-century religious customs among Algonquian- and Iroquoian-speaking groups in the Northeast. Not only does the seventy-three-volume *The Jesuit Relations and Allied Documents* (compiled 1610–1791; first published in 1896–1901; reprint in 39 vols., New York, 1959) contain accurate firsthand observations, but the scholarly training of these priests enabled them to engage in speculative comparative ethnology. The high point of Jesuit anthropology was reached by the priest Joseph François Lafitau in his two-volume *Moeurs des sauvages ameriquains comparées aux moeurs des premiers* (1724; translated by William N. Fenton and Elizabeth L. Moore as *Customs of the American Savages, compared with the Customs of Primitive Times*, Toronto, 1977). Lafitau offered a detailed overview of religious customs based on the works of his Jesuit predecessors and supplemented by his own inquiries. He systematically compared Indian religious practices with those of classical antiquity. Convinced that the Indians had emigrated from Asia, Lafitau argued for the unity of the human race, all of whom had in the remote past, he believed, shared a common God-given religion. Lafitau maintained that through migrations, local adaptations, and forgetfulness, primal beliefs and practices degenerated; yet vestiges of this original condition could still be discerned in the customs of contemporary savages, which presented clues for unraveling unwritten history. Lafitau's ideas were not unique, but the reliability of his documentation and his attempts at systematic comparison place him in advance of his times.

Spanish and English missionaries, with rare exceptions, fell far short of the high standards set by the French. The rigid religious orthodoxy of the Spanish and the notorious ethnocentrism of the English seemed to conspire in precluding sympathetic tolerance for native beliefs. Only in the late eighteenth century do missionary accounts of native religions begin to possess substantive worth.

Along with the records of enlightened missionaries, the reports of early travelers and traders offer valuable material on North American Indians. Travelers, by virtue of their experiences with a series of different groups, frequently were sensitive to religious variations. Lack of sustained observation tended to diminish the reliability of these reports, but this deficiency was overcome by exceptional traders and administrators who resided for long periods in Indian communities, learned Indian languages, and often married Indian women. For example, the trader John Long in his account of the Ojibwa (*Voyages and Travels of an Indian Interpreter and Trader*, 1791) is the first to refer to the concept of totem, which he describes as an association established with a guardian spirit during a vision quest. Later scholars misappropriated and universalized the term to denote names for descent groups and elementary forms of religion.

Much knowledge about traditional religion among Indians of the Southeast Woodlands derives from James Adair's *The History of the American Indian* (1775). Adair, who lived for forty years among the Cherokee and Chickasaw, believed that the Indians were descended from the lost tribes of Israel. To sustain his argument, he established twenty-three points of specific convergence between Indian and Israelite customs. Despite his erroneous thesis, Adair's mode of analysis forced him to ask questions and record important religious information that might otherwise have been ignored.

EMERGENCE OF A FIELD OF STUDY

Early theories about the indigenous people of North America revolved around questions of origin. Who were they? Whence did they come? Few theorists subscribed to an autochthonous origin; some, influenced by the foreshortened biblical chronology, attempted to link them with historically known Old World peoples. Such speculations encouraged the collection and analysis of ethnological materials, among which religious information was considered critical. Simple connections proved untenable, and the origins of North American Indians were pushed farther into the past. Many European and colonial philosophers and universal historians equated indigenous peoples with early stages of human development, as epitomized in Locke's famous phrase, "in the beginning all the World was America." Themes of native degeneracy and inherent inferiority were countered by the philosophical and literary image of the "Noble Savage," a convention that attained popularity in the mid-eighteenth century more as a critique of Western morality than as a serious effort accurately to portray Native Americans.

The post-Revolutionary consolidation of a national identity on the part of Americans provided another stimulus to the study of North American Indians. Intellectuals of the new republic sought to advance evidence proving that their continent was not inferior to the Old World and could support civilization. Under the influence of such leaders as Thomas Jefferson, Benjamin Barton, Peter DuPonceau, Lewis Cass, and Albert Gallatin, coordinated efforts were undertaken not only to "civilize" the Indians but also to preserve for posterity a record of their traditional cultures.

The career of Henry Rowe Schoolcraft (1793–1864) exemplifies the transition from amateur observer to professional ethnologist. Schoolcraft's younger years were spent on the frontier as a geological explorer and Indian trader. After taking up residence among the Chippewa of Sault Sainte Marie, he married an Indian woman, learned Chippewa, and became a governmental agent. In 1839 he published his influential *Algic Researches*, (New York, 1839) in which he sought to reveal the deeper levels of Indian mentality through the collection of myths and folklore and the analysis of subtleties in Algonquian linguistics. His scholarly reputation thus established, Schoolcraft deserted the frontier to promote the fledgling science of ethnology. He secured federal support and was responsible for compiling the mammoth, six-volume *Historical and Statistical Information Respecting the History, Condition and Prospects of the Indian Tribes of the United States* (Philadelphia, 1851–1860). This work is laced with important data from missionaries and Indian agents, but its cumbersome and disorganized format limits its utility.

ADVANCES UNDER THE BUREAU OF ETHNOLOGY

The founding of the Bureau of Ethnology in 1879 auspiciously launched formal government anthropology in the United States. The bureau's mission was primarily salvage ethnology and scientific systematization of knowledge about America's original inhabitants. Under the inspired directorship of John Wesley Powell, a dedicated group of scholars was assembled who left enduring contributions to the understanding of Indian religions.

The Southwest became an important area of investigation, since Apachean-speaking and Pueblo groups retained viable neoaboriginal religious systems. Such bureau-sponsored researchers as James Stevenson and Matilda Stevenson, J. W. Fewkes, Washington Matthews, J. G. Bourke, and Frank Hamilton Cushing produced papers and monographs on Southwestern ceremonialism that attracted international attention.

Other areas as well were attended to by the bureau. Clay MacCauley, James Mooney, and, later, John R. Swanton studied Southeast Woodlands religions. Research on Iroquois religion persisted through the works of Lewis Henry Morgan and Horatio Hale, whose *The Iroquois Book of Rites* (Philadelphia, 1883) represents the first modern monographic treatment of North American Indian ceremonialism. Such bureau scholars as Erminnie Smith and J. N. B. Hewitt contributed significant studies on Iroquoian myths and cosmology. Other aspects of Eastern Woodlands religion were documented by W. J. Hoffman's works on the Ojibwa and Menomini and later by Truman Michaelson's impressive corpus on the Fox.

The heyday of Plains culture still survived within living memory when bureau ethnologists entered the field. J. Owen Dorsey collected valuable information on Siouan religions; James Mooney reported on the Kiowa and Cheyenne; Alice Fletcher, in collaboration with native intellectuals Francis La Flesche and James Murie, produced classic monographs on Omaha and Pawnee religion. Mooney's brilliant description and analysis of the contemporary Ghost Dance remains a recognized masterpiece of religious ethnology. Very little bureau work was undertaken among tribes west of the Rocky Mountains until the twentieth century.

RISE OF UNIVERSITY SPECIALIZATIONS

By 1900 the center of American anthropology began to shift from museums and government agencies to universities. As gifted and resourceful as the early researchers of the Bureau of Ethnology were, none had received formal academic training in anthropology. The central figure in the movement toward professionalization was Franz Boas, a European-trained scholar, who exerted a dominant influence on American anthropology for the next half century. Boas developed the modern concept of culture, set new standards for fieldwork, and trained several generations of students destined to make decisive contributions to the study of Indian religions. Boas's own works on the Northwest Coast demonstrated a meticulous concern for ethnographic particularism aimed toward problems of cultural-historical reconstruction. Later he moved from an emphasis on trait analysis and diffusion toward interpretation of the dynamics of cultural integration. Reluctant to generalize and distrustful of grand theory, Boas assiduously collected native-language texts, many of which involve religious topics. Some have argued that Boas's strong positivistic empiricism inhibited theoretical development in North American anthropology; however, his insistence on obtaining the native viewpoint through texts provides a tangible legacy for modern anthropology.

Regardless of how one evaluates Boas's direct contributions to religious ethnology, his students and collaborators succeeded in filling out in fine descriptive detail the major lineaments of indigenous North American religions. Substantive works by such field-workers as Ruth Benedict, Ruth L. Bunzel, Roland B. Dixon, Alexander A. Goldenweiser, Esther Goldfrank, Erna Gunther, Herman Haeberlin, George L. Hunt, Melville Jacobs, A. L. Kroeber, Robert H. Lowie, Elsie Clews Parsons, Paul Radin, Gladys A. Reichard, Edward Sapir, Frank G. Speck, Leslie Spier, John R. Swanton, James A. Teit, Ruth M. Underhill, and Clark Wissler cannot be reviewed here. However, some brief comments on emergent trends can be mentioned. Increasingly, one finds concern with the nature of religious experience and religious meaning for the individual. Stylistic and literary features of myths and tales are given serious attention. Interest in culturally constituted worldviews becomes more apparent. Finally, there emerges an implicitly functional approach that relates religion to other aspects of culture, society, and the individual. Many of these scholars reached beyond ethnographic particularities to address problems of general theory and to impart the facts of native North American religions to a wider audience.

From the beginning, religious materials from North American Indian sources served as ammunition for the heavy artillery of European "armchair" theorists. These materials were employed in hit-or-miss fashion to support the global theories of such commanding figures as E. B. Tylor, James G. Frazer, Andrew Lang, R. R. Marett, W. J. Perry, Émile Durkheim, Marcel Mauss, Lucien Lévy-Bruhl, Wilhelm Schmidt, and Adolf E. Jensen. American reaction to these theories has typically been defensive and critical. It must be admitted that, with few exceptions, these theorists and subsequent European ethnologists, comparativists, and religious historians lacked direct

American field experience. Yet they have contributed significantly by viewing the American data from the broader perspective of world religions, by constructing typologies with which the American evidence can be analyzed and compared, and by probing deeply into the philosophical implications of these materials. Recent European scholars whose work deserves greater recognition by their American colleagues include Kaj Birket-Smith, Josef Haekel, Rolf Krusche, Werner Müller, Raffaele Pettazzoni, and Anna Burgitta Rooth. The prolific and more accessible works of Åke Hultkrantz, a Swedish scholar, deserve special comment. Hultkrantz conducted field research among the Shoshoni and Arapaho, but his principal eminence derives from his unparalleled grasp of the published literature on native North American religions, displayed in several comprehensive comparative monographs and in numerous topical essays.

RECENT TOPICS OF STUDY

The post-Boasian period from World War II to the present has witnessed an accelerating interest in the indigenous religions of North America, and many profitable approaches have been taken. Psychological anthropology, for example, has brought new insights into the nature of religious experience through the study of alternate states of consciousness induced through ritual use of hallucinogens and other means. Weston La Barre's *The Ghost Dance* (Garden City, N.Y., 1970) is particularly notable for its profound psychological interpretation of Native American religions.

Another approach is through environmental issues, which have stimulated considerations of the effects of religious ideology on ecological adaptation. Calvin Martin's *Keepers of the Game* (Berkeley, 1978), a historical account of Indian participation in the fur trade, has evoked a wide variety of responses on the role of religious motivation in hunting activities. Probably the most solidly crafted study to address this problem is Adrian Tanner's monograph on the Cree, *Bringing Home Animals* (New York, 1979).

The study of religious movements, too, commands much attention. Anthony F. C. Wallace's *The Death and Rebirth of Seneca* (New York, 1969), an eloquent account of the Handsome Lake religion, is a modern classic. Considerable study has been devoted to variations of the peyote religion. La Barre's enlarged edition of *The Peyote Cult* (New York, 1969) offers the best general overview of the subject, while David F. Aberle's *The Peyote Religion among the Navaho* (Chicago, 1982) and J. S. Slotkin's several publications on Menomini peyotism provide excellent accounts of specific manifestations. Homer Barnett's monograph *Indian Shakers* (Carbondale, Ill., 1957) stands as a definitive treatment of its subject.

The structuralism of Claude Lévi-Strauss has opened new vistas for the reinterpretation of North American totemism, art, myths, rituals, and the witchcraft-sorcery complex. Lévi-Strauss himself has utilized North American materials extensively in his provocative publications. Structuralism has inspired a whole generation of primarily younger scholars to think about previously collected data in interesting new ways.

Several noteworthy reworkings of important manuscript collections have recently appeared. Irving Goldman, synthesizing Boas's notes and scattered publications, has accomplished what Boas was never able to do—produce a coherent, theoretically informed account of Kwakiutl religion. Goldman's *The Mouth of Heaven* (New York,

1975) is complemented by Stanley Walens's symbolic analysis of Kwakiutl art and ritual, *Feasting with Cannibals* (Princeton, 1981). Raymond J. DeMallie and Elaine A. Jahner have made available the rich previously unpublished Lakota materials that were collected early in the century by James R. Walker (*Lakota Belief and Ritual*, Lincoln, Nebr., 1980; *Lakota Society*, Lincoln, Nebr., 1982; and *Lakota Myths*, Lincoln, Nebr., 1983). DeMallie has also assembled primary materials relating to the renowned Lakota medicine man Black Elk (*The Sixth Grandfather: Black Elk's Teachings Given to John G. Neihardt*, Lincoln, Nebr., 1984). William Power's *Oglala Religion* (Lincoln, Nebr., 1977) and his excellent descriptions of an Oglala curing ritual in *Yuwipi* (Lincoln, Nebr., 1982) amplify our understanding of Lakota religion. James R. Murie's account of Pawnee ceremonialism has been edited by Douglas Parks and published as *Ceremonies of the Pawnee* (Washington, D.C., 1981). Another important contribution to Plains research is Peter J. Powell's masterful, two-volume opus on Cheyenne religion, *Sweet Medicine* (Norman, Okla., 1969). Elisabeth Tooker has combed *The Jesuit Relations* to reconstruct Huron religion in her *An Ethnography of the Huron Indians, 1615–1649* (Washington, D.C., 1964), and she has also published a useful study entitled *The Iroquois Ceremonial of Midwinter* (Syracuse, N.Y., 1970). William N. Fenton has contributed mightily to Iroquois studies with his superb monograph on the Eagle Dance (*The Iroquois Eagle Dance*, Washington, D.C., 1953) and a continuing stream of research on Longhouse rituals. Information on several extinct Californian religions have been resurrected from the field notes of the remarkable J. P. Harrington and published in various books and articles.

The Ojibwa and the Winnebago remain two of the best-documented American religious traditions. The works of Alanson Skinner, John Cooper, A. Irving Hallowell, and Paul Radin have provided sturdy scaffolding for subsequent research. Ruth Landes's *Ojibwa Religion and the Midewiwin* (Madison, Wis., 1968) and recent historically oriented works on the Ojibwa by Christopher Vecsey (*Traditional Ojibwa Religion and its Historical Changes*, Philadelphia, 1983) and John A. Grim (*The Shaman: Patterns of Siberian and Ojibwa Healing*, Norman, Okla., 1983) illustrate this continuity. Landes's monograph on *The Prairie Potawatomi* (Madison, Wis., 1970) and James H. Howard's summary of Shawnee ceremonialism (*Shawnee: The Ceremonialism of a Native Indian Tribe and Its Cultural Background*, Athens, Ohio, 1981) enlarge our picture of Algonquian religions.

The Southwest continues as a focus of important research on religion. The complexities of Navajo religion, in particular, have been elucidated in the ethnographic and textual works of David F. Aberle, Leland C. Wyman, Berard Haile, David P. McAllester, Charlotte J. Frisbie, Louise Lamphere, and Gary Witherspoon, as well as in useful work by Sam D. Gill and Karl W. Luckert, both skilled historians of religion. Elsewhere in the Southwest, Alfonso Ortiz, a leading Tewa anthropologist, has written a sensitively informed account of Pueblo religion (*The Tewa World: Space, Time, Being and Becoming in a Pueblo Society*, Chicago, 1969), and Carobeth Laird, an affinal Chemehuevi, has recorded religious materials based on a lifetime of observation in her richly textured *The Chemehuevis* (Banning, Calif., 1976).

Knowledge of Southeast Woodlands Indian religion has been enriched by studies of religious continuities in modern Oklahoma (to which many Southeast Woodlands tribes were forcibly removed in the mid-nineteenth century); William L. Ballard's elegant analysis, entitled *The Yuchi Green Corn Ceremonial* (Los Angeles, 1978), and James G. Howard's *Oklahoma Seminoles: Medicine, Magic, and Religion* (Norman,

Okla., 1984) are notable in this regard. Howard also provocatively analyzed the ceremonial complex of the prehistoric Southeast Woodlands Indians in *The Southeastern Ceremonial Complex* (Columbia, Mo., 1968), in which he gains insights from surviving beliefs and practices. A collection of papers edited by Charles M. Hudson, *The Black Drink* (Athens, Ga., 1979), represents another effort to link prehistoric and ethnographic horizons.

The present surge in attention to native religions of North America derives from many sources. Most important is the growing recognition by Indians and non-Indians alike that religion constitutes a viable aspect of past, present, and future North American Indian societies, a point made in Vine Deloria's vigorous manifesto *God is Red* (New York, 1973). Not only have areas such as the Southwest enjoyed unbroken religious continuity, but elsewhere, once-moribund ceremonies—such as the potlatch in the Northwest, the Spirit Dance among the Salish, and the Sun Dance in the Plains—have been revivified. Syncretic and ecumenical native religions are achieving legitimacy, and in many areas Christianity has assumed a distinctively native flavor. These trends reflect changes in the political atmosphere toward native self-determination. Among other developments, passage of the Religious Freedom Act in 1978 has had far-reaching consequences in preserving sacred sites.

Academic concern with indigenous North American religions has grown dramatically in recent years. The establishment of special programs of study in many universities, the increased number of religion scholars of Native American descent, and the seriousness with which indigenous religions are now treated in many theological centers all testify to a new enlightenment. Yet despite the enhanced academic and popular visibility of Native American religions and the proliferation of publications in the field, much groundbreaking work remains. Only the surface has been scratched.

BIBLIOGRAPHY

Åke Hultkrantz's *The Study of American Indian Religions* (New York, 1983) has proved indispensable in preparing this entry. The same author's *The Religions of the American Indian* (Berkeley, 1979) and *Belief and Worship in Native North America* (Syracuse, N.Y., 1981) are valuable sources on native North American religions. A slightly older synthesis, Ruth M. Underhill's *Red Man's Religion* (Chicago, 1965), remains a useful introductory survey. A pair of works by Sam D. Gill, *Native American Religions: An Introduction* (Belmont, Calif., 1981) and *Native American Traditions: Sources and Interpretations* (Belmont, Calif., 1983), offer a lively introduction to the subject. Three anthologies with diverse contents are *Teachings from the American Earth,* edited by Dennis Tedlock and Barbara Tedlock (New York, 1975); *Seeing with a Native Eye*, edited by Walter H. Capps (New York, 1976); and *Native Religious Traditions*, edited by Earle H. Waugh and K. Dad Prithipaul (Waterloo, Ont., 1979). A carefully annotated areal selection of native texts is presented in Elisabeth Tooker's *Native North American Spirituality of the Eastern Woodlands* (New York, 1979). Other areal guides can be found in the available volumes of the new Smithsonian *Handbook of North American Indians* (Washington, D.C., 1978–). *Systems of North American Witchcraft and Sorcery*, edited by Deward E. Walker (Moscow, Idaho, 1970), and Virgil Vogel's *American Indian Medicine* (Norman, Okla., 1970) are useful sources. Harold W. Turner's *Bibliography of New Religious Movements in Primal Societies*, vol. 2, *North America* (Boston, 1978), is a major resource.

TWO
RELIGIOUS EXPRESSIONS

16 MYTHIC THEMES

Sam D. Gill

Enormous quantities of stories have been collected from the peoples native to North America, especially in the late nineteenth and early twentieth centuries. Still, the record is faulty in that the stories collected have rarely been adequately set in their cultural and historical contexts. Often, while the text of a story exists, little is known of the storyteller, the situation in which the story is told, and sometimes even the culture it comes from. A full description of a storytelling event, including the elements of performance style, motivating circumstances, and the audience composition and responses, is almost nonexistent. Furthermore, there has been remarkably little interest in the interpretive study of this literature.

MYTH, TALE, AND LEGEND

No standard exists for the use of the term *myth* to distinguish a segment or type of Native American oral tradition. Anthropologists and folklorists have not often discriminated between myth and the related term *tale*, using both simply to refer to narratives or stories. When a distinction is made several criteria are commonly used. Myths are sacred while tales are not. Myths are true while tales are not. The characters of myths are deities and primordial figures; humans and animals are the usual characters of tales. Myths deal with creation at the dawn of time or with cosmic transformations occurring in a prehuman era. Tales tell of fantastical and nonsensical events. Sometimes a subclass of tale or a wholly separate class of narrative is distinguished as *legend;* legend is closer to history and to human affairs. This threefold classification dates from distinctions made by Jacob Grimm in the early nineteenth century.

This manner of classifying Native American oral traditions focuses on story content considered in terms of external criteria. Other classificatory criteria include the context and function of a story since these may vary for the same story over time and from culture to culture. As early as 1915, Franz Boas insisted that native classifications be considered; however, a full-scale study of native classifications of oral traditions has never been done.

From the point of view of the academic study of religion, *myth* has come to be widely used to designate narratives that have major religious importance. It is also commonly, and more narrowly used to refer to, creation and cosmic transformation narratives. Such events are set in the primordium, a setting signaling that the narrative and the events of which it tells are fundamental.

In contrast, from the modern Native American point of view, the word *myth* has the meaning the word bears in common usage: it refers to a misconception or a story without base. To many Native Americans, *myth* is a pejorative term that indicates insensitivity and misunderstanding on the part of those who apply it to their stories. Concern for native sensitivity is all but entirely missing from studies and presentations of Native American oral traditions that use the terms *myth* and *mythology*.

STORY TYPES IN NORTH AMERICA

A great many of the stories in North America have to do with creation or with origins resulting from cosmic transformations; these stories often correlate with story types found throughout the world. Most tribes in North America have stories that tell of the beginning of the world that is presently lived in (not one of long ago); the origin of human beings; the origin of plants and animals; the origin of the sun, moon, and stars; and the origin of aspects of the human condition such as death, disease, laziness, and sexuality. I will summarize the types of these stories, with a discussion of their variant forms and geographic distributions.

Earth Diver. The distinctive feature of the earth-diver story type, as the term designating it indicates, is the attribution of the origin of the earth to the result of some figure diving to the bottom of primordial waters to get a bit of sand or soil from which to create the earth. The diver is most commonly animal, and usually there are a number of these divers who try in succession to dive for soil. Only the last diver succeeds, and this figure is usually gone a very long time, being dead or nearly dead when he or she surfaces. Beside the divers, there is a creator figure as well, and it is the work of the creator to take the bit of sand or soil and, through kneading, stretching, singing creation songs, or some other means, to expand this nascent earth to its present size. The created earth then floats upon the primordial waters. Sometimes it is not well anchored, and it shakes or wobbles. This condition is resolved by the erection of pillars in the cardinal directions or some other security measure usually associated with directional orientations.

Earth-diver stories commonly conclude with a post-creation inspection; the creator sends someone on a journey to inspect the newly made world and to measure its extent. Typically these figures do not attend only to the business assigned, but tarry to satisfy their own interests or desires. In consequence of this forbidden action, the figure is transformed in a way that explains his or her nature. In one story, for example, Buzzard is sent out but stops to eat. He is punished by being condemned to eat corpses; hence buzzards are carrion eaters.

This type of creation story is found throughout North America and is certainly the most common and widespread story type in the area. In some locations it appears only as an incidental theme, while elsewhere it has developed into long elaborate stories containing amazing detail and hundreds of elements. These stories are set in the beginning of time or following an era concluded by the cataclysmic event of a world destruction by deluge. [*For further discussion of earth-diver myths in North America, see* North American Indians, *article on* Indians of the Far North.]

Emergence. In emergence type creation stories, a world exists at the outset without its creation being described or in any way accounted for. There are also peoples living in a world below the present earth surface when the story begins. This story type is concerned with the ascent of these human beings and their search for or travel to a habitable world: it is more about finding the proper place in the world than the cosmic creation. Two major types of stories are commonly a part of emergence mythology: the story of the emergence journey onto the earth surface and the story of migrations from the emergence place to the current village site or homeland. The distinctive segment is the story of the emergence journey. Numerous elements are commonly found in that story. The plight of those in the depths of the earth is usually one of darkness, deprivation, filth, and ignorance. The pre-emergence peoples must await heroic figures, designated by a deity, to come to them and escort them on their emergence journey. The journey may be arduous, the way not well known. Sometimes there is no way out of the lower world; then, in a manner similar to the earth diver's diving for soil, various persons, or more typically animals, attempt to break through the earth's surface from below. Many may fail before one succeeds. The means of ascent may be a vine, a tree, a reed, or a mountain. It grows magically and bears the people upwards to the new world. The sequence of emergence sometimes establishes the universal social order: peoples of many tribes or clans, sometimes including European-Americans, emerge in a sequence that is correlated with status, material wealth, or character. Occasionally, the emergence channel is closed before all are able to emerge, often because someone defies a taboo; the result is that some people are left eternally in the lower world.

The story of the emergence is not always accompanied by one of migration, but such a pattern is very common. After emergence, the people discover that the place at which they have arrived is not suitable. The people must then migrate to the site of their present village or land. The migration may be a wandering in search of a suitable location, or it may be a prophetically directed journey to a designated place. There are also migration stories that are independent of emergence stories; either segment may be simple or elaborate, in any combination.

Emergence stories are not as common as earth-diver stories, but they are found widely throughout what is now the United States, with a few incidences recorded in southern Canada. [*See also* North American Indians, *article on* Indians of the Southwest.]

Two Creators. Another type of creation story that appears widely in North America, especially throughout the United States, is one that features two creators. The creator figures are usually antagonists and the creation of the world the result of their struggles. The two creators are often related, and they interact in a variety of ways. Often they are brothers, sisters, uncle and nephew, father and son, or simply powerful figures who meet in the act of making a world according to their respective styles and plans. The elements of contest, of the duality of good and evil, and of positive opposed to negative forces are usually present. A well-known example is the Iroquoian story in which brothers, one good and one bad, create the world. The good brother creates in a manner ideal for human beings, while the bad brother follows him and reverses some of the good, introducing elements that hamper human life, such as disease, plant blight, pests, and dangerous animals. In the climactic moment the brothers meet at the world's rim and engage in a final determining contest: the one who can move a mountain the farthest will be the winner. The bad brother tries first. After great effort he moves the mountain a little. As he turns toward the good brother the good brother effortlessly moves the mountain up against the back of the bad brother. Turning back to boast of his accomplishment, the bad brother smashes his nose against the mountain and twists it into a permanently deformed shape. The good brother then spares him his life at the cost of his becoming the model for the False Face society by devoting himself to the curing of illness.

Theft. Stories of the theft of light, fire, water, game, fish, and many other things necessary for human life are found widely, but especially in western North America from the Southwest all the way north through the Northwest Coast area. As with the emergence story, theft stories account not so much for creation as for a primordial transformation. The condition that motivates the action in this type of story is the loss or lack of something—such as light or game—that is necessary for human life. Often, it has been secreted by giants, monsters, or deities residing in an inaccessible place. The story centers upon a heroic figure who, through courage, tenacity, or magic, and sometimes aided by clever disguise, enters the place where the missing life-necessity is being kept. By theft, the hero achieves the release of this necessity and, consequently, life becomes possible. A moral twist is sometimes added when the returning hero is humiliated or shunned; the result is that the ideal conditions that would have existed are lost, resulting in turn in discomfort and inconvenience.

World Parent. The world-parent type cosmogony has been occasionally identified, particularly in the North American Southwest. Among the most common examples cited are stories of the Luiseño and Diegueño tribes of southern California. There is some suggestion of a sexual creation in these stories, yet a close consideration of the known examples suggests that they are more like the two-creator type of story. The primordial figures are brother and sister, and their struggles for dominance conclude with the brother sexually assaulting the sister (who later gives birth to some aspects of the world, usually including a small piece of earth). Another commonly cited example of world-parent creation is the Zuni story of creation recorded by Frank H. Cushing in the late nineteenth century. However, none of the many subsequently recorded accounts of Zuni creation involve the sexual creation by a sky father and earth mother that Cushing reported. It must be thus concluded that there is little, if any, evidence that world-parent cosmogony exists in North America.

Plant and Animal Origins. Throughout North America stories of the origin of plants and animals are very common, obviously correlating with the sustenance patterns of the respective tribes. Among the most widespread and complex of this type are the Corn Woman stories found throughout southern maize-growing portions of North America. A notable feature of many of these stories is the plight of Corn Woman during the events that introduce the plant to human cultivation. Particularly in Southeast Woodlands versions, Corn Woman produces corn by rubbing "dirt" from her flesh, or by defecating the kernels. People in this primordial era need not work for their food, they receive it as a gift from the Corn Woman. Several finally observe Corn Woman as she goes to gather food and they find out how she produces it. Being repulsed and disgusted by what they see, they accuse her of witchcraft and prepare to kill her. Through her prescience, Corn Woman knows her fate and tells her murderers what they are to do with her body; typically, her bleeding body is to be dragged about cultivated fields. Corn plants grow where her blood touches the soil, but now the people must cultivate the plants in order to receive the life-sustaining food.

Among the Pueblo tribes, Maize Women often appear in groups of four identified by the four colors of corn. The personified maize is identified as mother to the people, and so as identical with life itself. As Yellow Woman, Maize Woman is a character in an extensive range of stories about an adventuresome young woman. Yellow Woman may even suggest elements of a trickster figure.

Animal origin stories are widely known throughout North America. The Inuit (Eskimo) tell stories of Sedna, an unwilling bride who eventually marries a deceptive husband. Later, her father comes to visit her only to find her miserable in her husband's home. Attempting to rescue her, her father kills the husband and father and daughter flee by boat, but their flight is threatened by the husband's people. The father tries to sacrifice Sedna in order to save himself. He throws her from the boat, but she clings to the side by her fingers. Still trying to save himself, the father chops off Sedna's fingers, joint by joint. As these severed joints fall from her hands into the water, they are transformed into the game animals of the sea. Finally, as Sedna herself falls into the sea she descends to the bottom, where she takes up residence as the fearful mistress of the animals. [See Sedna.]

A very different sort of figure is White Buffalo Calf Woman of Oglala Lakota oral tradition. As Buffalo she reveals the ritual cycle to the people, thus sustaining both their physical and spiritual needs. [See Lakota Religion.]

In the many areas where both agriculture and hunting are important, the origin of animals and plants are often combined or conjoined in a single story. In the Plains area this is commonly a story of the origin of buffalo and corn. In other areas, the Southeast Woodlands for example, it is a story that tells of a primordial transformation resulting in the necessity of human labor in cultivation and hunting—that is, it is a story of the origin of planting and hunting.

Trickster Stories. The most widespread and best-known stories in North America center on a complex figure that has come to be known by the term "trickster." This figure takes various physical forms including Coyote, Raven, Mink, Blue Jay, and a variety of anthropomorphic figures. Although many collectors and interpreters of North American oral traditions have not considered trickster stories anything other than entertainment, more attention has been given in recent decades to the interpretation of these stories than perhaps to any other story type. It is important that the stories of the trickster are not all of a single type and the roles and characters the trickster plays are many and often complex. The trickster figure may also appear as the protagonist in many of the other story types we have discussed.

Basic human needs–sexuality, food, sense of self, sociability, and knowledge— almost always shape the character of the trickster, but by being exaggerated to their limits. The trickster is often grossly sexual. He has sexual relations with his daughter or mother-in-law, thus breaking the most unspeakable of taboos. He often has greatly exaggerated sexual organs, such as a penis so long that he must roll it up and carry it in a pack on his back. The trickster is often so concerned about satiating his hunger that he will eat anything (and assuredly food that is forbidden to him).

Furthermore, he is unsociable, antisocial, or falsely sociable. He plays tricks on people, resulting in their suffering, embarrassment, or death. He is slow to learn, but tenacious to the point of foolishness. The trickster is a lively character; stories about him are without doubt entertaining, if sometimes bawdy. Yet the stories are almost always highly valued by native North Americans. Doubtless this is because trickster stories are rarely simply stories about a prankster or buffoon; they are stories about the nature of the world and the nature of being human. In some stories the trickster is actually the cosmic creator, but more often he is a transformer or fixer. Because of the mythic actions of the character, such things as death, suffering, lust, and many of the seemingly negative aspects of being human are accounted for and their meanings are explored. Even physical features of the cosmos such as the Milky Way are attributed to acts of the trickster. In some ways the trickster is comparable to the culture hero type of figure, who steals fire, light, water, or game; in fact, the trickster is often portrayed in this very role. Trickster stories seem also to be related to the stories of creation that feature two antagonistic creator figures, for the trickster often plays opposite a spiritual creator-deity. The antagonism is clear in many cases, for the trickster is not a deity or even a spiritual being, yet through his actions he reverses andthereby reorders creation. [*For further discussion, see* Tricksters, *overview article and article on* North American Tricksters.]

"Orpheus." Another story type widely known among the peoples native to North America is one which depicts the death of one member of a close male-female relationship. Usually it is the woman who dies. The grief-stricken survivor ignores the interdiction that the dead are unreachable by the living and he (or she) departs on a journey seeking the dead loved one. This journey is often long and arduous, yet the tenacity of the seeker finally pays off and the place of the dead is reached. Contact with the departed lover is often contingent upon tests the seeker must pass; success leads to contact and renewed joy and happiness. An agreement is usually made establishing the conditions under which the lover may be taken back to the world of the living. Often this is an agreement not to touch the dead person or to look back until the pair is once again among the living. Sometimes the seeker must agree to treat the lover kindly after they return and to never strike or offend her. Invariably, the conditions are for some reason—eagerness, carelessness, or curiosity—not kept, and the loved one immediately disappears to return to the dead, closing forever the possibility of the dead returning to life. This story type, widely known throughout the world, is commonly identified by a reference to Orpheus, the male character of the version of this story in classical mythology. It is a story about the finality of death, but also more broadly about the human condition.

Speech. The idea that speech is a creative force is commonly found in the stories of peoples native to North America. These peoples commonly hold the view that the appropriate tellings of stories are creative acts, that is, acts that perpetuate the creative ordering powers of which the stories tell. In some cases the power of thought and speech is identified with the power of creation, as in the Achomawi and Acoma stories of creation. For the Navajo, thought and speech are personified as important figures in the stories of creation; more significantly, as a pair their conjoined names signify the most profound and central element of Navajo religious thought.

PERFORMANCE OF MYTH

Native American languages, with some significant exceptions in the historical period, do not have a written counterpart to utterance. Therefore, to write and read myths is alien to Native American cultures. The stories are kept alive in the minds and hearts of the living members of the cultures, who bear the constant responsibility of preventing their loss. The telling of many of these stories is restricted to particular seasons, to appropriate occasions, and to those who are qualified and deserve to tell them; in some cases stories are said to be owned by certain members of a community. Stories may serve as authority for, as interpretation of, or as directions for the performance of ritual, or they may have little if any relationship to ritual practices. Many Native Americans are reluctant to permit stories to be recorded either in written or taped form. More than anything, this reluctance is based on the extent to which such recording processes truncate and thereby violate the living dimensions of a story tradition, in which the telling of stories is a creative and nourishing act. In comparison, a written text extracted from a culture is a lifeless shadow of a story "event," and is inherently prone to misunderstanding and misuse.

INTERPRETIVE APPROACHES

What do we or can we learn of the religion and culture of a tribe from its stories? What can be learned from these texts about the story process and its formation, development, history, and function? One view holds that such stories are a culture's means for expressing fundamental social, cultural, and religious values. Another view maintains that they express feelings and structures common to all human beings. Clearly, the same story types and motifs are found over extensive geographic areas and on several continents, among disparate culture types, value systems, worldviews, ecological conditions, and sustenance modes, thus limiting the possibilities for culture-specific analyses of stories at the level of type, motif, or theme. The study of mythology in North America faces many challenges and obstacles.

A number of strategies have been adopted to meet the difficulties facing the task of interpreting the mythologies of North America. The most widely practiced approach, to use mythology as a measuring device for the diffusion of culture, largely avoids the matter of interpretation. Diffusionist studies are concerned primarily with the incidence of tale types and motifs identified according to a system devised by Antii Aarne and Stith Thompson. These studies are premised on the proposition that when a given tale type and motif appears incontiguous geographic areas, it is more likely accounted for by diffusion from one area to the other than by independent origins. The great majority of the collections and comparative studies of the stories of North America have been made with a concern for using them as a scale by which to measure the diffusion of culture over space and through time. Franz Boas and his many students provided the chief impetus behind this kind of study throughout the early part of the twentieth century.

Most strategies for interpreting Native American mythology are based on propositions about the nature of mythology that are meant to apply universally. Various sociological and psychological functions of myth have been articulated by Malinowski, Durkheim, Jung, and others. While some notable studies of North American mythology have been based on these models, these approaches have had surprisingly little general impact on the study of North American mythology. While often valid and illuminating, such approaches limit interpretation to the functional perspective assumed.

While studies based on a proposed function of myth interpret the content of a text in the light of this function, a deeper level of analysis is sought in structural analyses of myth. Certainly the most widely known, but not the only form of structural study, is that articulated by Claude Lévi-Strauss. He demonstrates his analytical approach in several studies of North American mythology (including work on the Zuni, Tsimshian, Pawnee, and Winnebago tribes), although the bulk of his study of myth, published in the multivolume *Mythologiques* (4 vols., 1964–1971; translated into English as *Introduction to a Science of Mythology,* 4 vols., 1970–1981) centers on South America.

Lévi-Strauss holds that the substance of a myth is in the story that it tells, not in the identification of its motifs and themes. The meaning of a story is revealed by discerning the interrelationships among the story elements, that is, by analyzing the structure of the story. This analysis is based on his proposition that mythical thought always progresses from the awareness of fundamental oppositions toward their resolution. For Lévi-Strauss the structural study of myths is focused on the discovery of the values shared among the elements of a story—elements that align in a pattern reflecting the fundamental binary opposition that the story serves to mediate. [*For further discussion of Lévi-Straus's work, see* Ge Mythology *and* Structuralism.]

Another form of structural analysis directed toward the study of North American mythology is presented by Alan Dundes in his *The Morphology of the North American Indian Folktales* (1964). Developing upon V. I. Propp's classic work, *Morphology of the Folktale* (1928). Dundes identifies the motifs of stories in terms of their intent or value (such as lack, lack liquidated, interdiction, and violation). One can describe and typologize the structures of stories in terms of these constituents, thus permitting study, comparison, and analysis of mythology in terms not restricted to simple content identity.

In the last quarter-century there have been developments in the study of mythology that are directed toward a deeper interpretation of the texts of stories, enhanced where possible by consideration of the details of particular storytelling events including the native languages in which the stories are told. This approach attempts to demonstrate that Native American mythology is equivalent to literature and that its texts should be studied with as much effort and theoretical concern as any literature. But this approach also goes further by recognizing that a key difference between literature and mythology is that mythology, by its nature, is told; it is exclusively oral, and therefore it must be studied as a social and cultural event as well as a text.

Dell Hymes has made a range of important contributions to this development of the study of North American mythology, working primarily with materials from Northwest Coast tribes. Hymes has effectively demonstrated that the free translations of stories, the "texts" that we often use, are frequently radically different from the stories as originally told. Subsequently directing his analysis to the native language texts, he shows that we cannot comprehend the deeper levels of their meaning if we are not aware of the untranslatable linguistic markers, repetitious language, tense, and other features, which are often observable only when considering the story in the language in which it is told and as it is actually told. He has also called attention to the different ways in which a story may be performed, from an outline demonstration of a story for an outside inquirer to a full performance including many elements of style, such as gesture, facial expression, timing, articulation, and voicing. Consideration of the elements of performance should include such features as the motivation for the storytelling, the relationship between a raconteur and the audience, the audience's reaction, and the expected and actual effects of the telling. Hymes describes his approach as listening to the text in all its details while looking for covariation in its form and meaning.

Based on almost any criteria, mythology is important to the study of religion, and the study of Native American religions is no exception. The study of the religious aspects of Native American mythology has scarcely begun within the academic study of religion. The potential for and importance of such a study is significant.

BIBLIOGRAPHY

For basic bibliographies and sample anthologies of North American mythology, see *Tales of the North American Indians,* edited by Stith Thompson (Cambridge, Mass., 1929), and Charles Haywood's *A Bibliography of North American Folklore and Folksong,* vol. 2, *The American Indians North of Mexico, Including the Eskimos,* 2d rev. ed. (New York, 1961). Important and representative studies focusing on the geographical incidence and diffusion of tales are Antti Aarne's *The Types of the Folk-Tale,* translated by Stith Thompson (Helsinki, 1928); Franz Boas's *Tsimshian Texts* (Washington, D.C., 1902); and Gladys A. Reichard's "Literary Types and Dissemination of Myths," *Journal of American Folklore* 34 (1921): 269–307. Gudmund Hatt collected North American Corn Woman stories and compared them with Indonesian stories about the Rice Mother in his "The Corn Mother in America and in Indonesia," *Anthropos* 46 (1951): 853–914. In "The Creation Myths of the North American Indians," *Anthropos* 52 (1957): 497–508, Anita Birgitta Rooth typologized three hundred texts and charted their geographic incidence in order to propose diffusion patterns from Asia to America. Her analysis is somewhat refuted by the evidence presented in Erminie Wheeler-Voegelin and Remedios Moore's "The Emergence Myth in Native North America," in *Studies in Folklore,* edited by Winthrop E. Richmond (Bloomington, Ind., 1957). Alan Dundes's "Earth-Diver: Creation of the Mythopoeic Male," *American Anthropologist* 64 (1962): 1032–1051, presents a psychological perspective on earth-diver mythology. Interpretations of trickster mythology are found in C. G. Jung's "On the Psychology of the Trickster Figure," in *The Trickster,* edited by Paul Radin (1956; New York, 1969); and in Mac Linscott Ricketts's "The North American Indian Trickster," *History of Religions* 5 (Winter 1966): 327–350. Åke Hultkrantz's *The North American Indian Orpheus Tradition* (Stockholm, 1957) is an expansive study of a single tale type.

Valuable accounts of the study of Native American mythology are Franz Boas's "Mythology and Folk-Tales of the North American Indians," in *Anthropology in North America,* edited by Franz Boas et al. (New York, 1915), pp. 306–349; Alan Dundes's "North American Indian Folklore Studies," *Journal de la Société des Américanistes* 56 (1967): 53–79; and Åke Hultkrantz's "Myths in Native American Religions," in *Native Religious Traditions,* edited by Earle H. Waugh and K. Dad Prithipaul (Waterloo, Ont., Canada, 1979), pp. 77–97.

Clyde Kluckhohn's "Myths and Rituals: A General Theory," *Harvard Theological Review* 35 (1942): 45–79, is an important theoretical discussion of the interrelationship of myth and ritual, which is illustrated by Navajo mythology.

For Claude Lévi-Strauss's study of North American mythology, see "The Structural Study of Myth," *Journal of American Folklore* 68 (1955): 428–444, reprinted in his *Structural Anthropology* (Garden City, N.Y., 1963), pp. 206–231, which focuses on Zuni mythology as an illustrative case; "La geste d'Asdiwal," in *L'annuaire, 1958–1959,* issued by the École Pratique des Hautes Études, Section des Sciences Religieuses (Paris, 1958), pp. 3–43, later published in English translation accompanied by several important critically evaluative articles in *The Structural Study of Myth and Totemism,* edited by Edmund Leach (London, 1967).

Alan Dundes's structural approach is developed in his book *The Morphology of North American Indian Folktales* (Helsinki, 1964) and is presented more briefly in his "Structural Typology of North American Indian Folktales," *Southwestern Journal of Anthropology* 19 (1963): 121–130.

Fortunately, many of the important articles by Dell Hymes have appeared together in a collection entitled *"In Vain I Tried to Tell You": Essays in Native American Ethnopoetics* (Philadelphia, 1981). Essays by Barre Toelken, Dennis Tedlock, and others who are also developing a more literary and contextual study of the Native American oral tradition can be found in *Traditional Literatures of the American Indian,* edited by Karl Kroeber (Lincoln, Nebr., 1981).

17 TRICKSTERS

MAC LINSCOTT RICKETTS

The most prominent and popular personage, generally speaking, in the varied oral traditions of the numerous Amerindian peoples living north of the Rio Grande is the figure known as the trickster. Although the trickster may be spoken of in the singular as a type, there are in fact many tricksters, of whom a great variety of stories is told across the North American continent. Some are purely tricksters, but the most significant and central mythic figure in many tribes is a trickster who is also the tribe's culture hero and the creator (usually by transformation) of the present world order. Sometimes he is the maker of the earth and its beings, or alternately the co-creator, often antagonistic to the principal creator.

With rare exceptions, North American tricksters are beings of the mythic age only; they are not believed to be living gods or spirits, and they have no cult (other than the semiritualistic narration of their stories). Their relationship to shamanism, the definitive religious form in most of the region, is debated. Tricksters' activities in myths often resemble shamans' journeys to the spirit world, but tricksters ordinarily employ no "helpers," and shamans do not seek help from "trickster spirits." Although a history of oral traditions can be only a matter of speculation, it appears that the trickster figure belongs to a very ancient stratum of Indian mythology, since certain universally disseminated motifs, such as the theft of fire and the origin of death, are regularly attributed to him.

The concept of the trickster as a type is based upon his most essential trait: his trickiness. Tricksters everywhere are deceitful, cunning, amoral, sexually hyperactive, taboo-breaking, voracious, thieving, adventurous, vainglorious—yet not truly evil or malicious—and always amusing and undaunted. Even though his activities are usually motivated by ungoverned desire, the trickster is capable of performing deeds that benefit others: releasing imprisoned game, the sun, the tides, and such; vanquishing and/or transforming evil monsters; and, like the shaman, journeying to the land of the spirits or the dead to rescue a lost loved one. The significant element in all these deeds is trickery. But the trickster's tricks are not considered evil: as a weak "animal-person" or mere human in a world of strange animals and spirit beings, the trickster must use strategy to survive. Moreover, as a being of insatiable appetites (for food and sex), he cannot afford the luxury of scruples. Thus he breaks incest taboos (rapes or marries in disguise his daughter or mother-in-law) and hoodwinks

167

small animals into dancing with eyes closed so he can kill them. His overweening pride prevents him from asking for help, or from acknowledging it when he receives it, and leads him into countless misadventures. Often behaving like a fool and coming to grief, he reacts invariably with buoyant good humor, refusing to accept defeat. Nothing is sacred in his eyes: all holy institutions may be mocked or mimicked with impunity by the trickster. Shamanism, especially, seems parodied in such continent-wide stories as those of a trickster's flight with geese or on the back of a buzzard, ending in his crashing to earth, often being fragmented, and his laughing it all off as a big joke.

In addition to humorous trickster folk tales, which are remarkably similar all over North America, each region has its own set of traditions about the mythic age, and in a majority of instances the leading personage of that time was a trickster.

Raven is the dominant mythic figure all along the Alaskan and Canadian Pacific coast. Some tribes attribute to him the creation of the land (e.g., by dropping pebbles on the water), probably following a world flood. The central myth of the Raven cycle is about his theft of the sun, which was being kept in a box by a "powerful chief." Making himself a tiny particle in the drinking water of the chief's daughter, Raven contrives to be reborn as a baby in the chief's house. He cries for the box and is given it, whereupon he resumes his raven form and flies away, bringing light to the world. (Theft of the sun is a mythic theme found over much of North America, attributed almost always to the principal trickster or to a group of animals headed by him.)

In the Plateau region of the northwestern United States, Coyote is usually regarded as the maker or procreator of the people, sometimes using the body of a river monster he kills, sometimes by cohabitation with trees after a flood. His principal cycle concerns his release of the salmon and his subsequent journey up the Columbia River, leading the salmon. He demands a "wife" at each village, and if his request is granted, he makes that place a good fishing spot. The cycle is prefaced with a tale of jealousy, lust, and deceit. Coyote, desiring his son's two wives, treacherously and magically causes his son to be taken into the sky world. Coyote pretends to be his son while the son in the sky is gaining supernatural powers, unbeknownst to Coyote. Later the son returns, reclaims his wives, and takes revenge by causing his father to fall into the river and be carried away. Thus Coyote arrives at the mouth of the river where the salmon are kept; by turning himself into a baby, he tricks the women who keep them and releases them to swim upstream.

In California and the Great Basin region, Coyote usually is involved in a dualistic relationship with a wise, benevolent creator (Eagle, Fox, Wolf, or an anthropomorphic figure). Set against the backdrop of a world flood (or fire), the earth is remade and repopulated by the two, with Coyote ordaining the "bad" things such as mountains, storms, and fruit growing out of reach. Coyote decrees death—and then his son is the first to die. So Coyote establishes mourning rites for people to "enjoy." He also decrees conception by sex and painful childbirth. Here and in the Plateau, where "spirit helpers" were commonplace in everyday life, Coyote too has his "helpers": two chunks of excrement that he voids when in need of advice, but to which he always replies, "Just what I was going to do anyway!"

The Paiute and Shoshoni of the Great Basin consider Coyote the progenitor of the people (through intercourse with a mysterious woman following the flood). But among the Pueblo, whose mythology centers on an emergence from the underground, Coyote plays a rather minor role in most tribes. The Navajo assign him a larger part than the others: he causes the flood that necessitates the emergence; then he scatters the stars in the sky haphazardly, ordains death, and establishes sex. On the Great Plains, Coyote is known primarily as a trickster only. Some northern tribes credit him with the re-creation of the earth after the deluge, and the Kiowa consider themselves the people of Sendah, a Coyote-like figure, who led them out of a hollow log in the beginning. Inktomi ("spider") of the Lakota is very similar to Coyote, except in the unique esoteric traditions reported from the Oglala Lakota. Here he is a veritable "fallen angel," who caused the first human family to be banished from their subterranean paradise and who subsequently induced the whole human race to emerge onto the earth by making them think life here would be better. The Oglala are one of the few groups in North America who consider the trickster genuinely evil, and almost the only tribe that believes the trickster to be a living spirit.

Hare, the chief trickster in the poorly preserved traditions of the Indians of the Southeast, seems not to be implicated in the emergence-origin traditions of these tribes. Rather, he is a culture hero (stealing the sun, fire, and such; transforming monsters), and he is the bungling rival of the youthful "blood-clot boy," a pure hero type. Siouan-speaking peoples seem to have brought a tradition of Rabbit stories to the Great Plains when they migrated there from the Southeast. Their Rabbit or Hare is a precocious boy, living with his grandmother, who by his foolish and/or heroic deeds makes the world habitable, as it is today. He is not, however, credited with any demiurgic activities.

The Algonquins, inhabiting a large part of eastern and midwestern Canada, New England, and the area around the three western Great Lakes, have mythologies centered on anthropomorphic culture heroes who were also tricksters, though seldom foolish, plus several minor theriomorphic tricksters. The leading figures are Gluskabe in Maine, Tcikapis in northern Quebec, and Manabush and Wisakejak (various spellings) in the most westerly tribes. The few Tcikapis tales recorded show him a monster-killing dwarf, whose greatest exploit was the snaring of the sun. Gluskabe, Manabush, and Wisakejak have much in common: they live with their grandmother and younger brother, Wolf—who is abducted and killed by water monsters and must be rescued and revived by the hero. (A remarkably similar tale is told of Coyote and Wolf far to the west, in the Great Basin.) The myth has been elaborated in the esoteric traditions of the Midewiwin, a secret curing society of the western Algonquins. Some investigators report a vague belief that the hero of this myth lives now somewhere in the north. The neighboring Iroquois make no place for their trickster, S'hodieonskon, in their dualistic creation myth.

In some tribes humorous trickster tales are relegated to a category apart from the more serious "myths," but because all these narratives are set in "myth times," they are never confused with quasi-historical legends or accounts of shamanic experiences. Thus, to some degree, a quality of sacredness adheres to the person of the trickster everywhere, despite the seemingly profane nature of many of the narratives.

The oral traditions of North America present a variety of combinations of trickster traits with others (culture hero, demiurge, etc.); but all are reducible to the idea of a being who lives by his wits and his wit, who represents a mythical perception of man making his cosmos and finding a place within it.

[See also North American Religions, article on Mythic Themes.]

BIBLIOGRAPHY

The term *trickster* was coined by Daniel G. Brinton in his *Myths of the New World* (Philadelphia, 1868). The only serious study of the American trickster to have been published in book form remains Paul Radin's *The Trickster* (1956; reprint, New York, 1969), which contains important essays by C. G. Jung and Karl Kerényi. It is not, however, a general study of tricksters in North America, but is mainly about those of the Winnebago tribe. My article "The North American Indian Trickster," *History of Religions* 5 (Winter, 1966): 327–350, is based on an earlier work, "The Structure and Religious Significance of the Trickster–Transformer–Culture Hero in the Mythology of the North American Indians" (Ph.D. diss., University of Chicago, 1965), which is a study of the entire continent north of the Rio Grande. Edward H. Piper sees the trickster as basically a child figure in his psychological analysis, "A Dialogical Study of the North American Trickster Figure and the Phenomenon of Play" (Ph.D. diss., University of Chicago, 1975). Laura Makarius has written several articles on tricksters from various parts of the world, viewing the trickster as a taboo-breaking magician; on the North American trickster, see her study "The Crime of Manabozo," *American Anthropologist* 75 (1973): 663–675. Barbara Babcock-Abrahams has published an interesting anthropological study, "'A Tolerated Margin of Mess': The Trickster and His Tales Reconsidered," *Journal of the American Folklore Institute* 2 (1975): 147–186. A recent popular collection of trickster stories, without significant interpretation, is by Barry Holstun Lopez: *Giving Birth to Thunder, Sleeping with His Daughter: Coyote Builds North America* (Kansas City, 1977). See also the February 1979 issue of *Parabola* (4, no. 1), which is devoted to the trickster. For the texts of the stories, one must resort to the hundreds of volumes of reports of pioneer American anthropologists published by the Bureau of American Ethnology, the American Folk-lore Society, and other organizations.

18 DRAMA

William K. Powers

In all regions of North America, indigenous peoples practiced various public rituals for the purpose of communicating with the supernatural spirits and powers that controlled their universe. The most ubiquitous and theatrical form of the dramatic performance was dance in which actors wore elaborate costumes and masks representing the supernatural beings they sought to appease. These dance dramas often involved a special performance area that included entrances and exits for the performers; a chorus of singers and dancers; principal dancers; scenic backdrops; special lighting effects; and, most importantly, plots revolving around myths of creation and supernatural beings and powers who were perceived to inhabit the everyday world. These dance dramas were characterized by masquerade, imitation, role reversal, burlesque, and reenactments of myths and personal visions.

American Indians relied greatly on their ability to mime the behaviors of those animals and birds that were important to their religious life. The environment played a great role in ritual performance, which was grounded empirically in knowledge of the seasons, flora, and fauna. As might be expected, hunters chose to emulate in their dances those animals that were important to their survival, while farmers performed rituals that focused on the agricultural cycle.

Dance drama was performed to the accompaniment of vocal music sung by an individual or chorus. The songs might contain meaningful text, sometimes short phrases that poetically captured the theme of the dance, or meaningless vocables that despite their lack of semantics were highly structured both melodically and rhythmically. The range of native musical instruments in North America was comparatively limited. Various sizes and shapes of drums served as the major accompaniment to song in all regions. Rhythmic patterns were characterized mainly by single unaccented beats, duple accented beats, and accented triplets. Only in the Pueblo Southwest do we find a highly structured sense of rhythm, particularly in some of the mimetic animal and bird dances, in which there is a perfect correspondence between song, drum, and dance steps without benefit of measured beats in the strict Western sense of time. [*See* Music, *article on* Music and Religion in the Americas.]

Costumes were both realistic and stylized. On the Plains, a Buffalo dancer would dress in the hides of a bull, complete with a headdress of horns, a robe over his shoulders, leggings made from the hairless part of the hide, and a buffalo tail hanging conspicuously from his waist. Similarly, Eagle dancers of the Pueblo Southwest soared gracefully in the dance plaza wearing costumes made from eagle feathers topped with a headdress representing the bald eagle's crown and golden beak. But in the Northwest Coast region, where wood sculpture reached its highest aesthetic form in all of North America, intricately carved masks, made to be manipulated by strings revealing masks within masks, and carved and painted dance houses and scenery frequently featured stylized representations of ravens, whales, bears, and other animals and birds significant to the coastal culture. [*See also* Iconography, *article on* Native American Iconography.]

All ritual performances were for the benefit of the general public as well as the principal performers, and all performances required a specially constructed performance area. Frequently, the public part of the performance represented only a small part of a longer ritual that sometimes took several days or weeks. For example, among the Lakota on the Great Plains, the vision quest was regarded as a personal and private form of mediation and propitiation. However, it was necessary for a medicine man to interpret the candidates' visions. Frequently, in order to legitimate the experiences, the supplicants were directed to reenact their visions before the entire village. This reenactment took the form of imitation of various animals or birds that had informed them, and appropriate costumes representing the buffalo, wolf, elk, bear, or eagle were worn.

On a larger scale, Plains Indians performed the Sun Dance collectively, after individual dancers had participated in private vision quests. An integral part of the ceremony, the elements of which were widely diffused to nearly all Plains tribes, was the erection of the medicine lodge, or sacred arbor, in which the performance occurred. Dancers wore special costumes including long kilts, necklaces representing sunflowers, and wreaths of sage around their wrists, ankles, and forehead. The segments of the dance in which the Sun was propitiated were directed by the Sun Dance leader. The performance lasted for several days and was accompanied by other intrusive dances prior to going on the buffalo hunt. [*For further discussion, see* Sun Dance.]

The Kwakiutl of the Northwest Coast were unsurpassed as dramatists with a full sense of lighting, scenery, costumes, and plot. The dance dramas were presented in cycles and depicted the kidnapping of the hero by a spirit who bestowed supernatural power upon him before returning the hero to the village. The hero was most frequently possessed by a "cannibal spirit" and therefore craved human flesh. In the reenactment, a frenzied hero was led back into the dance house by villagers and fed flesh believed to have been taken from a human corpse, although more likely it was animal meat. The dance house was replete with trap doors and tunnels, and performers could quickly appear and disappear magically. The dancers wore huge masks with movable parts, some representing the large beak of a bird, through which the dancers cried out "Eat! Eat!" Hollow stems hidden beneath the floor were used as microphones through which the voices of the actors could emanate from any part of the house. Dolls strung on ropes partly obscured by the dim firelight flew through the air for dramatic effect. Finally, the principal dancer, believing he had consumed human flesh, calmed down to end the event gracefully.

In the Northeast, the best-known Iroquoian sodality was the False Faces. The society was formed when a supernatural being called False Face appeared to the Iroquois in the form of detached faces and taught them the art of curing. The elaborate masks were carved and painted in grotesque ways, and when worn by the society, members were believed to frighten away malevolent spirits that caused sickness. The mask was carved from a living tree and was painted red or black depending on whether the carver began work in the morning or afternoon. Noses, mouths, and eye holes were twisted and contorted, and long shocks of horsehair fell over the wearer's shoulders. The False Faces performed during the midwinter festivals on the New York and Canadian reservations. Additionally, they visited every Iroquois house in fall and spring in order to exorcise evil spirits. Wearing the masks and tattered clothing, the False Faces carried turtle shell rattles and hickory sticks. When someone had contracted a disease over which the False Faces had power, the leader of the society was informed, and the troop of False Faces appeared at the patient's house, striking and rubbing their rattles against the house as they entered. Once inside they sang and danced, accompanied by the shaking of rattles. Some of the dancers would scoop up hot embers from the fire and blow them on the patient in order to cure him.

In the Great Lakes area the ritual of the Midewiwin was enacted by the Ojibwa and other central Algonquians. Translated as "Great Medicine Society," the Mide (the shortened form of the name) held its meetings once a year in a special lodge resembling a large wigwam varying in length from one hundred to two hundred feet and in width from thirteen to thirty feet. In height it was seven to ten feet with an open apex that was covered with cattail mats and birchbark during inclement weather.

The Midewiwin was a membership organization, and people were admitted on the basis of application, of having a suitable dream, or by replacing a deceased relative who had been a member. Both men and women could join, and the religious leaders of the Mide were elected by its membership. The main annual functions were initiatory, and curing rites were conducted by carefully trained Mide shamans.

The Mide priests determined which candidates would be accepted into the society, and candidates were expected to pay for the rites of initiation, which included knowledge of the myths, rituals, songs, and remedies of the society. All ceremonies had originated in revelations and were carefully transcribed on birchbark scrolls with a bone stylus and handed down pictographically from generation to generation.

The initiation rite was the most dramatic. The candidates knelt on mats surrounded by four posts inside the medicine lodge. Two members held the candidates' shoulders, while four others thrust their medicine bags at them. As the four leaders approached, the candidates were overcome by the power of the leaders' spirits and fell lifeless to the ground. When revived, each candidate spat out a small cowrie shell called *migis*, which was the sacred emblem of the Mide. The initiator then offered the shell to the four directions and sky after which it magically disappeared again into the candidate's body, and the candidate was fully resuscitated. All members were required to attend meetings once a year for the renewal of their spiritual powers, but smaller gatherings could be held for the treatment of the sick, singing songs, and strengthening their belief in the power of the Mide. A feast was an inseparable part of all Mide functions.

One of the most important ceremonies of the Southeast was the Green Corn Dance, a celebration of the harvesting of one of the major food staples of North America. Known among the Creek as the Busk (from the Creek word *puskita*, "to fast"), the ceremony of first fruits took place in August. The Busk was actually an aggregation of different ceremonies, including the drinking of *Ilex cassine*, or "black drink," used as an emetic to purge the participants and purify themselves. A sacred fire was built, and young initiates had their flesh scratched to make them brave. Both men and women performed various dances including the Stomp dance, which was performed in a serpentine pattern by a line of alternating men and women. The women wore turtle-shell shakers around their knees that accompanied the antiphonal singing of the group. At the end of the Busk, the various clans participated in a stickball game that marked the conclusion of the ceremony. Variations of the Green Corn Dance were found also among the Seminole, Cherokee, Choctaw, Chickasaw, and Yuchi of the Southeast, as well as among other tribes where corn was cultivated.

The Southwest is where the highest concentration of dance drama is found not only with the elaborate agricultural rituals of the Pueblos, but with the various curing rituals, puberty ceremonies, and mimetic animal dances. Literally hundreds of these rituals were performed by the Navajo, Apache, and Pueblo peoples each year. In many cases native rituals are still held in conjunction with feasts of the Catholic church. All provide colorful spectacles equal to any of the religious pageants of North America and Europe.

The Hopi of Arizona perform a number of masked dances on their mesas. The *kachina* dances, named after the spirits of the dead, are the most intriguing. The Hopi believe that in mythological times the *kachina*s came from their homes in the West to bring them rain and to ensure them long and happy lives. Later, the *kachina*s showed the people how to make masks and costumes and taught them their songs and dances with the understanding that if the people performed the ceremonies correctly, the supernaturals would continue to bring prosperity to the villages. There are over 250 named *kachina* spirits among the Hopi, each represented by a different mask and costume. It is believed that the men who impersonate the spirits at the *kachina* performances become the spirits they represent. Women and uninitiated youth are not supposed to know that the *kachina* dancers are really their clansmen. At each performance the *kachina*s bring gifts for the children and place them in the center of the village plaza. The *kachina* dances are performed during the first half of the year, when their appearance is supposed to ensure the successful planting of crops. The ceremonies represent intense periods of ritual performance in which all men and women in the village undergo instruction in their faith. It is also a time when the people entertain their spiritual benefactors.

At the time of the summer solstice, the Niman dance is performed in which all the *kachina*s appear en masse before the villagers who thank the supernaturals for the gift of a good harvest. It is believed that the *kachina*s then leave to return to their homes. When they return to their homes, they visit the dead, who are performing rituals of the winter solstice while similar ceremonies are being performed by the living during the summer.

In New Mexico among the Zuni the Shalako ceremony is held in November or December each year. Six dancers are dressed to represent giant birds, the messengers of the rain gods, with conical costumes attached to their waists measuring in height from ten to twelve feet. They have birdlike faces complete with beaks that are movable, protruding eyes, and upcurved tapered horns. At midnight, they enter special houses that have been built for their performance. They utter birdlike calls and clack their beaks in rapid succession. They dance and make speeches telling the people to pray for an abundant harvest and long lives for the villagers.

The Shalako dancers are joined in their ritual by the ten Koyemshi, or "Mud-heads," the children of a legendary incestuous union. These impersonators are appointed by the Zuni priests to serve for one year and are then free from further duties for another four years. The Koyemshi entertain at all public rituals when the *kachina*s are away from the village by providing comic, and sometimes obscene, interludes between the more serious dances. Sometimes they play Euroamerican games such as beanbag. The jokes, puns, and riddles that they cry out to the villagers are filled with scatalogical references, and they play pranks and make obscene jokes about the most respected and sacred aspects of Zuni religion. In this manner they make moral and ethical points by burlesquing those institutions and individuals with whom people come in contact every day. They also burlesque their most sacred beliefs through vulgar references that strongly contrast with appropriate Zuni behavior. For the duration of the ritual, the onlookers participate vicariously in what is temporarily socially approved behavior.

The Koyemshi appear as ludicrous figures. They wear formless baglike cotton masks that have bumps or knobs protruding from them. The knobs are filled with raw cotton seeds and earth or dust taken from the footprints made by the people in the streets around the village. Sometimes feathers are tied to the knobs, and the lower part of the mask is tied to the knobs with black cotton in scarflike fashion. Under the scarf they wear a small bag containing squash, corn, and gourd seeds. Their masks and bodies are painted with pink clay that comes from the sacred lake. These clowns also wear black homespun kilts, and the leader adds to his kilt a black tunic worn over his right shoulder. As is true with the Hopi, the Zuni dancers and clowns serve to underscore the religious values of the society by occasionally emphasizing the absurd. [*See* Clowns.]

Nearby in Arizona and parts of New Mexico and Oklahoma, numerous bands of Apache perform a ceremony used variously as a puberty ceremony, or to cure illness and avert catastrophe. The Mountain Spirits dance, or Gahan, as it is properly known, is an essential feature of the female puberty ceremony, in which the young initiate ritually represents White Painted Woman, the divine mother of the Apache culture hero, or in some cases, Mother Earth. The Apache believe that performance of the ritual brings good fortune to the initiate, her family, and to the entire tribe.

In this ceremony four male dancers represent the four directions, or Mountain Spirits, powerful supernatural beings who act as intermediaries between humans and the Great Spirit. The initiate is secluded in a special lodge. She is painted and dressed by a woman of impeccable reputation who also has received a vision from the White Painted Woman. Each day a male singer sings appropriate songs for her. Each night the masked dancers appear in spectacular and grotesque costumes. They are dressed and painted by a shaman in a special brush arbor before the evening ceremonies begin. The shaman paints their bodies with designs representing the sun, moon, lightning, planets, rain, and rainbow. After being painted and instructed, the dancers line up facing east. They then spin clockwise, spit four times into their headdresses, and put them on after feigning this action three times. A fire is made in the ceremonial lodge by rubbing sticks together, and each night the masked dancers enter the lodge and dance around the lodge in a prescribed manner. They wear wooden headdresses shaped like huge rainbows projecting from their black-hooded faces. Yellow buckskin kilts are tied from their waist, cuffed by long fringed boots. They carry wooden swords in each hand, and as they dance in rigid, angular patterns, bending and crouching in near- balletic movements, they slap their swords vigorously against their thighs and legs. On the fourth night, the candidate joins the dancers dressed in a yellow buckskin fringed dress with designs like those of the masked dancers. At the end of the four days, the young woman scatters pollen over the people who were brought to her to receive her blessings.

The Apache regard the dance as particularly powerful, and each of the aspects of the dance must be done properly lest harm befall the tribe. If the dance is not executed properly, it is believed that the dancers may have trouble with their eyes and noses, their faces will swell, or paralysis will set in.

Among one of the most vivid ritual performances of the Navajo of the Four Corners region of the Southwest is the Yeibichai, also known as Night Chant. The word *yeibichai* is partly a corruption of the Zuni word for "spirit" plus the Navajo term for "maternal grandfather," hence it literally means "grandfather of the gods." The ceremony was handed down by supernaturals and was thought to be particularly efficacious in curing both psychosomatic and somatic disorders, especially insanity, deafness, or paralysis.

The ritual is sponsored by one man and his clan relatives in winter and is performed outdoors on a barren plateau. A sacred hogan is built at the west and a brush arbor shelter for the dancers at the east. Between the two a row of bonfires is built.

The ceremony takes nine days, the first eight being composed of secret ceremonies, and the last day, a public performance. In the dance the Grandfather of the Gods is personified by the lead dancer, who wears buckskin hunting clothes. The other dancers wear masks and kilts and resemble Pueblo *kachinas*.

The ritual specialist in charge of the Yeibichai is the chanter, a person who has chosen to learn the sacred ritual. He pays to be taught and studies for many years learning by rote every detail. During this time he collects sacred objects such as prayer sticks, herbs, turquoise, white shell, abalone, and jet, which he will use in his ceremonies. The specialist also may learn a few lesser rites plus the Blessingway, a ritual that must follow every other ritual to atone for any possible mistakes in them.

During the first four days, the patient and his relatives purify themselves by sweating and taking emetics. The patient and the chanter pray to the supernaturals to aid them in the ceremony. Each supernatural must be named in the proper order lest misfortune befall them. The chanter sings sacred songs and administers potions and sacred pollen to help rid the patient of evil forces.

During the next four days, the chanter and helpers coax the supernaturals into the ritual area by constructing sand paintings of them. The final power will arrive when pollen has been sprinkled on the sand painting. In these paintings, male divinities are represented as having round heads, while females have square heads. The *yeis*, as these male and female divinities are called, are pictured as standing on clouds or lightning and guarded by rainbows. The completed painting forms an altar sometimes ranging in width from four to eighteen feet.

Next, the patients are bathed and dried with cornmeal and painted with the symbols of the supernaturals. They are then brought into the hogan to receive power from the supernaturals represented in the sand painting. Sand from various parts of the painted figures is pressed against their ailing parts, and they are made one with the supernaturals and share their power. Finally the sand is swept up so that it may not be contaminated. The Navajo word for the design means the "going away of the group" and the design itself is regarded as a temporary visit from the supernaturals. On the ninth night, both the chanter and the patient must stay awake until dawn while the power increases in them. The Yeibichai impersonators are dressed in grotesque masks and decorated kilts with as many turquoise and silver necklaces, bracelets, and bow guards as they can put on. They spend the night publicly dancing and singing. The patients must not sleep until sunset, when they enter the sacred hogan and stay there for four nights. The rite is ceremonially concluded with the Bluebird Song, sung in honor of the bird of the dawn that brings promise and happiness.

Although most dance dramas were performed by groups of singers and dancers, the Deer Dance of the Yaqui of the Southwest is a unique solo performance. The Yaqui believed that the deer had the power to cure or cause illness and also to bring thunder, lightning, and rain. Dancing to the deer deity also ensured food and fecundity for the people and animals.

A religious pageant announcing the Deer Dance, which took place just before Easter, was suddenly interrupted by the presence of four to six dancers and four singers striking gourds with sticks to create a rasping sound. All dancers were naked from the waist up and wore grotesque masks representing human faces. The lead dancer, however, wore small deer antlers attached to his head and a cocoon rattle, six to eight feet in length and filled with pebbles, wrapped around one leg.

The lead dancer performed most of the Deer Dance alone. His movements mimicked that of the deer with great realism, his head moving quickly and erratically from side to side as if he had picked up the scent of danger. His feet scratched the earth before he quickly bolted upward, leaping gracefully over some imaginary barrier. Then, as the dance came to a close, the dancer became hunter and hunted, imitating the actions of a man with bow and arrow carefully stalking his prey. Letting fly the arrow that mortally wounded him, he fell to the ground quivering as he breathed his last.

BIBLIOGRAPHY

Densmore, Frances. *Chippewa Music*. Bulletin of the Bureau of American Ethnology, no. 45. Washington, D.C., 1910. A classic work on the Chippewa with detailed discussion of the Midewiwin.

Densmore, Frances. *Yuman and Yaqui Music*. Bulletin of the Bureau of American Ethnology, no. 110. Washington, D.C., 1932. A good description of the Yaqui Deer Dance.

Drucker, Philip. *Indians of the Northwest Coast*. Garden City, N.Y., 1955. A discussion of various tribes of the Pacific Northwest with some emphasis on material culture and ritual drama.

Kurath, Gertrude P. *Iroquois Music and Dance: Ceremonial Arts of Two Seneca Longhouses*. Bulletin of the Bureau of American Ethnology, no. 187. Washington, D.C., 1964. A description of music and choreographic patterns of numerous Iroquoian rituals including the False Face society.

Ortiz, Alfonso, ed. *New Perspectives on the Pueblos*. Albuquerque, 1972. The section entitled "Ritual Drama and Pueblo World View," by Ortiz, himself an anthropologist and Pueblo, is one of the best theoretical introductions to ritual drama.

Powers, William K. *Oglala Religion*. Lincoln, Nebr., 1977. Includes a description and analysis of the vision quest, sweat lodge, and Sun Dance of the Lakota Indians of the Great Plains.

Powers, William K. *Sacred Language: The Nature of Supernatural Discourse in Lakota*. Norman, Okla., 1986. Contains descriptions and illustrations of various animal impersonators among the Lakota.

Reichard, Gladys A. *Navaho Religion*. New York, 1950. Perhaps the best work ever done on Navajo symbolism.

Roediger, Virginia More. *Ceremonial Costumes of the Pueblo Indians*. Berkeley, 1941. An excellent illustrated book of ceremonial costumes, including those described for the Hopi and Zuni.

Tyler, Hamilton A. *Pueblo Gods and Myths*. Norman, Okla., 1964. A good historical background to the Pueblo with an emphasis on cosmology and worldview.

Underhill, Ruth M. *Red Man's Religion*. Chicago, 1965. Although stylistically dated and somewhat patronizing, there are excellent descriptions of ritual drama from most parts of native North America.

19 ICONOGRAPHY

Armin W. Geertz

Iconography is a living force in North American Indian religious life, past and present. Rooted in mythical imagery, it informs the content of individual dreams and nourishes the themes of contemporary Indian art. A study of the iconography of a people provides a unique opportunity to gain insight into what Werner Müller calls the "pictorial world of the soul" (*Die Religionen der Waldlandindianer Nordamerikas,* Berlin, 1956, p. 57).

The following exposition of the major themes of religious iconography in North America is restricted to the evidence of the late-nineteenth and twentieth century of ethnographic research. As a result, the beautiful pottery and stone remains of the prehistoric peoples of the Southwest and Southeast are not represented here, nor are the remains of the Mound Builder cultures of the river regions.

The iconographical themes follow the general lines of myth and religious beliefs. As such, they can be cataloged in the following manner: the cosmos, supreme beings, tricksters/culture heroes, guardian beings, other mythic beings, astronomical beings, weather beings, animal beings, vegetation beings, human beings, geological beings, and abstract symbols. But it is not always the case that the verbal images of the myths are equivalent to iconographical images: one notorious example of divergence is the Ojibwa trickster, Rabbit, who, when pictured, is actually human in form.

Concerning the wide variety of media used, the following general distribution can be observed: in the Far North—ivory, bone, and stone; the Northeast and Southeast Woodlands—wood, bark, skin, quillwork, and beadwork; the Plains—skin, beadwork, pipestone, quillwork, and painting of bodies and horses; the Northwest Coast—cedar, ivory, argillite, blankets, and copper; California—baskets and some stone; the Southwest—sand painting, wood, stone, baskets, pottery, jewelry, and dolls.

THE COSMOS

Cosmologies vary from tribe to tribe in both content and imagery. But whereas the mythical image of the universe (its cosmography) may be highly detailed, the iconographical rendering is necessarily restricted. The cosmos is most often graphically limited to those elements that characterize its basic nature and structure, including its nonvisual aspects.

The most widespread symbol of the whole cosmos is the ceremonial lodge, house, or tent. The fundamental idea of the ceremonial lodge, such as the Delaware *xingwikáon* ("big house"), is that all of its parts symbolize, and in ritual contexts actually are, the cosmos. Usually the realms of this cosmos are interconnected with a central post, which is conceived of as extending itself like a world tree up to the heavens. Renewing such a house constitutes the actual renewal of the cosmos.

Similar ideas are found among the Plains Indians, for whom the sacred camp circle constitutes an image of the world, and the central pole of the Sun Dance tipi, the whole cosmos. In fact the Crow call this tent the "imitation" or "miniature" lodge, a replica of the Sun's lodge.

Representations of the cosmos can refer to the more subtle manifestations of the world, as in the sand paintings of the Luiseño of California, but they can also approach the reality of topographical maps, as in the sand paintings of the neighboring Diegueño. In a completely different approach to the visualization of the cosmos, the well-known Navajo sand painting of Father Sky and Mother Earth illustrates the anthropomorphic representation of the cosmos.

Concerning nonvisual aspects of the cosmos, it is not uncommon that ethical ideals or holistic images of proper human life, which are extensions of the theological bases of many cosmologies, are also visualized iconographically. The most common image of this type is that of the right, or the beautiful, path. The Delaware big house has a circular path on its floor, which the visionary singers and other participants in the big house ceremony walk and dance upon. This path is called the Good White Path, the symbol of the human life. It corresponds to the Milky Way, which is the path of the souls of the dead. The Ojibwa bark charts of the Midewiwin ceremony consist of illustrations of the degrees of initiation into the Mide secret society. All of the degrees are represented as connected by the path of the initiate's life, starting in the image of the primordial world and ending upon the island of direct communication with the supreme being. This path is pictured with many detours and dramatic occurrences.

SUPREME BEINGS

Among the myriad images found in North American Indian iconography are certain divine beings whose representations cut across taxonomic groups; these include supreme beings, tricksters/culture heroes, guardian beings, and other mythical beings. Since the majestic, all-encompassing supreme being is difficult to visualize, its morphology is relatively simple. When not visualized as some object or animal intimately associated with the supreme being, its form tends to be anthropomorphic. For example, the Ojibwa song charts visualize the supreme being, Kitsi Manitu, with a pictograph of a human head, belonging to an initiate in the Mide secret society (see figure 1).

On the other hand, the all-pervasiveness of the supreme being among the Plains Indians can result in the use of symbols of lesser deities to represent it. Thus Wakantanka, of the Oglala Lakota, has various manifestations such as the Sun, the Moon, Buffalo, and so on, all of which are pictured on hides or, as with Buffalo, represented by a buffalo skull.

FIGURE 1: Ojibwa Pictograph

TRICKSTERS/CULTURE HEROES

The most widespread iconographic trickster type is theriomorphic: Raven, Coyote, or Rabbit. The most well-known image is that of Raven among the Northwest Coast tribes, a character who encompasses all of the classical features of the trickster (see figure 2). He is pictured in raven-form on virtually every object throughout the Northwest, usually in the context of a mythical event that somehow affected the ancestor of the house in which the object is found, be it house pole, settee, or some other form. As part of shamanic paraphernalia, his image imparts one of his main characteristics: that of transformation. Even though the trickster is an animal, in mythical thought he can change to human form, and this process is often reflected iconographically, as with the Navajo Coyote and the Delaware and Ojibwa Rabbit.

The culture hero is a divine or semidivine mythic figure who, through a series of heroic deeds—especially the theft of such an important item as fire or light—starts humanity upon its cultural road. When he is not the theriomorphic trickster, he is often simply visualized as a human being. [See also Tricksters, *article on* North American Tricksters.]

GUARDIAN BEINGS

Guardian beings associate themselves most often on a personal level with single individuals, and they function as guardians who bring blessings to their human partners. In the Plains and Northern Woodlands cultures, to seek and receive a personal

FIGURE 2: Kwakiutl House-Front Painting

vision of just such a guardian is necessary in order to secure an individual's station in life. These guardians can appear in just about any form taken from the natural or the mythological world. Among the Oglala it may be necessary to paint a version of one's vision on the tipi in order to secure its validity, although generally images of the guardian are painted on shields.

In the cultures of the Far North and Arctic areas, the shaman and his guardians are a constant iconographic theme. His guardians are portrayed in several general ways: as diminutive human beings clustered near the shaman or as human faces clustered together, as a human visage under an animal visage such as seen in Alaskan masks, as an animal form reduced in size and resting on the head or shoulders of the shaman, as birdlike shamans or shamans in transformation, as flying spirits being ridden by shamans, as an animal or human being with skeletal markings, or as flying bears or other usually flightless beasts (see figure 3). These images are portrayed in contemporary drawings, ivory sculpture, masks, stone sculpture, bone sculpture, drumsticks, shaman staff, and so on. Throughout North America the shaman also uses organic parts of his guardians in his ritual paraphernalia, or else he can use the entire skin of his guardian animal to transform himself.

Guardians appear in nonvisionary and nonshamanistic cultures as well. The Pueblo deities of the six world regions are considered to be guardians of humanity. Another type of guardian is Rainbow Serpent, pictured on almost all Navajo sand paintings. This figure encircles the entire painting but remains open toward the east. Its function is to keep the evil spirits out of the reinstated cosmic region.

OTHER MYTHICAL BEINGS

Among the mythological figures who are pictured iconographically, one important group is that of monsters. The most common monster motif is an image of the primordial horned, flying serpent, the cause of floods and earthquakes. He is known all over the Americas and is generally pictured in exactly the form described. Another monster known all over North America is Thunderbird, usually pictured on shields, shirts, and beadwork as an eaglelike creature.

FIGURE 3: Inuit Stonecut Stencil Design

There is also a whole group of evil beings who, in one form or another, are believed to exercise a malignant and dangerous influence on humanity. Such creatures are usually theriomorphic but not necessarily so.

ASTRONOMICAL BEINGS

The sun, the moon, and the stars are pictured as beings throughout North America. The sun is portrayed most intensely where it is strongest, in southeastern and southwestern North America. The Hopi portray the Sun, Taawa, anthropomorphically but, in keeping with Hopi iconography, he wears a mask that consists of a circular disc fringed with radiating feathers and horsehair (see figure 4). This radial representation of the sun is the most common image known. The Ojibwa, on the other hand, have a completely different image, which is horned, winged, and legged.

The moon is usually represented in its quarter phase, although images of the full moon are sometimes found. The stars most often pictured are the Morning Star (Venus), the Pleiades, Orion, Altair, the constellation Ursa Major (which is invariably pictured as a heavenly bear), and the Milky Way. Stars are shown with four, five, and six points and are often associated with human figures.

METEOROLOGICAL BEINGS

This group consists of Thunder, Wind, Rain, and Lightning. Thunder is often pictured as the Thunderbird, but other birds can also be used. Wind, on the other hand, is generally associated with the cardinal regions and therefore not visualized directly. Cultures with anthropocentric morphology, however, such as the Navajo and the Ojibwa, picture even this being in human shape.

Rain is usually illustrated as lines falling from cloud symbols or as a being from which rain is falling. Lightning is always shown as zigzag lines regardless of the tribe

FIGURE 4: Drawing of a Hopi Kachina Dancer

in question. The lines usually end in arrowheads, for there is a conceptual link between lightning and arrows. Lightning and thunder are usually considered to be the weapons of the widely known Warrior Twins.

ANIMAL BEINGS

There are a number of animals which are known and visualized throughout North America, such as the bear, the deer, and the buffalo. However, other animals peculiar to a particular region are the more common iconographical subjects, such as the whales and seals of the northern coasts, or the lizards and snakes of the desert regions. The general rule is that the animal is depicted in its natural form.

Representations of animals may signify the spirit or master of their species or the form of some deity, guardian being, or primordial creature, or they may indicate the totem animal. All animal images used in ritual contexts have religious significance. But the most common use of animal images occurs in heraldry, which casts some doubt on the exclusively religious significance of its use and meaning.

The Northwest Coast Indians are the most conspicuous users of totem symbols. These symbols are represented in literally every conceivable medium: poles, house fronts, hats, aprons, spoons, bowls, settees, boat prows, spearheads, fishhooks, dagger handles, facial painting, masks, speaker staffs, paddles, drums, rattles, floats, bracelets, leggings, pipes, and gambling sticks. The question of religious significance may be resolved by the fact that the totem animal is considered either a direct ancestor of the clan or somehow associated with an ancient human ancestor. Thus the symbol at least, if not its use, has religious meaning.

VEGETATION BEINGS

Corn is the plant most commonly visualized. The representation can simply refer to the plant itself, but frequently a maize deity is being invoked. The latter is the case throughout the Southwest, whether among the Pueblo or the Athapascan peoples. The maize deity is usually clearly anthropomorphized. Hallucinogenic plants such as peyote, jimsonweed, or the strong wild tobaccos are more or less realistically pictured; such images refer to the deities of these potent plants. Others beings who somehow influence plant growth are also visualized iconographically; these include the Yuki impersonations of the dead, who have a decided influence on the abundance of acorns, or the Hopi impersonations of cultic heros and heroines whose rituals influence crop growth.

HUMAN BEINGS

This category concerns not only human ancestors but also a miscellaneous collection of beings that have human form. The first type are effigies of once-living human beings. These are most commonly figured on Northwest Coast mortuary poles, but they are also found elsewhere: the Californian Maidu, Yokuts, Luiseño, and Tubatulabal, for example, all burn effigies of prominent people two years after their deaths.

Human images can also be material expressions of the ineffable. During the Sun Dance the Shoshoni and the Crow each bring out a stone image in diminutive human shape, which is then attached to a staff or the center pole of the tent. It is said to represent the spirit of the Sun Dance. Human images, such as dolls, can symbolize or are actually considered to be small spritelike creatures who can have an array of functions and duties and who play a part in ceremonial contexts as well. Human representations can also signify the heroes or founders of cults; such is the case with many images on Pueblo altars and other representations on Northwest Coast poles.

GEOLOGICAL BEINGS

This category of images is based on a type of religious geomorphology. It is not a numerically dominant theme, but it is nonetheless of singular importance. The most prominent geological being envisioned is Mother Earth, although it is seldom that direct representations of it occur. In such anthropocentric iconographies as that of the Navajo, it is no problem to illustrate Mother Earth as a somewhat enlarged female human being. Usually, however, Mother Earth is symbolized by some fertility image, such as an ear of corn, or by a circle. Among the Delaware, the earth is symbolized by the giant tortoise who saved humankind from the flood and upon whose back the new earth was created by Nanabush (see figure 5). Sods of earth can also be used to represent Mother Earth, as in the Cheyenne buffalo-skull altar in the medicine lodge.

Another group of geological beings consists of images of mountains. Except for isolated pockets of flatlands and desert basins, most of North America is covered with mountains, and these are usually believed to be alive or at least filled with life, that is, they are the abodes of the gods. This feature of mountains is highly important and is also recognized iconographically.

Finally, some mention should be made of stones and prehistoric implements. Animacy or power is attributed to implements such as ancient pipe bowls, mortars, and blades, any odd-shaped stones, and stones resembling animal, vegetable, or human outlines. Such stones symbolize whatever they resemble.

ABSTRACT SYMBOLS

The dynamic and highly stylized geometric patterns on Southwest Indian pottery, which represent categories already discussed (such as clouds, rain, lightning, the sun, and so on), also belong to the category of abstract symbols. Cultures with highly developed artistic iconographies, such as those of the Northwest Coast, the Southwest, and the Woodlands peoples with their birchbark illustrations, also develop series of signs referring to abstractions inherent to their systems. On the Ojibwa Midewiwin scrolls, for example, the symbol of bear tracks in a particular context

FIGURE 5: Delaware Pictograph

represents a priest's four false attempts to enter the Mide lodge. These four false attempts can also be symbolized by four bars.

[*See also* North American Indians *and* Shamanism, *article on* North American Shamanism.]

BIBLIOGRAPHY

There is unfortunately no comprehensive work on the religious iconography of the North American Indians. Information about iconography is found in the original ethnographic data on various peoples published in the annual reports and the bulletins of the Bureau of American Ethnology. An ethnographic approach to art in North America, with emphasis on prehistoric art, can be found in Wolfgang Haberland's *The Art of North America,* translated by Wayne Dynes (New York, 1964). General works on the art of American Indians are numerous; the most comprehensive is Norman Feder's *American Indian Art* (New York, 1971). Another useful study is Frederick J. Dockstader's *Indian Art of the Americas* (New York, 1973).

For the Indians of the Far North, see Jean Blodgett's *The Coming and Going of the Shaman: Eskimo Shamanism and Art* (Winnipeg, 1979) and Inge Kleivan and Birgitte Sonne's *Eskimos: Greenland and Canada,* "Iconography of Religions," sec. 8, fasc. 1 (Leiden, 1984). Concerning the Northeast and Southeast Woodlands tribes, see Frank G. Speck's *Montagnais Art in Birchbark, a Circumpolar Trait,* "Museum of the American Indian, Heye Foundation, Indian Notes and Monographs," vol. 11, no. 2 (New York, 1937), and *Concerning Iconology and the Masking Complex in Eastern North America,* "University Museum Bulletin," vol. 15, no. 1 (Philadelphia, 1950). For the Plains Indians, see Åke Hultkrantz's *Prairie and Plains Indians,* "Iconography of Religions," sec. 10, fasc. 2 (Leiden, 1973), and Peter J. Powell's *Sweet Medicine: The Continuing Role of the Sacred Arrows, the Sun Dance, and the Sacred Buffalo Hat in Northern Cheyenne History,* 2 vols. (Norman, Okla., 1969). For Indians of the Northwest Coast, see Charles Marius Barbeau's *Totem Poles,* 2 vols. (Ottawa, 1950–1951), and Franz Boas's *Primitive Art* (1927; new ed., New York, 1955). Concerning the Pueblo Indians of the Southwest, see my *Hopi Indian Altar Iconography,* "Iconography of Religions," sec. 10, fasc. 4a (Leiden, 1986), and Barton Wright's *Pueblo Cultures,* "Iconography of Religions," sec. 10, fasc. 4 (Leiden, 1985). For the Navajo Indians of the Southwest, see Sam D. Gill's *Songs of Life: An Introduction to Navajo Religious Culture,* "Iconography of Religions," sec. 10, fasc. 3 (Leiden, 1979), and Gladys A. Reichard's *Navajo Medicine Man: Sandpaintings and Legends of Miguelito* (New York, 1939).

20 MUSIC

David P. McAllester

The record of human occupancy in both North America and South America begins with the hunting cultures of fifteen thousand to twenty thousand years ago. Evidences of agriculture and village life in Mesoamerica and South America are dated as early as 5000–3000 BCE, and with the invention of pottery the record of musical instruments begins. Instruments made of clay—whistles, panpipes, rattles, ocarinas and other flutes, and even trumpets and drums—are imperishable; they may be broken, but the fragments never decay and so the instruments may be reconstructed. Bone, antler, stone, and shell are other durable materials from which musical instruments were made.

We can infer from archaeological and ethnological evidence that the function of this rich inventory was largely religious and that much of the instrumentarium accompanied song. From the time of the earliest written historical record (the fifteenth century) it has come to be known, with increasing certainty, that the predominant native music in the entire hemisphere was vocal. Solo and ensemble instrumental playing developed widely in Mesoamerica and South America but hardly at all in North America.

SOUTH AMERICA

The early immigrants to the south, who spoke many different languages, developed an enormous variety of cultures over the millennia of their occupancy. Certain motifs seem to characterize the religious thought of the native peoples of South America and Mesoamerica: feline deities and a profound duality that includes paired male and female cosmic forces such as earth and sky or sun and moon. Hero twins, day and night creatures, and the contest between good and evil appear in the mythology and religious thought of both isolated tribal groups and the high civilizations of Mesoamerica and the Andes. Paired drums, horns, flutes, and other instruments often styled "male" and "female" carry this concept of duality into the realm of music. Other widespread cultural elements are puberty ceremonies with chanting to the accompaniment of rattles, and curing rituals in which supernatural powers are invoked in song with the percussive accompaniment of drums, rasps, rattles, or stamping tubes.

Scholarship on the native peoples of Mesoamerica and South America has until recently focused primarily on the civilizations of the Maya, Aztec, and Inca. As the result of field studies, some sense of the religious and musical life of the smaller and more isolated cultures has now begun to emerge. This research may also give a hint about the nature of urban cultures in their earlier stages. We learn that a complex priesthood is not essential to the development of a sophisticated view of the universe. The elaborate mathematical/astronomical/religious discoveries and speculations of the Maya in their temple cities may be matched by the psychological insights in the myth and religion of the Witoto deep in the jungles of Brazil. To convey a sense of the continuities and developments on this continent, I shall give brief sketches of the religion and music of a tribal group, the urban cultures that developed before the Spanish conquest, and the acculturative changes that took place after the European invasion.

The Tucano of the northwest border area of Brazil resemble, culturally, many of the other forest tribes that occupy the millions of square miles of river and jungle elsewhere in South America. They live by hunting, fishing, and agriculture; manioc, their staple, is a major food source and is fermented to make *chicha* beer. The Tucanos' mastery of chemistry is impressive: they can remove the prussic acid from manioc by a complex process; they hunt and make war with poison darts; and they make use of a wide range of narcotics, which they chew, drink, or inhale.

Tucano religious life emphasizes communication with ancestral spirits through music and dance to ensure human vitality and growth. Certain musical instruments are the properties of deities, such as Jaguar, Serpent, Fish, Butterfly, and Owl, and the fifteen-foot paired trumpets of wound bark used in their most important ceremonies are themselves deities. Called Grandmother and Grandfather, these deities were the first ancestors to die; they taught the people how to weep and how to make masks of bark cloth.

The Tucano's most important ceremony is the mourning ritual for an outstanding member of the *maloca,* the big communal house where extended families of more than a hundred persons may live. Immediately after death the body is buried under the floor of the *maloca* to the accompaniment of wailing, mourning songs, and the staccato chanting of the elders who recount incidents in the life of the deceased. A year later, visitors from many other *maloca*s come, by invitation, to perform the characteristic songs and dances of the various deities. The masked participants, who together represent every aspect of the cosmos, act out their roles for three days and nights. The great trumpets are brought by canoe, and their deep notes sound in concert with the singing, flutes, panpipes, bells, clay jaguar horns, turtle-shell friction blocks, and snail-shell trumpets. Great amounts of food and stimulants are consumed, and with the growing relaxation and intimacy the people are united both with each other and with their ancestors. Still another year later, a final day of songs and dances concludes with the burning of the masks and bark trumpets; that night there is more drinking, dancing, and music, and at dawn the departing spirit is honored with a farewell before it goes on to the home of the ancestors. The singing provides a low, melodic background for the repetitive formulas of the various pipes, whistles, and trumpets.

Eyewitness accounts of the performance of Aztec music have come down to us from sixteenth-century Spanish chroniclers. Even the famed Aztec calendar had a role in musical life, as it fixed the times for festivals. Every twenty days specific gods governing the seasons, agriculture, and war were venerated in a principal festival. Victories in war, the installation of new members of the nobility, marriages, and the commemoration of great moments in past history and the lives of deceased leaders were also celebrated.

Choirs of highly trained singers, often including the sons of the nobility, were maintained under the leadership of music masters in temples, courts, and private homes of the well-to-do. For private family rituals, singers with deep bass voices were highly regarded. The indispensable accompanying instruments were a pair of drums, the *huehuetl* and the *teponaztl;* these former deities had been banished from heaven for their sympathy to humankind. The *huehuetl* is an upright barrel drum in various sizes up to several feet high. It was played with the hands: the deerskin drumhead produced two notes a fifth apart. The *teponaztl* is a horizontal slit drum with two lamellae that produce two different notes. It was played with rubber-tipped sticks.

The shrilling of whistles announced the beginning of a performance under the direction of two music masters. The drums then began a soft introduction after which the chorus would begin slowly, in a low key. The songs were in rhymed couplets; in the pause following the end of a song the *huehuetl* was tuned to a higher pitch, then the next song would begin, faster and higher. Other instruments joined in: whistles, flutes, trumpets, flageolets. The performers wore brilliant mantles and carried flowers and fans of feathers and gold. For certain performances they were crowned or masked to represent deities. At times the whole audience would join in the dancing; some four hundred or even a thousand or more of them would perform movements said to be graceful and precisely in time with the music. Bernardino de Sahagún recorded that the correct performance of sacred material was so important that singers, dancers, or even song masters responsible for mistakes could suffer capital punishment.

Although the high culture of the Maya had passed away before the arrival of the conquistadores, their musical instruments were analogous to those of the Aztec. Murals and bas-reliefs on their deserted temple walls portray scenes similar to those described above.

The Inca of Andean South America had a highly regulated civilization with an even richer metallurgy than that of the Aztec and without the Aztec practice of human sacrifice. An extraordinary development of panpipes, coiled clay trumpets with shell or metal bells, end-notched flutes, and zoomorphic whistles sets their instrumentarium somewhat apart from that of other peoples of Mesoamerica. They also had schools for music training and observed calendrical festivals. In three principal celebrations of thanksgiving and purification they sang fables of their past, invoked local deities, and honored the sun, the ancestor of their divine rulers. There was music to revive the dying moon at the time of an eclipse.

Mourners went in procession to localities that had been frequented by their deceased; they played drums and flutes and sang sad songs that recounted the life of the departed. Among the skulls, shells, and horns that served as resonators for trumpets the giant conch was particularly prized. The first European ship to sail in Peruvian waters (in 1526) intercepted an oceangoing raft loaded with fabrics, gold, silver, and jewels, all to be exchanged for conch shells from the Caribbean.

A major goal during the colonial period was conversion of the Indians to Christianity, and early on excellent choirs were singing masses and other liturgical music.

Of the more than two hundred books published in Mexico in the sixteenth century, thirteen dealt with sacred music. So great was the native enthusiasm for church music that in the 1560s royal and ecclesiastical decrees set limits to the number of musicians in the churches lest too many natives be withdrawn from the work force.

In the rural areas the music of the folk religions mixed indigenous instrumentation and musical ideas with European elements. Today a wide variety of native instruments, such as panpipes and notched flutes in the Andes, and flutes, drums, and whistles in Mexico, are played along with violins, harps, and other European instruments.

In the revolutionary era a new interest in indigenous music developed as twentieth-century composers sought to create national styles. However, the widespread use of native instruments and melodies in modern Latin America has been largely confined to popular music and art music.

NORTH AMERICA
Certain elements of the high civilizations to the south made their way to North America. Temple villages developed throughout the vast Mississippi drainage, and as far back as two thousand years ago pyramidal and zoomorphic mounds, vast in extent, bespoke obedience of large populations to powerful rulers or priesthoods. But the great inventory of musical instruments is missing from the archaeological record, and the accounts by Spanish and French explorers and conquerors of the seventeenth and eighteenth centuries tell us little about the music here or elsewhere on the northern continent. The account that follows refers to present-day practice, some aspects of which may have had their beginnings many generations ago.

Over the whole area the native music is almost exclusively vocal, usually with the percussive accompaniment of drums, rattles, or both. The only traditional melody instruments are flutes and flageolets used for courtship and a few small fiddles that provide social music in two or three tribes. Nevertheless, the drums and rattles are myriad in form and number. Many are used for a particular ceremony in only one tribe and have deep symbolic meaning. An Iroquois rattle made from a snapping turtle *(Chelydra serpentina)* is used only in the midwinter False Face ceremony; no other tribe makes that particular kind of rattle. Water drums made on a clay pot, a wooden barrel, or an iron or aluminum pot are also specific in form and use. In addition, various kinds of whistles and bull-roarers (a flat stick whirled at the end of a thong) represent voices of deities or mythical creatures and signal important ritual moments.

Religious observances among the Indians of North America range from purely private ceremonies inherited, or obtained in dreams, to complex performances supervised by religious societies or priesthoods. The religious function of ceremonies varies according to tribe and geographic region. Among Eastern Woodlands Indians the focus is on thanksgiving; the Athapaskan of the Southwest emphasize curing; the agrarian tribes of the southwestern Pueblo seek rain and a good harvest. Hunting cultures, such as the Inuit (Eskimo) of the Arctic and the Indians of the Northeast Woodlands and central Plains, practiced ritual to ensure a plentiful supply of game. The music ranges from brief songs to long chants composed of many song series that require a number of days and nights for their performance. The songs may have texts that are entirely in vocables (untranslatable syllables), or they may include a few lines of meaningful text, or they may have many lines of cosmic poetry relating the story of creation.

Some of the better-known large ceremonies of the North American tribes are the *kachina* dances of the Pueblo peoples of the Southwest, the healing chants of the Navajo, the Midewiwin of the Chippewa and other tribes of the Great Lakes region, the Sun Dance of the Plains tribes, the potlatch of the Northwest Coast tribes, and the midwinter feast of the dead of the Iroquois in the Northeast.

The *kachina*s are ancestral deities who spend half the year in the sacred mountains or a sacred lake and the other half in the villages of their descendants. At the autumn homecoming ceremony, masked dancers represent the deities, and for the next six months they appear in a round of ceremonies designed to bring rain and a good harvest. Priestly societies are responsible for the ceremonies and the public dances associated with them. The melodies of *kachina* songs are some of the longest and most complex to be found in native North American music. There are occasional breaks in rhythm and many verses concerning clouds, rain, and the fruits of the fields. The dancers sing in deep powerful voices to the accompaniment of a large barrel drum.

The Navajo healing chants exemplify their belief that the voice is wind, the greatest cosmic force, made articulate. Deities of mountains, sky, earth, and the animal and vegetable kingdoms are invoked to bring harmony and restorative power to a sick person. The deities are also made manifest in the famous Navajo sandpaintings and, in some ceremonies, in the persons of masked dancers or actors. The music contrasts markedly with that of the Pueblo Indians. The melodies are relatively short and repetitive; the texts may comprise as many as fifteen or twenty verses. The ceremonial practitioner, who learned the songs in a long apprenticeship, leads the participating friends and relatives of the sick person. The tone is high and nasal, and the melodies have wide leaps in the choruses and a narrow range in the verses.

The Midewiwin is healing in emphasis, and it also serves as a teaching and grading society in supernatural knowledge and power. As the members advance to higher levels of training, their ability to heal and their repertory of songs increase. There are many of these songs to be learned, but they are short; often they are made up of downward transpositions of only one or two musical phrases. The texts are cryptic references to the various deities that bring power to the ceremony: "In form like a spirit / It appears." The Chippewa sing in a robust emphatic voice much like that in European folksinging, but in the Midewiwin an exaggerated vibrato is a part of the vocal style.

The isolation of North American Indians on their reservations did much to preserve the traditional cultures; recent decades, however, have brought increasing influences from outside that have touched every aspect of their lives, including religious music. In the late nineteenth century, as armed resistance proved inadequate against whites, nativistic religions spread from tribe to tribe. For example, the Ghost Dance religion looked to a second coming of Christ and a return of indigenous powers to help the Indians. It featured group dancing and plaintive songs with the paired phrases of the Plateau region where the religious movement originated. The peyote religion (Native American Church) has a large pantribal membership today. The nightlong ceremony includes extended prayers to native and Christian deities for health and the solution of personal problems. The songs, which come in sets of four, are sung to the loud, rapid beating of a water drum made on a metal pot. The songs, performed with a rapt, inward quality, also address Christian or native deities or describe visions induced by the intense feeling of the ceremony and the sacramental ingestion of the hallucinogenic peyote plant *(Lophophora williamsii)*.

As Christianity has spread among the North American Indians a hymnody of a unique sort has been added to the traditional music. Standard hymns, often with Indian texts, are sung with much feeling in a slow, dragging meter. Some of the Southeast Woodlands tribes, such as the Cherokee, have created an improvised harmony that resembles Sacred Harp singing. In recent years, gospel rock has caught the imagination of young Indians as have country and western, rock, and other forms of popular music.

Other new forms of music that express present-day Indian religious values are produced by composers using guitars, electric rock ensembles, and other Western instrumentation to accompany songs about nature, family feeling, and friendship, all part of an Indian "sacred way." As they adapt to increasing exposure to the outside world, North American Indians will continue to express a valuable aspect of the general culture in the continuation and development of traditional religion and music in new, syncretized forms. North American Indian activists have begun making common cause with Indians of the continent to the south in the struggle against discrimination and expropriation. The exchange of religious and musical ideas may well be among the more predictable results of this new extension of pan-tribalism.

[*See also* Drama, *article on* Native American Religious Drama.]

BIBLIOGRAPHY

Chase, Gilbert. *A Guide to the Music of Latin America.* Washington, D.C., 1962.

Densmore, Frances. *Chippewa Music,* 2 vols. Bureau of American Ethnology Bulletin, nos. 43 and 53. Washington, D.C., 1910 and 1913.

Herndon, Marcia. *Native American Music.* Norwood, Pa., 1980.

Izikowitz, Karl Gustav. *Musical and Other Sound Instruments of the South American Indians.* Gothenburg, Nebr., 1935.

Kurath, Gertrude P. *Iroquois Music and Dance: Ceremonial Arts of Two Seneca Longhouses.* Bureau of American Ethnology Bulletin, no. 187. Washington, D.C., 1964.

Martí, Samuel. *Canto, danza y música precortesianos.* Mexico City, 1961.

McAllester, David P. *Peyote Music.* Viking Fund Publications in Anthropology, no. 13. New York, 1949.

Nettl, Bruno. *North American Indian Musical Styles.* Memoirs of the American Folk-lore Society, vol. 45. Philadelphia, 1954.

Stevenson, Robert M. *Music in Aztec and Inca Territory.* Berkeley, 1968.

Taylor, Donald. *The Music of Some Indian Tribes of Colombia.* London, 1972. Background notes (100 pp.) with three twelve-inch LP records.

21 SUN DANCE

JOSEPH EPES BROWN

Sun Dance is currently used as a generic term having reference to a rich complex of rites and ceremonies with tribal variations specific to at least thirty distinct tribal groups of the North American Plains and Prairie. Although tribal variations of beliefs, traits, and the structuring of ceremonial lodges are significant and of great importance to the groups concerned, there are nevertheless sufficient similarities to justify use of the generic term. Since these distinct tribal groups represent at least seven mutually unintelligible language families, understandably there is also present the once-universal sign language, a rich means by which even subtle and complex matters could be communicated to all the tribes. Traditionally the peoples have been divided into four major groupings: the northern tribes; the southern tribes; the village, or eastern, tribes; and the Plateau, or western, tribes. Each tribe within these groups gives the Sun Dance its own specific term, which has reference to particular ritual emphases. The Shoshoni and Crow, for example, refer to the complex as the Thirst Lodge, or Thirst Standing Lodge; for the Cheyenne it is the Medicine Lodge; and for the Siouan peoples it is known as the Dance Gazing at the Sun.

The precise tribal origin of the Sun Dance within the North American Plains groups cannot be determined with certainty, in part because calendric rites of world and life renewal involving sacrificial elements and shamanic-type acts of healing are very widespread throughout North America. Leslie Spier's extensive yet inconclusive study (1921) suggested that the complex possibly originated among—or diffused from—the Arapaho and Cheyenne. In terms of more ancient origins outside North America there are compelling parallels with the Tunguzic peoples of Siberia, who had new year festivals of renewal with ritual emphasis on a world tree as axis joining heaven and earth; offerings made of ribbons and sacrificed animal skins were made to this tree. Other shamanic elements described by A. F. Anisimov involve the rhythmic power of drums, the inducing of trances, visions, and curing ceremonies, all of which are strongly reminiscent of the North American Plains Sun Dance traits (Anisimov, 1963).

It is unfortunate that the early anthropological accounts of Native American religious practices were usually flat, ignoring or paying insufficient attention to the spiritual realities underlying religious beliefs and practices as the peoples themselves understood them. The rich values and sacred meanings encoded within cultural forms such as the arts, crafts, and architecture were also largely ignored. Even Robert Lowie, who was very familiar with the early history of the Crow Sun Dance, was able to write in 1915 that the Sun Dance "in large measure served for the aesthetic pleasure and entertainment of the spectators." The Swedish scholar Åke Hultkrantz, commencing his early studies in 1947, challenged these prevailing reductionist perspectives; by giving proper recognition to religious beliefs and practices of primal origin and by integrating the perspectives and methodologies of both anthropology and the history of religions, an approach now found increasingly within current ethnohistorical studies. It is essentially this approach that is respected in the following descriptions.

The rich diversity of beliefs and traits specific to the Sun Dance traditions in some thirty distinct tribal groups, each of which manifests varying levels of acculturation and creative adaptions, can hardly be encompassed within a brief essay. Judicious selection must therefore be made of essential elements across a fair sampling of tribal groups. Attention will also be given to contemporary movements among many Native American peoples for revitalization of traditional sacred values and practices. Indeed, it is primarily the Sun Dance that, as its popularity increases, is acting as model and stimulus for traditionalist movements extending even to non-Plains tribes and to disenchanted non–Native Americans who are seeking examples of what true religious traditions really are.

GENERAL DESCRIPTION

The major Sun Dance celebrations take place for all the tribal groups in late June or early July, "when the sage is long" and "the chokecherries are ripe," or, as some put it, in "the moon of fattening." In the times when these peoples were nomadic pasturalists, the grasses of the prairies would during these months be sufficient to feed the great herds of horses belonging to the tribal bands, who often were joined in the circles of camps with allied tribes. These springtime ceremonies (in the past they may have been held earlier than June) were actually the climax of an annual cycle of minor rites and meetings of many types. Among the Crow, for example, "prayer meetings" take place regularly at the time of the full moon; among all the tribes, groups of singers meet periodically around their drums in order to practice and to instruct younger singers in the extremely difficult and subtle Sun Dance songs, many of which have been faithfully transmitted from ancient times. There are also contemporary songs that have come out of an individual's sacred experiences or that have been learned from other tribes, for today there is much exchange of songs and other cultural elements in the course of the more popular pan-Indian summer powwow circuit. However, all songs that are used in the Sun Dance lodge must accord with particular styles and rhythms, since clear distinctions are made between ceremonial and social dance songs.

Given the complex logistics of the Sun Dances, with encampments of large numbers of people, many people volunteer or are selected during the year to fulfill a wide range of duties. Usually a sponsor coordinates the many details and materials for the construction of the sacred lodge or the provision of the feast at the end of the ceremonies, both of which are accomplished at considerable expense and sacrifice. The most important person however, is the spiritual leader, a "medicine person," who is guardian of the sacred lore and who usually has received special powers through the vision quest (or who may have received the authority to lead the ceremonies from a retiring elder who has passed on his sacred powers). These spiritual leaders have traditionally been recognized as holy people, for they know and live the sacred traditions and have powers for curing those who are ill in body or spirit. Such shamanic figures have been greatly respected as leaders within the tribe, or they have been feared because of the great strength of their mysterious powers. Such leaders should not be considered as belonging only to the past, however, for new leaders are taking their places and are living into the present-day among most of the tribes. Indeed, there are today a growing number of such leaders, including younger men and women who have attempted to become acculturated within the dominant society but, often finding this to be a process of diminishing returns, have gone back to the wise elders for help in reestablishing traditional values in their contemporary ways of life.

Those who participate in the actual ceremonies within the sacred lodge are often individuals who were previously in situations of extreme danger, perhaps as members of the armed forces in wars the United States has conducted overseas, and who vowed that if they should survive they would participate in the next Sun Dance upon returning home. Paradoxically, their experiences in foreign wars have acted as a stimulus for the continuation, and indeed intensification, of the Sun Dance traditions into the present.

To those sacrificing in the lodge for the first time are assigned mentors who are experienced in the Sun Dance rituals and who—having known the suffering of being without food or water for a period of three or four days—are able to counsel and give support to the novice in the lodge. Other camp duties are taken care of by special "police" who see that proper conduct and respect for sacred matters are observed, functions once fulfilled by the warrior societies. A camp crier is also named, who has the responsibility of encircling the camp on horseback in the very early mornings and in the evenings, of chanting instructions to the people, or of giving useful information concerning the day's activities. On occasion such criers might relate humorous incidents, intending to bring great laughter from the circles of lodges, or from the wall tents used today. For in Plains life, now as in the past (and even in the context of the most serious affairs), humor has a legitimate and effective purpose—not just the momentary relief of tensions accompanying the enactment of sacred rites, but also the opening of the human person to deeper modes of understanding.

LODGE CONSTRUCTION

Once the Sun Dance encampment has been established at an appropriate place where there is good water and pasturage, the first ritual act is to select a special cottonwood tree with branches forking at the top. The tree is then cut in a ceremonial manner, the first blow of the ax often being given by a young woman who has been chosen for her virtue and purity (if any man present knows that she has been unfaithful he has the right and obligation to denounce her publicly). The tree must be felled in a specific direction and is not allowed to touch the ground; it is then carried on poles, with songs, ritual acts, and prayers performed along the way. The cottonwood tree is finally placed in a hole prepared at the center of what will be the sacred lodge, which is itself at the center of the encampment. The selected tree is now understood as the axis at the center of the world. It links heaven and earth, thus giving the people access to spiritual realities and conveying the images of the center and the heavens above, together with their larger implications. For most peoples who practice the Sun Dance, this special tree is understood as a "person." In a way akin to human participation in the sacrifice, the tree transmits to those who sacrifice in the lodge the cooling powers of the moisture it has gathered from the stream near which it grew, and then it dies.

The tree thus recapitulates the major themes of the Sun Dance, which involve the alternations of dry and moist, ignorance and wisdom, and death and life—for if there is to be life there must also be death. Once the tree has been ceremonially raised, offerings are placed at its base, and in its fork is put a nest of cherry or willow branches in which may be placed sacred offerings or, often, rawhide effigies. Colored ribbons, signifying heaven and earth, may be tied high on the tree's forking branches. Each tribal group has its own color symbolism and specific manner of dressing the tree. Among the Crow, for example, the head of a bull buffalo is placed, facing east, on the tree, and in the branches there is an eagle, both symbols recapitulating the theme of heaven and earth. Around the tree as spiritual center the circular lodge is then constructed in accord with symbolical variations specific to each of the tribal groups.

The general architectural design for most tribal Sun Dance lodges is the central tree around which are twenty-eight vertical, forked poles associated with the twenty-eight days of the lunar month. This circle of forked poles is then joined together by horizontal poles laid into the upright forks. In addition the Shoshoni, Crow, and Arapaho lodges have twenty-eight very long poles extending from the forks at the circumference and then all laid into the crotch high on the central tree, a structure that resembles a spoked wheel. The Siouan lodges do not have poles radiating out from the center; a distinctive feature of their lodge, in accord with their ceremonial usage, is the construction of a continuous overhead shade arbor around the inner periphery of the lodge. All styles of lodges, however, have entryways facing the east, the place of the rising sun, and brush is usually placed loosely around the outer walls for the greater privacy of the participants within. For all tribal groups, the lodge is not merely understood as a "symbolic model" of the world, but rather it *is* the world, universe, or created cosmos. Since construction of the lodge recapitulates the creation of the world, all acts in this process are accompanied by prayers and powerful songs associated with ancient myths of origin and creation. The occasion, reminiscent of a primordial time, is solemn, dignified, and of great beauty.

Around the sacred lodge in concentric circles the camps of family units are set up in accord with long-established protocol. At Sun Dance encampments the doorways of many tipis or wall tents are not toward the east, as is customary in daily usage, but rather toward the sacred lodge and tree at the center of the circle. To the west of the sacred lodge there are usually special tipis in which private ceremonies take place exclusively for those who will sacrifice in the lodge. Sweat lodges are also set up, but apart from the camp circle, so that those who have made their vows may be purified before entering the lodge.

TYPICAL PERFORMANCES

Even though there are many commonalities in all Plains Sun Dance ceremonies, there are also tribal variations that are of great importance to the peoples concerned. In the Siouan form, for example, which has been described by the Lakota Black Elk in *The Sacred Pipe* (Brown, 1952), there are at least two distinctive and central sacrificial elements, one of which is described by the Lakota term for the Sun Dance, *wiwanyag wachipi* ("dance gazing at the sun"). Here, during one complete daylight cycle, the dancers, who are also observing a total fast, move periodically around the inner periphery of the lodge in sunwise manner so that they are always gazing at the sun—a cause, no doubt, of intense suffering.

A second Lakota or Siouan emphasis, also involving sacrificial elements, is the practice of certain dancers, in accord with earlier vows, to have the muscles of the chest pierced by the presiding spiritual leader, who inserts wooden skewers by which they are tied with rawhide thongs to the central tree. These people then dance, encouraged by the drums and the songs of warriors (brave songs), pulling back on the thongs until the flesh and muscles tear loose. In addition to elements of self-sacrifice, there are spiritual implications of being physically tied to and thus identified with the tree as sacred center. A similar theme is also expressed by the ceremony wherein individuals have skewers inserted into both sides of the shoulders and into the muscles of chest and back. The thongs are then attached to posts set up to represent the four directions. The individual is thereby identified with the center in relation to the four horizontal directions of space. Such sacrificial acts are not just of former times, but are in increasing use today among a number of Siouan peoples. In distinction from prevailing traits and themes of the Siouan Sun Dance, which are strongly reminiscent of elements from earlier military complexes, the Arapaho, the Cheyenne, and the tribes of the Blackfeet Confederation place emphasis on rites of world and life renewal, employing ritual objects that include sacred medicine bundles whose contents have reference to the origins of the tribes.

Finally, emphasis should be given to critical elements in the history of the Sun Dance and to a present-day modified Sun Dance movement that originated among the western Shoshoni and has been transmitted to the Crow. In 1881 the United States government attempted to ban all Sun Dances, believing that they were "demoralizing and barbarous." It was not until 1904, however, that the dances were rigorously prohibited by the Commissioner of Indian Affairs. However, because these ceremonies were central to spiritual needs, they continued to be practiced in secret or in modified forms by almost all the Plains tribes with the exception of the Crow, who had already abandoned the ceremonies in 1875. One of the still continuing modified Sun Dances was that of the Wind River Shoshoni, whose version spread to the Northern Ute in 1890, to the Fort Hall Shoshoni and Bannock in 1901, and to the Shoshoni of Nevada in 1933. With the Indian Reorganization Act of 1934, however, open practice of the dances commenced, but now in forms that gave greater emphasis to spiritual elements rather than to the extreme tortures associated with the earlier military societies.

In 1941 the charismatic Shoshoni Sun Dance leader John Truhujo brought the Sun Dance back to the Crow through the support of the tribal superintendent Robert Yellowtail. A tradition that had been abandoned for more than sixty-six years was thereby reinstated. In January of 1985 Truhujo died at the age of approximately 105, having transferred his sacred powers to Thomas Yellowtail, brother of the former superintendent. It is the Sun Dance in this particular form, faithfully led by Thomas Yellowtail to the present time, that has become for the Crow, as well as for many other tribes, an example and stimulus giving continuity and viability to the essentials of the spiritual heritage of the Plains peoples.

In this Shoshoni/Crow Sun Dance the dancers take positions in arbors that surround the inner periphery of the lodge, with the presiding spiritual leader, or "medicine man," always at the west. Women, who are allowed within the lodge to fast, take places slightly to the north of the east-facing entrance. The large ceremonial drum and the alternating teams of drummers and singers have their place a little to the south of the entrance, and they are surrounded by strong-voiced older women who help to sing the sacred songs. The dance's spiritual force resides in the movements of the fasting participants, who for the three or four days' duration of the ceremony are always oriented to the central tree, toward which they dance as often or as little as they wish. They blow on eagle-bone whistles tipped with eagle down, as if they themselves were eagles; then they dance backward to their stalls, still facing the central tree. The rhythmic movements of the dancers are dignified, and their concentration on the tree is continual and intense; for them this is the center and source of life, and the lodge symbolizes the totality of creation. In the course of the ceremonies, participants often receive sacred visions; when they sleep—never for more than a few hours at a time—dreams of special meaning may come.

An especially powerful and beautiful ceremony central to the Sun Dance takes place every morning just before sunup, when all the dancers, under the direction of the group's spiritual leader, face the direction of the rising sun, moving slowly to the beat of the drum and blowing softly on eagle-bone whistles. As the sun rises the drum and the sunrise greeting-song come to a crescendo. Eagle plumes tied to the wrists of the dancers are held out to the sun's first rays and are then touched to parts of the body so that the dancer may receive purifying blessings. Once the sun is above the horizon, the dancers sit wrapped in their blankets while very ancient sacred songs are sung and communal prayers are offered. On the second or third day of the dance, people who are ill come into the lodge and stand at the sacred tree to receive help from the spiritual leader, who prays over them and often draws out the illness with the aid of an eagle-wing fan. Accounts of cures are legion. At the conclusion of the Sun Dance, water that has been blessed is ceremonially passed around among the participants, who have taken no food or water since they first entered the lodge. Thereafter, many people from the camp bring valuable gifts into the lodge, sometimes even horses loaded with blankets and beadwork, which are given away to particular persons who are called forward to receive them. The dancers themselves usually complete the ceremonies with a purifying sweat bath at a nearby creek or river, and in the evening there may be a special feast for all.

The power of sacred traditions of primal origin cannot be compromised by time, place, or number of participants, for in themselves the values and realities concerned are of timeless and universal validity. Though a world of other priorities ignores or neglects such values they may nevertheless be rediscovered as still enduring, even increasing in meaning into the present day. The history of the Plains Sun Dance is continuing witness to this reality.

BIBLIOGRAPHY

Anisimov, A. F. "The Shaman's Tent of the Evenks and the Origin of the Shamanistic Rite." In *Studies in Siberian Shamanism,* edited by Henry N. Michael, pp. 84–123. Toronto, 1963. An excellent example of Siberian shamanic elements reminiscent of shamanic phenomena in North America.

Brown, Joseph Epes, ed. *The Sacred Pipe.* Norman, Okla., 1953. An especially useful work; chapter 5 presents descriptions of the Lakota Sun Dance by the sage Black Elk.

Dorsey, George A. *The Arapaho Sun Dance.* Chicago, 1903.

Dorsey, George A. *The Cheyenne,* vol. 2, *The Sun Dance.* Chicago, 1905. Dorsey's books define in great ethnographic detail and with excellent plates and diagrams most elements of the Arapaho and Cheyenne Sun Dance as they obtained at the turn of the century.

Hultkrantz, Åke. *Belief and Worship in Native North America.* Syracuse, 1981. Chapter 4 presents an excellent treatment of the symbolical language encoded in the Wind River Shoshoni Sun Dance Lodge.

Jorgensen, Joseph G. *The Sun Dance Religion.* Chicago, 1972. This work contains much valuable information on the Ute and Shoshoni Sun Dances, but its theory that these were redemptive movements following the collapse of the Ghost Dance of 1890 is open to question.

Lowie, Robert H. *The Sun Dance of the Crow Indians.* New York, 1915. Good ethnographic documentation of the early forms of the Crow Sun Dance; omits many of the religious and spiritual elements.

Powell, Peter J. *Sweet Medicine.* 2 vols. Norman, Okla., 1969. One of the best accounts of the Cheyenne Sun Dance rites and beliefs, with close attention given to religious symbolism and the people's sacred history.

Spier, Leslie. "The Sun Dance of the Plains Indians: Its Development and Diffusion." *Anthropological Papers of the American Museum of Natural History* 16 (1921):451–527. An early, inconclusive study of the origins of the Sun Dance.

Voget, Fred W. *The Shoshoni-Crow Sun Dance.* Norman, Okla., 1984. The best account of the renewal of the Crow Sun Dance under the influence of the Shoshoni Sun Dance leader, John Truhujo.

Walker, James R. *The Sun Dance and Other Ceremonies of the Oglala Division of the Teton Dakota.* New York, 1917. The best and most comprehensive account of the early forms of the Sun Dance among the Lakota.

22 GHOST DANCE

Åke Hultkrantz

The Ghost Dance was the major revivalist movement among nineteenth-century North American Indians. Dating from about 1870, it had its culmination in the 1890–1891 "messiah craze" of the Plains, which caused the last Indian war in the Dakotas. The name *Ghost Dance* refers to the ritual round-dances that were thought to imitate the dances of the dead and were performed to precipitate the renewal of the world and the return of the dead. There were other American Indian ceremonial dances that were called ghost dances—for instance, a ritual dance among the Iroquois. However, it was the messianic Ghost Dance of 1890 that attracted general attention because of its message and consequences. It has been considered prototypical of other revivalist movements among North American Indians, so much so that most later movements have been classified as "ghost dances" (La Barre, 1970).

HISTORY

Strictly speaking, there have been two Ghost Dances, closely connected with each other and almost identical in form and cultic performance.

The 1870 Ghost Dance. The Ghost Dance movement of 1870 was introduced on the Walker Lake Reservation in Nevada by a Northern Paiute Indian, Wodziwob ("gray hair," 1844–1918?). During a trance he was conveyed to the otherworld, where he learned that the dead were soon to return, that the disappearing game animals were to be restored, and that the old tribal life would come back again. In order to hasten this change, people had to perform round dances at night, without fires. This Ghost Dance lasted some few years among the Paiute, several middle and northern California tribes, and some Oregon Indians.

Wovoka and the Ghost Dance of 1890. One of Wodziwob's inspired adherents was Tävibo ("white man"), who despite his name was a full-blooded Northern Paiute. He had a son, Wovoka ("the cutter," 1856–1932). Wovoka lived in Mason Valley, Nevada, where he served as a farmhand to a white family named Wilson, and because of this association he went under the name of Jack Wilson. During an eclipse of the sun, probably in January 1889, he fell into a trance and was transported to the supreme being in the sky. In this vision the supreme being showed him the land of the dead and the happy life there, and promised that the living would have a reunion with the deceased, providing a series of rules were followed.

At this point our information divides. To the whites, Wovoka said that the reunion would take place in the otherworld if people behaved correctly (i.e., did not lie, steal, or fight) and performed the round dance. To the Indians, he announced the speedy coming of the dead (who would be guided by a cloudlike spirit that was interpreted as Jesus) as well as the return of game and a lasting peace with the whites. The round dance would more quickly bring about this change. The scene was to be on earth, not in the otherworld. It is obvious that, to the Indians, Wovoka presented the same message, in many ways, as Wodziwob.

The round dance was the same as well. It was conducted on four or five consecutive nights. Men and women danced together in a circle, interlacing their fingers and dancing round with shuffling side steps. The dance was exhausting, although not continuous, and no fainting spells or visions were reported.

This second Ghost Dance appeared when the Plains tribes had been subjugated and their old style of living was on the wane. The freedom-loving Plains Indians looked for an escape, and in their desperation they found it in the Ghost Dance. Emissaries were sent over to the "Messiah," Wovoka (who in fact had claimed only to be a prophet, not a messiah), and were instructed in his doctrine. However, the Plains delegates misinterpreted the message to mean that the whites would be driven off or exterminated. The Ghost Dance spread like fire among the Plains Indians, and in particular the Arapaho, Cheyenne, Lakota, Kiowa, and Caddo became staunch believers. Dancing songs expressed the wishes of the arrival of the dead and praised the Father above.

The Lakota added several new traits that were in line with their visionary and militant ethos: they became entranced while dancing; they pondered military action against the whites; and they covered their upper bodies with white "ghost shirts," decorated with spiritual emblems. The ghost shirt was supposed to protect the wearer magically against enemy bullets. It was probably patterned on Mormon garments worn by the Paiute for protection from bodily harm.

Although the Lakota plans for action were very vague, their frenetic dancing in the summer and fall of 1890 released countermeasures from the suspicious white authorities in the Dakotas, resulting in the so-called Ghost Dance Uprising. Highpoints of this development were the arrest and assassination of the famous Lakota leader Sitting Bull and the massacre at Wounded Knee at the end of December 1890, when Hotchkiss guns indiscriminately killed men, women, and children in Big Foot's camp.

After these catastrophic events, enthusiasm for the Ghost Dance ebbed. Some groups continued dancing, but their expectations of the coming of the dead were projected to a distant future. The last Ghost Dances were held in the 1950s, among Canadian Dakota and Wind River Shoshoni.

THREE MAIN ROOTS

It is possible to find three main roots of the Ghost Dance: earlier religious movements stimulated by Christian missions, shamanic experiences, and indigenous rituals. Of these sources, the impact of earlier syncretic movements has been thoroughly analyzed, beginning with James Mooney's famous study (1896). The import of native religious development has been properly studied only relatively recently. Scholars have, of course, been aware of changes in the Indian's spiritual, cultural, and military background that may have triggered the outbreak of the Ghost Dance. There is no unanimity of opinion, however, as to whether readjustment to a new sociopolitical situation or predominantly religious drives steered the development. The overwhelming majority of scholars, all of them anthropologists, favor the first view, whereas historians of religions prefer the latter.

The impetus for the Ghost Dance revivalism was the Indians' enforced contact with an expanding white civilization beginning in the 1860s. Because of growing white settlements, the white military takeover, and the introduction of white jurisdiction, there was no more room for the continuation of the old native existence, in particular for the hunters and gatherers of the West. Their independent cultures ceased rapidly, sometimes even abruptly, as on the Plains: the whole culture of the northern Plains tribes, built on hunting buffalo, collapsed when in 1883 the last herd of buffalo was exterminated. The Indians had to adjust to white man's culture and, in part, to his values, in order to survive. At the same time they drew on their past to mobilize a desperate spiritual resistance against the overwhelming white influence. In this reactive effort they combined Christian or Christian-derived elements with indigenous ideas and rituals to form a resistance ideology.

Earlier Religious Movements. The formation of mixed ("acculturated") ideologies is part of American Indian religious history since the beginning of European colonization: the restitutional ("nativistic") doctrines launched by the Tewa Indian Popé (1680–1692) and by Neolin, the so-called Delaware Prophet (around 1760), are among the better-known early instances. These prophets proposed an ethical and religious program. In many respects Neolin set the pattern for subsequent prophets, including those of the Ghost Dance: an inspired person who suffers from the ways of the white man enforced upon him and his people, who longs for a return to the good old Indian ways, and who experiences an ecstasy or similar state. In his vision he is brought to the Master of Life, from whom he obtains instructions about a right life. Provided this road is followed, he is told, the game will return, the whites will be driven away, and the old life will be restored. No wonder that such enchanting messages fostered Indian wars, like Pontiac's uprising, which was inspired by Neolin's prophecies.

While the messages of the prophets reflected a yearning for old value patterns, they were in fact deeply dependent on Christian missionary teachings. Exhortations to believers to refrain from liquor, adultery, lying, and murder and to show brotherly friendliness, even beyond tribal boundaries, reveal more or less Christian ethical precepts. Where the abandonment of traditional fetishes and rituals was propagated, as by the Shawnee prophet Tenskwatawa, Christian value judgments are easily recognizable. The very idea that the Supreme Being had to introduce the new religious program through revelation to a prophet also speaks of Christian influence. The hope for the day of salvation, or the coming liberation, implies a linear view of history and an eschatological goal, ideas that were never American Indian, but are thoroughly Christian.

Shamanic Experiences. The second root of the Ghost Dance is shamanic experience. Although the instigators of the revivalist movements were prophets (i.e., ecstatics who had received their calling from God) and not shamans (i.e., vocational ecstatics acting on behalf of their fellowmen), the difference is a minor one, for shamans often receive their calling from spirits. There was definitely a Christian background to the Indian conception of the prophet, his reception of an eschatological message after a comatose experience, and his direct contact with a more or less christianized God. However, the pattern of spiritual communication is very much shamanic. Wovoka, for instance, was himself a medicine man, and fell repeatedly into self-induced trances. It was during these séances that he visited the otherworld and received his messages. Of course, the destination of his soul was the heaven of God, not the spirit land of the dead; these were two different realms in most Native American beliefs.

The Ghost Dance had its precursors in movements that crystallized around shamans. Leslie Spier (1935) retraced the Ghost Dance ideology to an older "Prophet Dance" founded on the intense relations of the living with the dead on the Northwest Coast and the Plateau. The Prophet Dance ideology contained such elements as a world cataclysm, renewal of the world, and the return of the dead. World renewal and the return of the dead could be hastened by the performance of the "dance of the dead." The Prophet Dance had its basis, according to Spier, in the periodic cataclysms (earthquakes) to which the region is subject and in the shamanic visits to the dead made to restore the lost soul of a sick person.

Round-dance Ritual. The third main root of the Ghost Dance is, as Michael Hittman (1973) has observed, the indigenous round dance. The latter has been interpreted by some scholars as simply a dance for entertainment, but there is much evidence that the Basin round dance, performed around a pole or cedar tree, was a religious ceremony—the Father Dance, offered with thanksgivings to the Master of Life for food, rain, and health. In the Ghost Dance this old ceremony was given a new, eschatological meaning.

[*See also* North American Religions, *article on* Modern Movements; Shamanism, *article on* North American Shamanism; *and the biographies of Wovoka and Neolin*.]

BIBLIOGRAPHY

The classic in the field is still James Mooney's *The Ghost-Dance Religion and the Sioux Outbreak of 1890* (1896; reprint, Chicago, 1965). It is a reliable account of Mooney's field visits, just after the Lakota conflict, to a number of tribes that performed the Ghost Dance. Other general works, but less professional, are Paul Bailey's *Wovoka: The Indian Messiah* (Los Angeles, 1957) and David H. Miller's *Ghost Dance* (New York, 1959). In a wider setting of so-called crisis cults, the Ghost Dance religion has been discussed in, among other works, Weston La Barre's *The Ghost Dance* (Garden City, N.Y., 1970).

The discussion of the Ghost Dance has, in comparative works on prophetism, messianism, and millenarianism, concentrated on terminological, psychological, and acculturation problems, whereas the specialized works on the Ghost Dance have paid attention primarily to its origins. Pathbreaking has been Leslie Spier's *The Prophet Dance of the Northwest and Its Derivatives: The Source of the Ghost Dance* (Menasha, Wis., 1935). Spier's idea of an exclusively aboriginal origin of the Ghost Dance religion is today in doubt, but much of his work remains extremely useful.

The grounding of the 1890 Ghost Dance in Wodziwob's movement of the same name twenty years earlier has directed scholars' attention to the latter. The details of the 1870 movement have been excellently clarified in Cora Dubois's *The 1870 Ghost Dance* (Berkeley, 1939). A new orientation, which argues for the mutual independence of the 1870 and 1890 movements, is represented in Michael Hittman's "The 1870 Ghost Dance at the Walker River Reservation: A Reconstruction," *Ethnohistory* 20 (1973): 247–278.

The connection of the Ghost Dance with the Father Dance has been worked out in my book, *Belief and Worship in Native North America,* edited by Christopher Vessey (Syracuse, N.Y., 1981); see especially "The Changing Meaning of the Ghost Dance as Evidenced by the Wind River Shoshoni," pp. 264–281.

23 POTLATCH

Stanley Walens

Potlatch is any of a disparate variety of complex ceremonies among the Indians of the Pacific Northwest Coast of North America, associated with the legitimization of the transfer or inheritance of hereditary aristocratic titles and their associated rights, privileges, and obligations. Potlatches are characterized by the reenactment of the sacred family histories that document the legitimacy of the claimant to the rank, by ritual feasting, and by the formal distribution of gifts by the host group to its guests, each according to his rank. Though the wealth distributed at a potlatch may be quite substantial, the amount distributed is much less important than the requirement that it be distributed according to the correct social protocols and moral prescriptions.

Potlatches have traditionally occurred at points of social stress accompanying any part of the process of ascension or succession to rank: investiture into a new name; the building of a house; erecting of a totem pole or other emblem of hereditary prerogative, such as a marriage or a child's coming of age; or alternatively as a mortuary feast for a previous rankholder, as a means of acquiring prestige; and sometimes even as a means of discrediting rival claimants. The legitimacy of the rankholder's claims is proven by his dual ability to command the allegiance of his family group in putting together such a complicated ceremony and to perform correctly the formal display of his family's origin myths and ceremonial objects. The acceptance of gifts by the guests signals their acceptance of the validity of his claim.

Anthropologists have focused on the secular, social aspects and functions of the potlatch—on the way in which potlatches maintain social equilibrium, consolidate chiefly power over commoners, provide for the orderly transfer of wealth and power, provide a measure of group identity and solidarity, redistribute surplus wealth and level economic imbalances, provide outlets for competition without recourse to violence, and provide an occasion for aesthetic expression and dramatic entertainment. Irving Goldman has suggested in his *The Mouth of Heaven* (1975) that, since in Northwest Coast philosophy all status, power, and wealth are considered to be a gift from the beneficent supernatural beings who provide the materials that humans need to survive, the potlatch is inherently a religious institution, fundamentally endowed with a sacramental quality. Each of the family origin myths, whose retelling is such an important part of the potlatch, tells of how one of a particular family's ancestors was able to make a covenant with a supernatural being. In return for the right to collect food of a specific type at a specific location, to possess an aristocratic name, to impersonate (and thus become) the supernatural being in ceremonies, and to invoke the aid of that being in times of distress, the ancestor accepted the responsibility of performing the rituals that would ensure the reincarnation of that supernatural being. This covenant expresses the mutual dependency of human and supernatural, and the potlatch is the ceremony through which the aristocrat fulfills his responsibilities to the supernatural being.

The chief is the representative of his house to the spirits and in his person are brought together all the historical, social, and spiritual aspects of his group's identity. He is the being who links the spiritual world to the social world, and his costume and behavior at potlatches clearly state the duality of his role as spirit in human form. Indeed, since chiefs are the representatives of particular supernatural beings, the distribution of wealth to other chiefs at potlatches can be seen as a metaphorical distribution by one supernatural being to others, and as such it represents the flow of substance throughout the entire universe.

The potlatch, obviously a rite of passage for human beings, a death of an old identity and a rebirth into a new one, is also a rite of passage for the supernaturals. The supernatural beings sustain human beings not only by giving them power and knowledge, but by being their food—when supernatural beings come to the human world, they put on costumes that transform them into animals. The objects displayed, transferred, or distributed in potlatches are manifestations of the bodies of supernatural beings: the flesh and skins of animals (which, since they are thought to be the animals' ceremonial costumes, imply that humans survive by ingesting the ceremonial, spiritual essence of their prey); the coppers (large, ceremonial plaques that represent repositories of captured souls awaiting reincarnation); and the feast dishes (which are the coffins for the animal substance before the humans who partake of that substance begin the process of its reincarnation). Potlatches, in a sense, are funerals for the supernaturals and inherently involve the reaffirmation of the eternal moral covenants between mankind and the other inhabitants of the universe. As animals sacrifice their flesh that humans may eat it and live, so humans must sacrifice themselves or their wealth, which is a symbol of themselves, that the dead may be reborn.

In Northwest Coast thought, moral order and spiritual purity are achieved through acts of self-sacrifice, and the giving away of possessions places humans in harmony with the moral order of the universe. The universe is imagined to have been originally a place of self-interest and possessiveness, that is, until culture heroes started the process of distribution. Northwest Coast peoples believe that the universe will collapse back into the primordial chaos of selfishness unless humans continually reaffirm their willingness to disburse their possessions, to pass out wealth to their fellow men, and to pass on rank to their children. The potlatch provides the ceremonial realization of that commitment to the cosmic moral order and is a reaffirmation by all its participants—hosts, guests, ancestors, the unborn, and supernatural beings—of the system of moral covenants and mutual dependencies that lie at the basis of Northwest Coast society. The potlatch reenacts myth, and then, through redistribution, recreates its processual nature, thereby becoming a graphic representation of the continuing reality and salience of those myths, linking the past to the present, the dead to the living, the sacred to the mundane, the human to the supernatural, the local to the cosmic, and the momentary to the eternal.

It should be noted that the potlatch underwent substantial change during the nineteenth century. Heavy governmental and missionary pressures contributed to the abandonment or secularization of many Northwest Coast Indian rituals. Potlatches and all other native ceremonies were illegal in Canada between 1876 and 1951, and though some ceremonies were carried out in secret, Northwest Coast religion was irreparably altered. The potlatch and other ceremonies have played an important role in the native renaissance of the 1960s, 1970s, and 1980s, but few studies of the potlatch in contemporary Indian life have been conducted, and very little can be said of the particulars of its role in Indian society today.

BIBLIOGRAPHY

Philip Drucker and Robert F. Heizer provide a lucid review of the literature and a discussion of the potlatch as a social institution in *To Make My Name Good* (Berkeley, 1967); Helen Codere's *Fighting with Property: A Study of Kwakiutl Potlatching and Warfare, 1792–1930* (New York, 1950) deals with the issue of historical changes in the potlatches of the Kwakiutl; Irving Goldman's *The Mouth of Heaven* (New York, 1975) reexamines many of the Kwakiutl materials collected by Franz Boas and argues for a new religio-philosophical interpretation of Northwest Coast culture.

24 MODERN RELIGIOUS MOVEMENTS

JOSEPH G. JORGENSEN

Throughout the initial 270 years following the establishment of the Jamestown colony in what is now Virginia, North American Indians engaged in wars and rebellions against colonial and United States governments. Often these same Indian societies, as well as other groups that had not engaged in warfare, fled from the settlers and the military. Religious movements frequently preceded, accompanied, or followed these direct physical attempts to preserve native lands and ways of life. During the twentieth century such religious movements have come to dominate native responses to oppression and deprivation, sometimes through the pursuit of litigation, involvement in public demonstrations, and even in occasional rebellions. Participants in these movements have attempted to rectify Indian grievances and to maintain Indian culture in the face of overwhelming obstacles.

EARLY REBELLIONS

Early events in the eastern and western portions of the North American continent provided harbingers for the sweep of European-Indian relations and the religious movements that have emerged in the wake of those relations. The initial Indian responses to European expropriation and exploitation were to accommodate and, less frequently, to fight. Yet protracted contact with Europeans often provoked the Indians to fight—and not necessarily as a result of special religious messages.

In the East, for example, the Pamunkey Algonquians, under Powhatan (1550?–1618), welcomed the Virginia Company's Jamestown settlers in 1607, supplying them with food. But by 1622 the Pamunkey rebelled against land expropriations, taxes, and pressures to convert to Christianity. As a consequence the Pamunkey were defeated in war and subjected to a policy of harassment and extermination; neither flight nor reservation confinement was useful in protecting them (Tyler, 1959).

In the West, Pueblo Indians residing in what are now Arizona and New Mexico came under the domination of the Spanish in 1598. The Puebloans suffered nearly a century of precipitous population decline and oppression in the forms of forced labor, land expropriation, and forced attendance at Catholic church services. On 10 August 1680, the Great Pueblo Revolt, headed by a San Juan Tewa religious leader, Popé, was successful in driving the Spanish from all of the Pueblo villages. However, the Spanish reconquered the Pueblos twenty years later. Following a subsequent abortive revolt and with no place to retreat to, the Puebloans were forced to take their traditional Indian religious practices underground, enabling them to put a spiritual distance between themselves and their oppressors (Dozier, 1970; Sando, 1979).

MESSIAHS AND WARRIORS

In the eighteenth century, as colonial populations grew, Indian struggles were often prompted by prophets—visionaries who received spiritual messages prescribing acts, beliefs, and observances that would effect imminent transformations. The Delaware of the Atlantic seaboard were defeated in numerous contests with colonists over land; the Indians gradually moved west. Prophets began emerging among them and closely related tribes, such as the Shawnee, in the 1750s and continued to appear for the next sixty years. The visionaries of the early period preached that total transformation of the world was nigh and that Indians would be restored to their former state. Later prophets preached redemptive messages that prescribed the total transformation of persons. Both groups, however, taught that white ways must be eschewed and that the oppressors could be defeated in war through spiritual forces that would accompany Indian warriors.

The most prominent of the early visionaries was Neolin, known as the Delaware Prophet. [*See the biography of Neolin.*] His message was acted upon by Pontiac, an Ottawa leader. Pontiac's unified forces experienced early successes in battle against the British, but gradually his supporters began to divide, and finally they withdrew in the face of stiff resistance at Detroit and Fort Pitt (Newcomb, 1956; Wallace, 1956).

During this same period visionaries with messages similar to that delivered by Neolin arose among the Iroquois in the area that is now western Pennsylvania and New York. The Iroquois prophets are not known to have influenced Iroquois war leaders. Nevertheless, Iroquois leaders conspired with Pontiac, who was himself acting on Neolin's message, and carried out relatively successful warfare against the British in 1763.

In 1799 Handsome Lake, a debauched erstwhile war leader among the Seneca, received the first of several visions that were eventually shaped into the *gaiwiio* ("good word"), a social and moral code traditionally recited over a four-day period. Handsome Lake's visions proposed religious and secular, moral and material solutions to Seneca poverty and humiliation. [*See the biography of Handsome Lake.*]

In 1811 Tenskwatawa, a Shawnee prophet, preached that redemption would come through strict avoidance of white practices, drunkenness, racial intermarriage, the release of Indian land to whites, and witchcraft. This redemptive message was soon joined with the belief that spiritual assistance would help the Shawnee and Delaware overcome the United States in battle. The prophet's brother Tecumseh and their followers joined forces with the British in the War of 1812, only to lose and eventually to be removed to Kansas and Oklahoma (Newcomb, 1956; Wallace, 1956). [*See the biography of Tecumseh.*]

PROPHET DANCE AND GHOST DANCES

Between 1847 and 1858, war and violence raged throughout the Columbia River drainage area and along the Pacific Coast of contemporary Washington and Oregon as whites extended their dominance over Indian communities and continued to expropriate Indian land. Around 1855 a Wanapum from the Columbia Plateau known as Smohalla claimed to have returned from the dead and began to preach from visions he had experienced. Smohalla preached that agriculture and mining defiled Mother Earth, that land should not be conveyed to whites, and that all of nature should be held in common by those who lived within it. Smohalla's religion, which came to be known as the Prophet Dance, consisted of a formal set of rituals and symbols (some derived from Christianity) integrated with these beliefs. Adherence to his code and performance of the ritual would result in the elimination of all white men, the resurrection of all deceased Indians, and the restoration of the Indians' former way of life (Spier, 1935). The Prophet Dance spread throughout the Columbia Plateau. The famous Chief Joseph of the Nez Perce and his band were also followers. In 1877 they refused to be pushed from their land. At first they fought off the Army, but were finally forced to flee on a one-thousand-mile retreat toward Canada. Eventually they were removed to Oklahoma, then moved again to Washington, but were not allowed to return to their homeland. The Prophet Dance, although stripped of its transformative message (which has been replaced by promises of personal redemption and the acquisition of curative powers), persists in the 1980s as the Pom Pom religion on the Warm Springs reservation in Oregon and the Yakima Reservation in Washington State.

In the late 1860s a Northern Paiute known as Wodziwob or Fish Lake Joe received visions instructing him to create and proselytize the Ghost Dance religion. Visions obtained by participants in the Ghost Dance hastened the day, perceived to be imminent, when the resources from which Indians once culled their livelihoods would be restored, when deceased Indians would be resurrected, when whites would be removed, and when a new and happy existence would be created for all Ghost Dance adherents (Mooney, 1896; Gayton, 1930; DuBois, 1939; and Hittman 1972, 1973). The Ghost Dance of 1869 swept southwest and northwest through California; the northwestern movement carried to the northern Oregon coast.

The Earth Lodge cult, which grew out of the Ghost Dance, emphasized the catastrophic end of the world from which adherents would be spared by sequestering themselves in huge subterranean earth lodges. Several years later a redemptive movement, the Bole-Maru, evolved from the Earth Lodge cult. The Bole-Maru cult focused on coping with obstacles in the here and now to achieve a happy afterlife.

In 1889, well after the Ghost Dance religion as a transformative movement had died among most California, Oregon, and Great Basin societies, a second Ghost Dance movement was started. Wovoka ("the cutter"; also known as Jack Wilson), a Northern Paiute from Mason Valley, Nevada, received a series of visions instructing him to revive the Ghost Dance religion. Redemption rather than transformation was Wovoka's message, but interpretation of his message varied outside the Northern Paiute area.

The Ghost Dance religion spread throughout the Plains from Canada to Oklahoma. After a year-long period of intense participation in the dance by Indians at Pine Ridge, South Dakota, the infamous "Sioux Outbreak of 1890," the Wounded Knee massacre, occurred in which 370 Indians, 250 of which were women and children, were killed by government troops and state militiamen. These Ghost Dance adherents had believed that their "ghost shirts" were immune to bullets (Mooney, 1896). Partially because of the overwhelming influence of the Ghost

Dance, the federal government enacted legislation prohibiting all native Indian religions. [*See also* Ghost Dance *and the biography of Wovoka.*]

INDIAN SHAKERS AND THE SUN DANCE

Many of the Salish and Quileute Indian communities of the Puget Sound region (in present-day Washington State) engaged in the Prophet Dance in the 1860s and 1870s. In 1881 three severe epidemics hit the area; the Indians suffered from confinement on the reservations as well as domination by federal officials, settlers, and Christian missionaries. Also in 1881, a new prophet from among the Puget Sound Salish, John Slocum (1840?–1898?), claiming to have returned from the dead, was resurrected in a fit of shaking and incomprehensible speech before the eyes of many of his Salish relations and friends. Slocum, a logger who worked irregularly, had assumed many of the white man's vices, such as drinking and betting on horses. He was instructed by one of God's angels to follow Christ's guidelines for salvation.

After some initial interest in his vision's message, which instructed him to return to earth, to bear witness to his personal transformation, and to lead other sinners into the Christian way of life, Slocum stumbled over some of the obstacles in his worldly path, fell ill, and was expected to die. Yet after his wife—praying, sobbing, and trembling uncontrollably—approached his prostrate form, Slocum began to improve; his recovery was attributed to divine power manifested by his wife's shaking (Barnett, 1957).

As had also been the case for the Ghost Dance, missionaries spread the Shaker message, and investigators journeyed to Slocum's residence on Puget Sound to learn how to receive the gift of redemption, the new state of grace. The cult spread in all directions, spilling into British Columbia and northern California. In the latter area it was syncretized with the Bole-Maru and eventually with Pentecostal-charismatic practices. The religion continues to flourish throughout this wide area (Barnett, 1957; DuBois, 1939; Schultz, 1968; and Amoss, 1979).

The Indian Shaker participants repudiated their Christian heritage, refusing to accept the status of an affiliate of the established religions. The Shaker religion encourages individual variation and provides for it through "gifts" received in individual religious experiences. Some participants become cured, some become curers, some do both.

In the late 1880s several shamans among the Wind River Shoshoni in Wyoming had become disillusioned with the Ghost Dance. The tribe had already participated in a prereservation form of the Plains Sun Dance, and in the late 1880s they began making significant modifications to its ideology and purpose, dropping warfare and hunting themes and emphasizing concern for illness and community misery (Shimkin, 1953). By 1890 a new Sun Dance religion emerged among the Wind River Shoshoni; the new religion sought solutions to illness, death, oppression, and the factionalism that had become pervasive on the reservations during the preceding twenty years.

By about 1904, the Sun Dance had become the principal religion practiced among the Shoshoni of Idaho and Wyoming and the Ute of Utah and Colorado. It continues to be the dominant religion of these peoples in the 1980s, much as misery and oppression continue on all of the reservations. At Sun Dances a communitarian ethic is preached that eschews narrow, individualistic behavior of all kinds. Each participant—dancer, singer, chief, committeeman, and spectator-adherent—sacrifices pleasures and endures hardships so that living and dead Indians might have happier conditions (Jorgensen, 1972). [*See also* Sun Dance.]

PAN-INDIAN REDEMPTIVE MOVEMENTS

The peyote religion is a pan-Indian redemptive movement; its ritual adherents eat the peyote cactus *(Lophophora williamsii)*. Although some Indian societies in Mexico employed peyote in their religious practices for centuries, as did some Indian societies of the southern Plains, the peyote religion that spread like wildfire throughout the Plains in the 1890s and throughout much of North America during the next few decades was then, and remains now, distinct from eighteenth-century practices. Known as the Native American Church, the peyote religion has syncretized some Christian content—such as God, Mary, the heavenly angels, and Jesus—with Indian symbolism, the latter dominating and also varying among different tribes. In the course of its first century, the Native American Church has had to struggle against federal opposition, state opposition, Christian opposition, and the strong opposition of tribesmen on many, if not all, reservations. It has nevertheless endured and grown throughout North America (Aberle, 1982; Stewart, 1980; and Slotkin, 1956). [*See* North American Indians, *article on* Indians of the Plains; *see also* Psychedelic Drugs.]

Charismatic Christianity, in the form of Pentecostal sects, has spread widely and rapidly on North American Indian reservations since the early 1960s, as has Mormonism (the Church of Jesus Christ of Latter-day Saints). These religions emphasize the accessibility and power of the Holy Ghost, and make believers aware of the evil spirit. These various sects provide explanations of the world and ethical codes that are meant to change the relations of the believers to one another and to nonbelievers, and they demand that believers seek a state of grace invested with the power of the Holy Ghost. Such movements are not fertile sources of rebellion. Rather, they allow believers to challenge evil, explain calamities, and to heal themselves and the sick. They do so by explaining why Indians have experienced grief and dissatisfaction in the past, and they provide a new ideology and the spiritual power that enable adherents to recognize and to cope with evil in this world while preparing for the next world (Jorgensen, 1984; Aberle, 1982).

On the other hand, at certain times and places in the past two decades North American Indians have shown their willingness to resist tribal governments as well as the federal government, to learn more fully their cultural traditions, and to fight, even to take up arms against superior forces. Many rebellious acts occurred in the 1970s, including the ransacking of the Bureau of Indian Affairs offices in Washington, D.C., in 1972, and the occupation of a store and a church in Wounded Knee in 1973. Beginning in the mid-1970s, however, acts such as those perpetrated by the American Indian Movement (AIM) were reduced dramatically as activist Indian leaders were taken to court, some being indicted, convicted, and imprisoned.

Because of the acts of protest and the resulting litigation of the 1970s, a new understanding of Indian problems emerged among many Indian activists across the continent, as they joined with elder traditional religious leaders to learn the ideology and rituals that comprise the Dream Drum, peyote, Sun Dance, sweat lodge, and Ghost Dance religions. Younger leaders have joined with older religious leaders to participate in these religions, and to spread the practice of them to all Indian people so as to better explain the evil in the system and persons that dominate them, while creating social distance from that system. In 1981 the Dakota ("Sioux") American Indian Movement established a religious settlement known as the Yellow Thunder Camp in the Black Hills of South Dakota. The United States Forest Service controls the land, but the AIM participants in this action, claiming self-determination and freedom to worship under the Indian Freedom of Religion Act of 1978, seek title to the land so that all traditional Indian peoples can unify in spiritual pursuits. As the movement evolves, spreading principally from the Pine Ridge and Rosebud Sioux reservations in South Dakota, it focuses on an analysis of evil in the world, and on the benefits of good health, community well-being, and spiritual power that can be gained from a combination of Indian religious practices—all of which are treated as "traditional."

A combination of ritual practices, performed serially, has occurred. Some of these practices are of precontact origin, others are of postcontact origin. Some were once part of transformative movements, others of redemptive movements, and still others were traditional. All have been modified. The combination includes ritual sweating (a precontact practice) in small sweat lodges created specifically for the ritual; the Sun Dance (of precontact origin but modified to accommodate contemporary pledges for health, well-being, and the acquisition of spiritual power); peyotism (a postcontact redemptive movement); and the Ghost Dance (a latter-day redemptive version of the transformative dance that promotes good health by driving away evil). This new amalgam of nativistic practices is seen as unifying and traditional by its adherents. They are seekers of spiritual power who have recognized the enormous material, economic, and political power possessed by the opposition.

This Traditional Unity complex has spread through the American Indian Movement network to help guide sweating rituals and Sun Dance performances on the Navajo Reservation and the McDermitt Northern Paiute Reservation (both possess peyote traditions), and even to the D-Q University campus in Davis, California. D-Q University, supported by federal funds, is operated by and for American Indians and Mexican-Americans. Practitioners of the Dream Drum, peyote, and Longhouse religions of the Eastern Woodlands are also compatible partners in this loose religious confederacy (Jorgensen, 1984).

BIBLIOGRAPHY

Aberle, David F. *The Peyote Religion among the Navajo* (1966). 2d ed. Chicago, 1982.
Amoss, Pamela. *Coast Salish Spirit Dancing: The Survival of an Ancestral Religion.* Seattle, 1978.
Barnett, H. G. *Indian Shakers: A Messianic Cult of the Pacific Northwest.* Carbondale, Ill., 1957.
Dozier, Edward P. *The Pueblo Indians of North America.* New York, 1970.
DuBois, Cora. "The 1870 Ghost Dance." *University of California Anthropological Records* 3 (1939): 1–151.
Gayton, A. H. "The Ghost Dance of 1870 in South-Central California." *University of California Publications in American Archaeology and Ethnology* 28 (1930–1931): 57–82.
Hittman, Michael. "An Ethnohistory of Smith and Mason Valley Paiutes." Ph.D. diss., University of New Mexico, 1972.
Hittman, Michael. "The 1870 Ghost Dance at the Walker River Reservation: A Reconstruction." *Ethnohistory* 20 (1973): 247–278.
Jorgensen, Joseph G. *The Sun Dance Religion: Power for the Powerless.* Chicago, 1972.

Jorgensen, Joseph G. "Religious Solutions and Native American Struggles: Ghost Dance, Sun Dance, and Beyond." In *Religion/Rebellion/Revolution: An Interdisciplinary and Cross-Cultural Collection of Essays,* edited by Bruce Lincoln. London, 1985.

Mooney, James. "The Ghost Dance Religion and the Sioux Outbreak of 1890." *Fourteenth Annual Report of the Bureau of Ethnology, part 2* (1896): 641–1136.

Newcombe, William W., Jr. *The Culture and Acculturation of the Delaware Indians.* Ann Arbor, 1956.

Sando, Joe P. "The Pueblo Revolt." In *Handbook of North American Indians,* vol. 9, *Southwest,* edited by Alfonso Ortiz, pp. 194–197. Washington, D.C., 1979.

Schultz, John L. "Deprivation, Revitalization and the Development of the Shaker Religion." *Northwest Anthropological Research Notes* 2 (1968): 92–119.

Shimkin, Demitri B. "The Wind River Shoshone Sun Dance." *Bureau of American Ethnology Bulletin* 151 (1953): 397–484.

Slotkin, J. S. *The Peyote Religion: A Study in Indian-White Relations.* Glencoe, Ill., 1956.

Spier, Leslie. *The Prophet Dance of the Northwest and Its Derivatives: The Source of the Ghost Dance.* Menasha, Wis., 1935.

Spindler, George, and Louise Spindler. *Dreamers without Power: The Menomini Indians.* New York, 1971.

Stewart, Omer C. "The Native American Church." In *Anthropology on the Great Plains,* edited by W. Raymond Wood and Margot Liberty, pp. 188–196. Lincoln, Nebr., 1980.

Tyler, L. G., ed. *Narratives of Early Virginia.* New York, 1959.

Wallace, Anthony F. C. "New Religious Beliefs among the Delaware Indians, 1600–1900." *Southwestern Journal of Anthropology* 12 (1956): 1–21.

Wallace, Anthony F. C. *The Death and Rebirth of the Seneca: The History and Culture of the Great Iroquois Nation; Their Destruction and Demoralization, and Their Cultural Revival at the Hands of the Indian Visionary, Handsome Lake.* New York, 1969.

CONTRIBUTORS

JOSEPH EPES BROWN, University of Montana

THOMAS BUCKLEY, University of Massachusetts at Boston

RAYMOND D. FOGELSON, University of Chicago

ARMIN W. GEERTZ, Aarhus Universitet

SAM D. GILL, University of Colorado at Boulder

JOHN A. GRIM, Sarah Lawrence College

HOWARD L. HARROD, Vanderbilt University

CHARLES HUDSON, University of Georgia

JOSEPH G. JORGENSEN, University of California at Irvine

ÅKE HULTKRANTZ, Stockholms Universitet

INGE KLEIVAN, Københavns Universitet

LOUISE LAMPHERE, Brown University

DAVID P. MCALLESTER, Wesleyan University

WERNER MÜLLER, Eberhard-Karls-Universität Tübingen (emeritus)

MORRIS EDWARD OPLER, University of Oklahoma

WILLIAM K. POWERS, Rutgers, The State University of New Jersey, New Brunswick Campus

MAC LINSCOTT RICKETTS, Louisburg College

DONALD P. ST. JOHN, Moravian College

STANLEY WALENS, University of California at San Diego

PETER M. WHITELY, Sarah Lawrence College

LAWRENCE E. SULLIVAN is professor of the History of Religions and acting director of the Institute for the Advanced Study of Religion at the University of Chicago.

FINDING LIST OF ARTICLE TITLES

The following table lists the article titles (in parentheses) as they originally appeared in *The Encyclopedia of Religion*. Titles not listed below are unchanged.

The Religious Life of Native North Americans (North American Religions: An Overview)

The Plains (North American Indians: Indians of the Plains)

Blackfeet (Blackfeet Religion)

Lakota (Lakota Religion)

The Southwest (North American Indians: Indians of the Southwest)

Apache (Apache Religion)

Navajo (Navajo Religion)

California and the Intermountain Region (North American Indians: Indians of California and the Intermountain Region)

The Northwest Coast (North American Indians: Indians of the Northwest Coast)

The Far North (North American Indians: Indians of the Far North)

Inuit (Inuit Religion)

The Northeast Woodlands (North American Indians: Indians of the Northeast Woodlands)

Iroquois (Iroquois Religion)

The Southeast Woodlands (North American Indians: Indians of the Southeast Woodlands)

History of the Study of Native North Americans (North American Religions: History of Study)

Mythic Themes (North American Religions: Mythic Themes)

Tricksters (Tricksters: North American Tricksters)

Drama (Drama: Native American Religious Drama)

Iconography (Iconography: Native American Iconography)

Music (Music: Music and Religion in the Americas)

Modern Religious Movements (North American Religions: Modern Movements)